Paul ON THE Cross

reconstructing the apostle's story
of redemption

David A. Brondos

Fortress Press
Minneapolis

Cover art: Cross against Red Background © André Burian/CORBIS. Background scroll image is 1QpHab, col. 7 © Dr. John C. Trever, Ph.D.
Cover and interior design: James Korsmo

Unless otherwise indicated, all Scripture quotations are from the New Revised Standard Version Bible, copyright © 1989 by the Division of Christian Education of the National Council of the Churches of Christ in the U.S.A. and used by permission. All rights reserved.

Scripture is from the Revised Standard Version of the Bible, copyright © 1946, 1952, 1971 by the Division of Christian Education of the National Council of the Churches of Christ in the USA. Used by permission. All rights reserved.

Library of Congress Cataloging-in-Publication Data

Brondos, David A, 1958–
  Paul on the cross : reconstructing the Apostle's story of redemption / David A. Brondos.
    p. cm.
  ISBN-13: 978–0–8006–3788–0 (alk. paper)
  ISBN-10: 0–8006–3788–7 (alk. paper)
  1. Redemption. 2. Jesus Christ—Person and offices. 3. Bible. N.T. Epistles of Paul—Criticism, interpretation, etc. 4. Bible. N.T. Epistles of Paul—Theology. I. Title.
  BS2655.R3B76 2006
  232'.3—dc22

                                                              2006024542

The paper used in this publication meets the minimum requirements of American National Standard for Information Sciences—Permanence of Paper for Printed Library Materials, ANSI Z329.48-1984.

Manufactured in the U.S.A.
  10   09   08   07   06   1   2   3   4   5   6   7   8   9   10

Contents

Abbreviations

ABC	Anchor Bible Commentary
ABRL	Anchor Bible Reference Library
AnBib	Analecta Biblica
ANTC	Abingdon New Testament Commentaries
BGBE	Beiträge zur Geschichte der biblischen Exegese
BNTC	Black's New Testament Commentaries
BZNW	Beihefte zur *ZNW*
ExpT	*Expository Times*
HDR	Harvard Dissertations in Religion
HNTC	Harper's New Testament Commentaries
ICC	International Critical Commentary
Int	Interpretation, a Bible Commentary for Teaching and Preaching
JBL	*Journal of Biblical Literature*
JSHJ	*Journal for the Study of the Historical Jesus*
JSNT	*Journal for the Study of the New Testament*
JSNTS	*JSNT* Supplement Series
JSOTS	*JSOT* Supplement Series
JTS	*Journal of Theological Studies*
KJV	King James Version
LBS	Library of Biblical Studies
LCL	Loeb Classical Library
MBT	Münsterische Beiträge zur Theologie

NCBC	New Century Bible Commentary
NICNT	New International Commentary on the New Testament
NIGTC	New International Greek Testament Commentary
NovT	*Novum Testamentum*
NovTSup	Supplement to *NovT*
NRSV	New Revised Standard Version
NTG	New Testament Guides
NTL	New Testament Library
NTR	New Testament Readings
NTS	New Testament Studies
NTT	New Testament Theology
NTTS	New Testament Tools and Studies
RelSt	*Religious Studies*
RSV	Revised Standard Version
SB	Stuttgarter Bibelstudien
SBLAB	SBL Academia Biblica
SBLDS	SBL Dissertation Series
SJLA	Studies in Judaism in Late Antiquity
SNTSMS	Society for New Testament Studies Monograph Series
TANT	Texte und Arbeiten zum neutestamentlichen Zeitalter
TNTC	Tyndale New Testament Commentary
TPINTC	Trinity Press International New Testament Commentaries
TSAJ	Texte und Studien zum antiken Judentum
WBC	Word Biblical Commentary
WMANT	Wissenschaftliche Monographien zum Alten und Neuen Testament
WUNT	Wissenschaftliche Untersuchungen zum Neuen Testament
ZNW	*Zeitschrift für die neutestamentliche Wissenschaft*

Introduction

For Christian theologians and biblical scholars alike, few questions have proven more problematic than that of the New Testament teaching concerning the relationship between Christ's death on the cross and human salvation. Over the centuries, seemingly endless attempts have been made by theologians to define this relationship in satisfactory fashion, resulting in an abundance of what are commonly known as "theories of the atonement." In many cases, such "theories" or explanations have gone quite a bit beyond anything in the New Testament, and thus they can scarcely be considered to be grounded in the thought of its writers. Nevertheless, certain ideas associated with a number of these explanations have been widely adopted not only by theologians but also by biblical scholars as well, who claim that they faithfully reflect New Testament teaching on the subject. Thus, for example, even though New Testament writers like Paul never employ terms such as *satisfaction, substitution,* and *representation* in relation to Christ's death nor speak explicitly of Christ's undergoing divine judgment, suffering the penalty or consequences of human sin, exhausting God's wrath, or healing our fallen humanity, it is common to claim that ideas such as these are in fact behind the language we find in Paul's letters and elsewhere in the New Testament concerning the redemptive significance of the cross.

The main argument of the present work is that all of this has led to a misreading of Paul, and that Paul's understanding of the role of Jesus' death in the salvation of human beings is fundamentally different from that which has generally been attributed to him by his interpreters from at least the late second century to the present. For Paul, Jesus' death did not save anyone or reconcile anyone to God; it did not have "redemptive effects." According to his letters, while Paul regarded Jesus' death as sacrificial, he did not teach that it expiated sins, propitiated God, or exhausted God's wrath at sin, or that human sin was judged, taken away, or atoned for on the cross. Nor did Paul maintain that Jesus' death liberated humanity from sin, death, the devil, or the power of evil. Paul did not regard Jesus as a corporate or representative figure who summed up or included others, so that what was true of him was thereby true of them as well. Nor did he believe that Jesus had died as humanity's substitute or representative, or in order to make it possible for God to forgive sins while remaining righteous. Jesus' death, for Paul, was not the basis upon which people were justified or their sins forgiven; neither was it some type of cosmic event that put an end to the world as it was and ushered in a new age. Our sinful humanity was not destroyed, put to death, renewed, or transformed when Jesus was crucified. In Paul's thought, Jesus did not die for the purpose of setting an example for others to follow; revealing some truth about God, humanity, or the world; enabling people to participate in his death and resurrection; or providing them with a means of transfer from this age into the new one. Believers are not saved by trusting in the efficacy of Christ's death for their salvation.

All of these ideas are foreign to Paul's thought, and they lead to a distorted image of the apostle. This is not Paul, nor is it his thought on the cross. In reality, the reason biblical scholars and theologians have never been able to reach any consensus regarding the way in which Paul understood the significance of the cross is that they have been looking in his letters and elsewhere in the New Testament for something that is simply not there, namely, an answer to the question of how Jesus' death saves and redeems human beings. This question reflects the mistaken assumption that Paul taught that Jesus' death *effects* human salvation and redemption in some way. In fact, Paul did not.

Instead, what Paul *did* teach is that *by means of* Christ's death God has saved and redeemed human beings and has reconciled them to himself. This is not a matter of splitting hairs. There is a vast difference between saying that "Christ died for our sins" (1 Cor 15:3) and saying that his death takes away sins, effects forgiveness, or makes atonement. To say that believers have died and been crucified and buried with Christ (Rom 6:3–8; Gal 2:20) is not the same as saying that they participate in his death, crucifixion, and burial. To say that Jesus "gave himself for our sins to deliver us from the present evil age" (Gal 1:4*) is not the same as saying that his death has effected that deliverance or inaugurated a new age. Similarly, to say that believers are justified *in* or *through* Christ's blood (Rom 5:9) is different from saying that Christ's blood or death justifies them.

In other words, for Paul, Jesus' death is certainly salvific and redemptive, but not *in itself*, and not through any "effects" it has. Rather, *it is salvific and redemptive only in that it forms part of a story*. This story, however, is quite different from the stories of redemption that the vast majority of theologians and biblical scholars have attributed to Paul, including those who have recently taken a "narrative" approach to his epistles. For the most part, those stories continue to place at the heart of Paul's soteriological thought concepts, words, and phrases that never appear in his epistles, such as many of those mentioned above. The result is that the story of redemption ascribed to Paul ends up looking quite different from the relatively simple, straightforward story told about Jesus in the Gospels and Acts.

Here I will argue that the story behind Paul's language regarding the cross is essentially the same simple story we find in the Synoptic Gospels and Acts, which in turn developed out of the foundation story running throughout the Hebrew Scriptures and other ancient Jewish writings.[1] This involves the claim that Paul understood Jesus' death primarily as the consequence of his dedication and faithfulness to his mission of serving as God's instrument to bring about the awaited redemption of Israel, which would also include Gentiles throughout the world. In this case, for Paul, Jesus' death is salvific not because it satisfies some necessary condition for human salvation in the way that most doctrines of the atonement have traditionally maintained nor because it effects some change in the situation of human beings or the world in general; rather, it is salvific because God responded to Jesus' faithfulness unto death in seeking the redemption of others by raising him so that all the divine promises of salvation might now be fulfilled through him. Through Jesus' death, a new covenant-community (the church) has been established, in which people from all nations may now find salvation and forgiveness of sins as they live under his lordship, led by the Holy Spirit. For Paul, this is what Jesus lived and died for, and what he attained by giving up his life and consequently being raised and exalted to God's right hand. It is *in this sense* that Jesus died for others and for their sins. In short, Paul regarded Jesus' death as salvific because for him it formed part of an overarching story culminating in the redemption of Israel and the world; it is *this story*, and in particular *what precedes and follows* Jesus' death on the cross, that makes that death redemptive.

In order to develop this argument, it will be necessary briefly to review several of the most influential interpretations of Jesus' death found in the writings of Christian theologians and biblical interpreters from the time of Irenaeus of Lyons (ca. 130–200 C.E.) to the present, so as to identify some of the basic ideas and assumptions associated with them. This will be our task in chapter 1. In the following two chapters, we will look at the foundation stories found in first-century Judaism and early Christianity, considering at the same time the question whether certain of the central ideas and assumptions identified in chapter 1 are present in these stories. In chapter 4, we will begin to examine Paul's soteriology in the light of the Jewish and Christian foundation stories so as to determine the extent to which his thought is in continuity with those stories. All of this will provide the background necessary to look more closely at Paul's allusions to the cross in chapters 5 and 6, where we will consider respectively his so-called cultic or juristic language and participatory language. Finally, a brief summary of the main conclusions of this study will be presented.

Due to the historical nature of the present work, I will employ masculine pronouns to speak of God in accordance with the usage of the writings under consideration. I believe it is important to separate the theological question of how we should speak of God today from the historical question of how God was spoken of in these writings; in order to represent faithfully the thought of the authors of these texts, I believe it is preferable to use their own language and concepts rather than placing limitations on ourselves due to present-day theological concerns. On occasion, in order to refer to a particular conception of humanity and human nature found in the writings of the theologians discussed in chapter 1, I will use the word "man" in quotes rather than some gender-inclusive term for human beings. Where I consider it necessary to depart from the text of the New Revised Standard Version and translate certain phrases directly from the Greek New Testament, an asterisk will appear following the reference.

I would like to express my profound gratitude to all of those at Fortress Press who have contributed to the publication of this book, including particularly Acquisitions Editor Neil Elliott and Assistant Managing Editor James Korsmo. Above all, however, I would like to thank Editor-in-Chief Michael West for his patience, support, and encouragement.

CHAPTER 1

Stories of Redemption
in the Christian Tradition

Every doctrine of redemption is in essence a story. Jewish people of Jesus' time told a story of redemption that for the most part has remained intact among them to this day. This story revolves around figures such as the patriarchs, Moses, and David and tells of the election of Israel, the exodus from Egypt, the conquest and settlement of the promised land, the monarchy, the period of exile, the diaspora, and, ultimately, the restoration and redemption of this people in fulfillment of the promises made to them by their God. According to the New Testament, when the apostles and first Christian believers spoke of redemption, they built upon this same story to tell the story of Jesus of Nazareth, a Galilean Jew who had been crucified after carrying out a ministry of teaching and healing, but had been raised by God three days later and exalted to heaven.

Yet precisely *how* did the first Christians, such as Paul, believe that people were saved and redeemed by these events? While countless answers have been given to this question in the history of Christian thought and biblical interpretation, several in particular have found widespread acceptance.

Paul and the Interpretations
of Christ's Work from Past to Present

Among the oldest interpretations of Christ's work is the *Christus Victor* or "classical" idea of the atonement, as it was labeled by Gustav Aulén in the book of that name, first published in English in 1931. Aulén summarized the basic idea thus: "Christ—*Christus Victor*—fights against and triumphs over the evil powers of the world, the 'tyrants' under which mankind is in bondage and suffering, and in him God reconciles the world to himself."[1] Aulén traced this idea back not only to Irenaeus and other church fathers, such as Athanasius and Gregory of Nyssa, but to Paul himself, who included sin, death, and the law among the "tyrants" defeated by Christ.

While this understanding of Christ's work was widely accepted during the first centuries of the church's existence, a second and similar understanding also became quite popular, commonly referred to as the "physical" doctrine of redemption. Here the word "physical" is used not in contrast to "spiritual" but to refer to the human nature or *physis* (embracing body, soul, and spirit) that is healed and restored through its union with the divine nature or *physis*. This idea is generally found alongside the *Christus Victor* view in the church fathers, including particularly those just mentioned. The difference, however, is that whereas the forces of evil in the *Christus Victor* view are seen as being above and external to human beings, the physical doctrine of redemption speaks of evil forces such as sin and death as having become inherent to human nature in its present fallen condition, and it generally conceives of them in impersonal terms. In Athanasius's words, "The corruption which had set in was not external to the body, but had become attached to it."[2] Christ thus saves human beings by taking upon himself the fallen nature or humanity all people share and restoring it to incorruptibility and immortality. According to Irenaeus, the Son of God "became what we are, that he might bring us to be even what he is himself."[3] Irenaeus, like many of the other church fathers, repeatedly uses the word "man" to refer simultaneously to human beings collectively and to the human nature in which all share. Thus, for example, when he affirms that Christ "caused man to cleave to and to become one with God," he means that human nature has been joined to God, together with all human beings who participate in that nature.[4] At times both ancient and modern, proponents of this type of view have argued that not only human nature but nature in general, that is, the entire created order, has been healed by Christ through his incarnation, death, and resurrection. Ideas such as these form the background to the interpretation of Paul's language regarding redemption and reconciliation with God found in the writings of many of the Fathers.[5]

A third type of explanation as to how human beings are saved through Christ revolves around the notion of "satisfaction" and is associated particularly with the name of Anselm of Canterbury. In his *Cur Deus Homo,* completed in 1098, Anselm argued that human beings were unable to pay the debt of honor and obedience that they owed to God on account of their sin. God's justice, however, demanded either satisfaction or punishment. Because no mortal human being could make the satisfaction required, God's Son became incarnate so that through his passion and death he might offer up on behalf of human beings the honor and obedience necessary to satisfy divine justice. In this way human beings were released from their debt; the divine punishment was averted by satisfaction.

In the centuries following the appearance of *Cur Deus Homo,* the distinction Anselm made between satisfaction and punishment came to be lost, and it became common to equate the two: because God's justice (or law) would not allow human sin to be left unpunished, the only way satisfaction might be made was for Christ to undergo the necessary punishment in the place of others. We find this idea in the writings of John Calvin, who looked to a variety of passages from Paul's epistles to argue that human beings "could not escape God's dreadful judgment." Because of this, it was necessary for "the penalty to which we were subject" to be imposed on Christ, who frees us "both by transferring our condemnation to himself and by taking our guilt upon himself" as our substitute.[6] This understanding of Christ's work is generally referred to as a "penal substitution" view: Christ came to "pay the penalty that we had deserved," and "bore the punishment and vengeance due for our sins" in our place by suffering in full the terrible consequences of humanity's sin, thus delivering human beings from suffering those consequences themselves.[7] Many New Testament scholars continue to interpret Paul's thought along these lines.[8]

While the views of redemption in Christ that revolve around the notions of satisfaction and substitution became widely accepted in the West, they also met with a great deal of criticism. Among the first to object to Anselm's type of teaching was Peter Abelard, who argued in his commentary on Romans that the purpose of Christ's life and death had been to bring about a greater righteousness in human beings by revealing God's love to them: "His Son has taken upon himself our nature and persevered in teaching us by word and example even unto death—he has more fully bound us to himself by love; with the result that our hearts should be enkindled by such a gift of divine grace, and true charity should not now shrink from enduring anything for him." According to Abelard, this is what St. Paul meant when he wrote that "we have been justified by the blood of Christ and reconciled to God."[9] This understanding of Christ's work became popular among many of the liberal theologians of the late nineteenth and early twentieth centuries, who sought an alternative to the views of redemption centered on the notions of satisfaction and penal substitution. Generally this was referred to as the "subjective," "exemplary," or "moral influence" doctrine of atonement. This kind of interpretation of Christ's death has remained popular up to the present: the cross and resurrection of Christ are said to be salvific because of what these events *teach* or *reveal* to human beings.[10]

In recent decades, however, an alternative view of Christ's work has gained popularity. According to this view, human beings are redeemed through *participation* in Christ's death and resurrection. The widespread adoption of this view can be attributed especially to the influence of Karl Barth and Rudolf Bultmann. Drawing on ideas and language taken from the church fathers, Anselm, Calvin, and others, Barth argued that God's Son assumed the humanity common to all, that is, "sinful man" in his "fallen and perishing state,"[11] so as to effect the destruction of that "old man" and bring a "new man" into existence through Christ's resurrection and exaltation: "The life of a new man lived by Jesus is preceded by the dying of an old man suffered by him, the rising of the true man in his existence and death by the destruction of a false and perverted [man]. . . ."[12] Because in Christ God "assumed the human being of all men,"[13] it can be said that what happened "in the history of Jesus Christ" has also happened "in the history of all other men."[14] "In the history in which he became and is man, and suffers and acts as man, there took place an exaltation of the humanity which as his and ours is the same."[15] "Man in general . . . is like the man Jesus and thus participates in the history enacted in him."[16] In passages such as these, Barth's use of the word "man" is similar to that of Irenaeus and the church fathers, in that it refers not only to humankind collectively but also to the nature or essence in which all men and women share. Barth combined the notion of substitution with that of participation or representation to claim that the reconciliation of God and humankind took place once and for all on Calvary: "For then and there, in the person of Christ taking our place, we were present, being crucified and dying with him. . . . We died: the totality of all sinful men. . . . His death was the death of all."[17]

Like Barth, Rudolf Bultmann traced the idea of participation in Christ's death back to Paul. According to Bultmann, while Paul followed the tradition he received in interpreting Christ's death in terms of a substitutionary sacrifice, at the same time he borrowed from the mystery religions the idea that "participation in the fate of the mystery-divinity through baptism and sacramental communion grants the *mystes* (initiate) participation in both the dying and the reviving of the divinity."[18] Similarly, Paul found in the Gnostic myths the belief that human beings constitute a unity with the Redeemer by sharing the same substance or body with him; thus, "what happens to the Redeemer, or happened while he tarried in human form on earth, happens to his whole *soma*—i.e. not to him alone but to all who belong to that *soma*." Influenced by such ideas, Paul viewed Christ's death and resurrection as "cosmic occurrences, not incidents that took place once upon a time in the past."[19] Believers die and rise with Christ by virtue of their union with him and with the Christ-event. In contrast to Barth, however, Bultmann insisted that Paul did not conceive of this union in terms of sharing in a common substance or essence, arguing instead that what was involved was the possibility of a new type of existence in faith. The cross of Christ is "recognizable as salvation-event" by virtue of the "decision-question which the 'word of the cross' thrusts upon the hearer: whether he will thereby acknowledge the demand to take up the cross by the surrender of his previous understanding of himself" or not.[20] On the basis of these ideas, Bultmann also rejected Barth's heavily objective understanding of redemption, according to which Christ's death and resurrection had brought about "the alteration of the situation of the men of all times."[21] In spite of their different understandings of participation, however, the two agreed in speaking of Christ's death and resurrection as an "event" or "occurrence" that has an "effect" on human beings by virtue of their *participation* in that event.[22]

This idea of participation has come to be regarded by many New Testament scholars as central to the thought of Paul. Particularly influential in this regard has been E. P. Sanders, who drew on the work of Bultmann and others so as to argue that the notion of participation in Christ or in his death is "the heart of [Paul's] soteriology and Christology," and that the "real bite of his theology lies in the participatory categories."[23] Since then, other scholars, such as Morna Hooker, James Dunn, Richard Hays, and N. T. Wright, have further developed the argument that "Paul's notion of participation in Christ is fundamental, not only for his Christology, but for his understanding of salvation,"[24] although their interpretations of Paul's teaching on the subject vary in important regards. Nevertheless, most would concur with the summary of this understanding of Christ's work provided by T. L. Donaldson, who describes the pattern of "(eschatological) salvation by representation and participation" in the following terms:

> (i) Christ's death and resurrection is the eschatological crisis event. In this event, the 'powers of this age' are defeated (1 Cor 15.24–28; Rom 8.3f., 31–39; Col 2.15), and Christ himself makes the passage from 'this age' to the 'age to come' (1 Cor 15.20). (ii) Christ functions in this event not as an individual but as a representative figure (e.g. 2 Cor 5.14). He fully identifies with the sinful human condition, even to the point of death (e.g. Gal 4.4; Rom 8.3f.; 2 Cor 5.21; Phil 2.6–8), with the result that all can share in the implications of his resurrection, viz. vindication (i.e. justification) and the life of the age to come (e.g. Gal 2.20). (iii) The way to receive these benefits is to be 'in Christ' (e.g. Gal 2.17; 3.26, 28), i.e. to participate with Christ in death and resurrection.[25]

While many Pauline scholars today agree that Paul continued to understand Jesus' death in substitutionary terms, some have followed Bultmann and Sanders in seeing this as a secondary aspect of Paul's thought. In fact, many of the passages Bultmann regarded as reflecting a substitutionary understanding of Christ's death have now come to be interpreted in participatory terms. Thus, Sanders, for example, argues that "even the foundation stones of the substitutionary theory—Rom. 8.3f.; II Cor. 5.21; Gal. 3.16 [*sic*]—do not really convey the doctrine of redemption by substitution. They are primarily participationist."[26] Others, however, have chosen to follow Barth by claiming that Paul's doctrine of redemption *combined* the notions of participation and substitution.[27] For their part, some German scholars have come to distinguish between these two ideas by contrasting an "inclusive" type of representation (*einschließende* or *inkludierende Stellvertretung*) with an "exclusive" one (*ausschließende* or *exkludierende Stellvertretung*); the former corresponds more closely to the notion of participation, and the latter to that of substitution.[28]

Nevertheless, Pauline scholars also continue to interpret Paul's thought on the basis of the other understandings of Christ's work mentioned above, often combining them with each other, as Donaldson does above in attributing to

Paul the *Christus Victor* idea that "the 'powers of this age' are defeated" together with the notion that believers "participate with Christ in death and resurrection." James Dunn's interpretation of Paul draws not only on the concepts of substitution and participation but also on ideas taken from the physical view found in the church fathers: Christ's work consisted of overcoming the malignant powers of sin and death in our humanity through his death and resurrection, thereby replacing the old fallen humanity with a new one.[29] In fact, Dunn states explicitly that in his view Irenaeus and Athanasius faithfully represent Paul's "theological logic."[30] David Seeley argues for what is in effect a "moral influence" interpretation of Paul's thought, yet also incorporates ideas from the *Christus Victor* view: to be saved, one must "reenact" the obedience shown by Christ in his death and imitate his example; in this way "one gains liberation from and shares in a victory over the evil tyrant Sin."[31] Thus, all of these different understandings of the salvific significance of Christ's death continue to be attributed to Paul by Pauline scholars.

Common Assumptions

In reality, each of the understandings of salvation in Christ just outlined constitutes a story of redemption. According to the story told by many of the church fathers, for example, through Adam and Eve human beings had fallen from their created condition into bondage under powers such as the devil, sin, and death, but had consequently been liberated by Christ, either by the payment of a ransom to the devil or by the uniting of the human nature to the divine that had taken place in him. The same type of story can be discerned in Anselm's *Cur Deus Homo*, John Calvin's *Institutes*, Karl Barth's *Church Dogmatics*, and even T. L. Donaldson's summary of the participatory understanding of Christ's work presented above.

While these stories of redemption differ on many points, for the most part they share a number of common assumptions. Among the most important of these is the idea that Christ's death has some type of salvific "effect" on God, human beings, or the human situation. Calvin, for example, writes, "The *effect* of his shedding of blood is that our sins are not imputed to us."[32] The church fathers even speak of some type of ontological change produced in humanity by Christ's incarnation, death, and resurrection. According to Irenaeus, Christ performed "all kinds of healing" on "man" so as to "restore man sound and whole in all points"; "The righteous flesh has reconciled that flesh which was being kept under bondage in sin, and brought it into friendship with God."[33] For Gregory of Nyssa, Christ took "the concrete lump of our nature" and then, by dying and rising, bestowed on that nature "the principle of the resurrection." "As the principle of death took its rise in one person and passed on in succession through the whole of humankind, in like manner the principle of the Resurrection life extends from one person to the whole of humanity."[34] Often views such as these have been labeled "mechanical," in that they posit some type of "cause-and-effect mechanism" whereby Christ's incarnation or death "works" to produce some salvific consequence. At times, this consequence is said to affect all people, "the whole of humanity," as Gregory states. *Christus Victor* views, such as that of Irenaeus, generally claim that humankind in general has been delivered by Christ from Satan's power,[35] while satisfaction and penal substitution understandings of Christ's death tend to claim that he has obtained forgiveness "for the sins of the whole world," as Anselm taught.[36] In theological language, this has usually been referred to as the "objective" redemption that embraces all people potentially or "in principle," in contrast to the "subjective" redemption that takes place when an individual actualizes that salvation personally by coming to faith.

When Christ's death is said to "effect" human salvation or atonement in some way, it is generally claimed that both his incarnation and his life had his death as their goal. In Anselm's words, "He became man for the purpose of dying."[37] Furthermore, precisely because no other human death could produce the same "effect" of saving human beings from their subjection to sin and death, Christ's death is considered to be unique in human history, essentially distinct in nature from the death of any other person. Often this has involved claiming that in his passion and death Christ underwent some experience of suffering or divine abandonment that no other person in human history has ever undergone, such as going through "all the abysses and hells of God-forsakenness, of the divine curse and final judgment" on the cross.[38]

One further assumption common to virtually all of these stories of redemption is that, for various reasons, human salvation was impossible without Christ's incarnation and death. Irenaeus, for example, argued that God could not act unjustly toward Satan in redeeming humanity, and because Satan could be rightfully overcome and "legitimately vanquished" only if a human being effected that redemption, God's Son had to become human.[39] Elsewhere he argued for the necessity of Christ's incarnation on the basis of a physical under-standing of redemption: "Unless man had been joined to God, he could never have become a partaker of incorruptibility. . . . For *by no other means* could we have attained to incorruptibility and immortality, unless we had been united to incorruptibility and immortality."[40] This kind of argument for necessity is particularly associated with Anselm, who wrote *Cur Deus Homo* precisely to "prove by rational necessity" that no one "can possibly be saved without [Christ]."[41] Anselm's argument for necessity, like that of Irenaeus, is based on a certain understanding of God's righteous nature: because God is perfectly just, "either satisfaction or punishment must follow upon every sin."[42] And since no one could offer up the necessary satisfaction except one who was both divine and human, God's Son had to assume human nature and die on the cross.

In attributing versions of these various stories of redemption to Paul, Pauline scholars have at the same time attributed to him the assumptions associated with these stories. Christ's death is said to "effect" salvation in some way, producing salvific "consequences." E. P. Sanders refers to the "effect of Christ's death,"[43] while T. L. Donaldson speaks of "the (universally) redemptive effect of Christ's becoming a curse 'for us (all)' on the cross."[44] This reflects the assumption that Christ's death in some way affects all human beings, or brings about some change in the condition of humanity as a whole in relation to God. James Dunn even asks, "How did Jesus' death 'work' to deal with the power of sin entrenched in human flesh?"[45] thereby attributing a mechanical idea of redemption to Paul. The claim that Paul regarded Christ's death as *nec-essary* for human salvation also runs throughout the writings of these scholars: Sanders affirms explicitly that for Paul Jesus' death "was necessary for man's salvation," and that "salvation cannot come in any other way,"[46] while Richard Hays speaks of the "necessity for the Son of God to die on a cross."[47] Similarly, Dunn argues that Christ's death, "so far as Paul was concerned, was *the only way* God could deal with the power of sin and death,"[48] and N. T. Wright claims that Christ's death and resurrection provided "the pattern of exile and restoration" that "Israel *needed* if she incurred the curse of the law."[49]

But are these ideas and assumptions really those of Paul, or are they instead those of his later interpreters? And is the story of redemption told by Paul really a version of one or more of the stories outlined above, or are such stories being read back into his writings? These are the questions that will be addressed in the following chapters.

CHAPTER 2

The Jewish Story of Redemption
Known to Paul

As N. T. Wright has recently shown, the worldview common to most Jews in the first century was based on a foundation story that was essentially the same story we find in the Hebrew Scriptures, out of which it developed.[1] Because this story undoubtedly formed the background for the story of redemption told by the first Christians, including Paul himself, if we wish to understand Paul's soteriology, it is there we must begin.

The Story of Israel in the Hebrew Scriptures

The basic elements of the first-century Jewish foundation story are well known and not a subject of controversy, and thus can be summarized fairly quickly.[2] It speaks of the creator God YHWH's election of Abraham, Isaac, Jacob, and their descendants ("Israel") to be his special people, and his promise to bless them in many ways, particularly by giving them a land. These promises are framed in the context of a covenant established under Moses after God had led Israel out of Egypt. Of course, not only the exodus but also the establishment of this covenant and the giving of the commandments to Israel were regarded as acts of divine grace and mercy. Particularly important in this story is the idea that the promised blessings are contingent on Israel's obedience to those commandments. As passages such as Lev 26 and Deut 28 affirm, obedience is to bring prosperity, but disobedience is to bring suffering, hunger, devastation, illness, and death, as well as oppression and exile at the hands of other nations. This belief formed the basis for the interpretation of Israel's history consistently found throughout the Hebrew Scriptures and other ancient Jewish writings, where the various disasters the people suffered are seen as God's reaction to Israel's sins and God's attempt to discipline and purify the people so that they might come to practice the justice and righteousness commanded of them in the covenant.[3] Nevertheless, due especially to the influence of the prophetic writings, it was thought that sooner or later Israel's God would act to redeem his people and restore their fortunes in the land he had given them, inaugurating a new age marked by abundance, prosperity, long life, and freedom from the nations that oppressed them.[4] Undoubtedly, there were differences among Jews regarding many aspects of this story, for example, regarding the role that a "Messiah" figure might play, whether there would be a resurrection of the dead, and the extent to which Gentiles might participate in the coming redemption.[5] In broad terms, however, such was the Jewish story of redemption being told in Jesus' day.

As N. T. Wright stresses at several points throughout *The New Testament and the People of God*, this Jewish foundation story differs in various regards from the later Christian stories of redemption, such as those outlined in the previous chapter. Above all, it is first and foremost a story about *the redemption of Israel*. The promises of salvation were made to this particular people in the context of a covenant in which no nation but Israel lived. This covenant brought with it concrete hopes for the restoration of Israel and its capital, Jerusalem, in the land God had given them, together with the people's deliverance from oppression at the hands of foreign powers such as the Romans.[6]

By contrast, the Christian stories of redemption outlined in chapter 1 employ Hellenistic modes of thought so as to posit some objective redemption or transformation affecting all human beings by virtue of their belonging to a common humanity or human nature ("man"). According to these stories, individuals are saved only to the extent that they participate in the universal salvation of humanity accomplished through Christ. Rather than proceeding from the universal to the particular, however, Jewish soteriology begins with the particular, namely, the patriarchs and the people descended from them, in order then to proceed to the universal, the fate of the nations as a whole. God's design is primarily to redeem his chosen people Israel rather than to redeem "man" in general. Of course, according to many passages from the Hebrew Scriptures and later Jewish writings (as well as the New Testament), it was thought that righteous non-Jews might also share to some degree in this redemption. Yet *it is not the Jewish people who share in the universal salvation of "man" but rather the nations in general who share in the salvation of a particular people, Israel.* As Wright observes, in Jewish thought the salvation of the Gentiles was linked to the salvation of Israel and dependent upon it: "That the fate of the nations was inexorably and irreversibly bound up with that of Israel there was no doubt whatsoever. . . . What happens to the Gentiles is conditional upon, and conditioned by, what happens to Israel."[7] Furthermore, it is important to stress that in Jewish thought, God's promises of salvation had to do first and foremost with a *nation* or a *people* as a whole rather than with isolated individuals: "Individual Jews would find their own 'salvation' through their membership within Israel, that is, within the covenant; covenant membership in the present was the guarantee (more or less) of 'salvation' in the future."[8]

A second difference between Jewish soteriology and that of later Christian thought is that, as Wright has stressed, the hope of Israel was not that the world and human history might come to an end but that the new age of redemption might arrive. Salvation was defined not in terms of a "*post mortem* disembodied bliss*" but as the fulfillment of the promises made by God of old regarding a new historical reality in which his people would enjoy freedom, peace, abundance, and happiness in the land he had given them.[9]

The manner in which the Jewish people conceived of the forgiveness of sins also reflects this different understanding of redemption. In Christian thought divine forgiveness tends to be defined in relatively abstract terms, usually having to do with assurance of eternal salvation after death and some sort of inner peace with God in the present. For ancient Jews, however, divine forgiveness was tied to concrete events in the history of individuals or the people as a whole. The common belief was that when things went well for people, either they were free from sin or God had forgiven them their sins. In contrast, when people suffered, it was often thought that God was chastising or disciplining them for some sin as yet unforgiven. Those who offered sacrifices, for example, were not merely seeking some inner spiritual assurance that they were "right with God" or that God would overlook their sins at the final judgment, but that God might deliver them from hardships in their everyday life and grant them concrete blessings, often of a material sort. As Wright observes, the same understanding of the forgiveness of sins applied to the nation as a whole: the people of Israel would know that God had forgiven their sins when he redeemed them from the plight they were suffering on account of those sins. Thus *redemption* and *forgiveness* of sins were virtually synonymous terms.[10]

Finally, it should be stressed that the idea of some type of objective salvation that might be accomplished "in principle" or "potentially" before becoming an "actual" reality was foreign to the first-century Jewish worldview. There we do not encounter the kind of realized eschatologies often found in later Christian theology, according to which some type of redemption of humanity or creation has already taken place in some hidden or invisible sphere—fallen human nature has been renewed, forgiveness of sins has been attained definitively, the powers of evil have been vanquished, or people have been transferred into a new age. It was obvious to all that God had not yet forgiven Israel's sins or acted to redeem Israel; nor had the awaited transformation of the world and the ultimate defeat of evil taken place. The dead had not yet been raised, those living in the diaspora had not yet been brought home, and Israel had not yet been delivered from its foreign oppressors. None of these things can readily be spoken of as having occurred "potentially" but not "actually," or in an objective, universal manner that now calls for a subjective response. In first-century Jewish thought, the people and the world in general remained in the "present age" *(ha-'olam hazeh),* characterized by suffering, sin, and evil; the "age to come" *(ha-'olam haba')* had not yet arrived in any sense.[11]

Obedience as the Condition for Salvation

According to the understanding of salvation just outlined, what was necessary for the Jewish people to attain the blessings promised to them in the covenant was that they be obedient to the commandments God had given them. This idea runs throughout the Hebrew Scriptures and the ancient Jewish writings from beginning to end. Yet does this mean that the ancient Jews believed they could *earn* their salvation by keeping the commandments? In

Paul and Palestinian Judaism, E. P. Sanders maintains that although obedience was consistently believed to be the *"conditio sine qua non* of salvation,"[12] the Jewish people did not believe that they could *earn* their salvation through that obedience.

Precisely how to reconcile these apparently conflicting affirmations, of course, is problematic. It appears to be said at one and the same time that in Jewish thought salvation *does* depend on whether the people obey God and that it *does not*. Sanders attempted to resolve this problem by making a distinction between "getting in" and "staying in." According to Sanders, "getting in" depends entirely on divine grace and election in Jewish thought, and "staying in" on obedience to the commandments. In their minds the Jewish people were not attempting to obtain salvation through "works of the law" done in obedience to God's commands; instead, the common Jewish view was that "obedience maintains one's position in the covenant, but it does not *earn* God's grace as such. It simply keeps an individual in the group which is the recipient of God's grace."[13] Sanders calls this "covenantal nomism," which he defines as "the view that one's place in God's plan is established on the basis of the covenant and that the covenant requires as the proper response of man his obedience to its commandments, while providing means of atonement for transgressions."[14]

Yet, while all would agree with Sanders that in Jewish thought divine grace is operative *prior* to the people's response of obedience to God's will, once obedience is made the condition for "staying in," it appears that salvation is ultimately dependent on that obedience.[15] Members of God's people had to respond properly to the grace of God shown to them in election by doing God's will to the best of their abilities; those who refused to do so would lose their place among the elect and thus fail to attain salvation. This would mean that works of obedience are not just the *result* of God's gracious salvation, as Sanders affirms,[16] but also *merit* salvation.

Yet it is important to note that the idea Sanders consistently rejects is not that good works *merit* or *deserve* salvation, but that they *earn* salvation; his choice of the word "earn" seems to be deliberate. At first glance, there may seem to be no real difference between these terms. To speak of "earning" salvation, however, implies the possibility of making some rightful claim on God on the basis of good works, as if Israel's God had set up a system in which he put himself under *obligation* to save those who would do the prescribed works, or in which fulfillment of the commandments would *automatically and in itself* bring about justification and salvation. In that case, people could now save themselves, and God's mercy and grace would cease to be operative; salvation would be simply a matter of fulfilling the necessary requirements, and once those requirements had been fulfilled, salvation would be ensured or "earned."

Sanders is certainly correct to insist that such a view runs contrary to Jewish thought. The Hebrew Scriptures and extant ancient Jewish literature consistently present Israel's God as *intensely personal, absolutely sovereign,* and *constantly active in human history.* Virtually everything that happens can in some way be attributed to God, either because God himself carries out certain acts, or because he allows certain things to happen. In the latter case, the fact that God has the power to prevent anything from happening means that even when God merely *allows* something to happen, it must be regarded as taking place according to God's will.[17] Thus, if an individual or a people in general suffer, it is because God has willed it to be so; were it not God's will, God would put an end to it. In Jewish thought, therefore, there is no independent, self-governing system to which God has subjected either himself or the world; God always remains free and sovereign and acts as he wishes in the world. If any kind of "natural laws" are said to exist, God is still believed to be above them and has the power to suspend them or act contrary to them; thus, whatever happens must still be attributed to God's will.

Precisely because of this understanding of God and God's relationship to the world, in Jewish thought the law was never seen as some autonomous system established by God, automatically meting out rewards and punishments. Much less is God himself subject to that law, as if God had put himself under obligation to reward acts of obedience and punish acts of disobedience. At times, if it serves God's purposes, God may not reward obedience but instead temporarily send suffering for the righteous, just as God often refrains from punishing sins or overlooks them; and when God does these things, he is not regarded as acting contrary to justice. Undoubtedly, because God is just, one can trust that in the end God will reward obedience and punish disobedience, but how and when he will do this are ultimately for God alone to decide.[18] In Jewish thought, therefore, human deeds do indeed *deserve* or *merit* certain responses from God (even though they do not *earn* any reward); ultimately, acts of obedience merit reward from God, but disobedience merits chastisement. Nevertheless, it is always up to God to decide precisely what rewards and punishments those deeds merit. This depends on God's sovereign and inscrutable will, which human beings cannot always understand. Of course, any degree of obedience is far below what God really desires and commanded, so that even when God deems certain acts of obedience as "deserving" or "meriting" salvation or some other reward, God was being gracious, merciful, and forgiving, accepting as "good" works those that are never entirely so.

In fact, as Sanders demonstrates, in Jewish thought what ultimately matters to God is not perfection, which is impossible for human beings, but the commitment of the individual to doing God's will; in Rabbinic language, this is referred to as "confessing the commandments."[19] The general consensus among Jews was that all who were committed to remaining in the covenant relationship and obeying the law would be saved; those who did so were counted among the "righteous" and regarded as "true Israel."[20] No one could keep the commandments perfectly, nor was one expected to do so in order to be justified before God and saved. Had God expected and demanded absolute perfection in keeping the commandments, God would never have made provisions for atonement to be made so that the people might seek forgiveness when they had sinned.

This, however, leads us back to the question of what was necessary for Israel to be redeemed. If Israel's redemption depended on the people's obedience to the commandments, then the fact that this redemption had not come meant that their obedience was not yet adequate or sufficient in God's eyes; if it had been, then God would already have delivered his people. Evidently, God had not yet forgiven their sins but was still disciplining them and attempting to purify them from their sinful ways. What was required, therefore, was that the people become *more* obedient, observing the commandments more diligently, and perhaps that a greater *portion* of the Jewish people become obedient; in this case, God was "delaying in order to give time for more people to repent."[21]

This way of thinking led to a program of what Wright has labeled "Torah-intensification." This involved studying the law more meticulously to make sure that each and every commandment was being interpreted correctly so as to be kept properly, as well as striving to bring about in others a greater observance of the law by calling them to repentance (*teshubah*) and obedience and instructing them as to what proper law-observance involved. Groups such as the Essenes and the Pharisees practiced a stricter obedience to God's commandments, evidently hoping that this would move God to act to redeem his people; the Pharisees, scribes, and others may also have been concerned about bringing about the proper observance of Torah in their fellow Jews.[22] Nevertheless, while all agreed that God would rescue from their enemies those who were faithful to YHWH's covenant and the Torah, [23] there was much disagreement as to precisely how the commandments of the Torah were to be interpreted, and as to which Jews were actually being faithful to the Torah.

Yet the fact that even though the people had been striving for centuries to observe the commandments, the awaited redemption had not yet come led some to the conclusion that something else was necessary: an act of divine grace. God had to *give* Israel the obedience he required of them. This idea is found already in the prophetic writings, most notably Jeremiah, who spoke of God's putting his law within his people and writing it upon their hearts (31:33–34), and Ezekiel, who promised that God would remove the hearts of stone from his people and replace them with hearts of flesh, and would pour out his Spirit upon them (36:26–27). The same idea runs throughout the literature of the Second Temple period.[24] Generally, however, the expectation seems to have been that this would take place in the coming age rather than in the present one.

This meant that in the end, all the Jewish people could do was keep the commandments to the best of their abilities and wait, trusting that their God would eventually keep his promises. God had not yet chosen to redeem his people because they were "riddled with corruption, still undeserving of redemption," and needed to be purified and refined further; what was expected on their part was simply "to be patient and faithful, to keep the covenant with all their might, trusting him to act soon to vindicate them at last."[25] To trust in God, of course, meant submitting to God's will, both in the passive sense of accepting with a spirit of humble resignation whatever God determined and in the active sense of doing what God commanded. This means that in Jewish thought, the people of Israel would be saved *by faith*, that is, merely by putting their future in God's hands. It was not a question of faith versus works, as if the two were mutually exclusive, but a question of faith and trust in God manifested in lives dedicated to doing the works God commanded and having confidence that sooner or later God would fulfill his promises.

Atonement and Sacrifice

If, in Jewish thought, obedience to the commandments was the condition for salvation, was anything else required as well? Virtually all of the stories of salvation considered in chapter 1 posit another condition as necessary for salvation, namely, the work of God in Jesus Christ, particularly his death and resurrection. According to these stories, without Christ it was impossible for sin, death, and evil to be overcome and for human beings to be saved. In order to claim that such an idea is in continuity with Jewish thought, Christian scholars have often maintained that in addition to obedience to the law, there was a further condition for salvation in Judaism, namely, that atonement for sins be made, particularly through some type of bloodshed or death. The basis for such a claim has generally been located in Jewish beliefs concerning sacrifices as well as in the death of righteous persons such as martyrs.

Whether consciously or not, discussions among Christian scholars on the meaning of and need for atoning sacrifices have generally taken as a starting point one or more of the explanations of redemption considered in chapter 1. This is to work backwards: ideas that form the basis for certain interpretations of Jesus' death are read back into the biblical texts regarding sacrifice so as to argue that the same ideas are behind ancient Jewish beliefs concerning sacrifice. Thus, if Jesus' death is understood according to the categories of satisfaction and substitution, it is argued that in ancient Israel, sacrifices were understood as involving the death of an animal as a substitute for the persons who had sinned and thus deserved death: sinners themselves were spared this penalty when the animal victim endured it in their place.[26] Although such an understanding of sacrifice is never articulated explicitly in the Hebrew Scriptures, those who argue in favor of it support their view by appealing to the ritual in which the sinner laid hands on the animal to be sacrificed, as well as the rite of the scapegoat on the Day of Atonement. They also claim that Isaiah 53 suggests this idea in speaking of the suffering servant bearing the sins and chastisement of God's people. These same ideas are then applied to Christ's death: like the scapegoat, the sacrificial victims, or the suffering servant, Christ is said to have taken upon himself the penalty or consequences of human sin as humanity's substitute, thus delivering human beings from that penalty or those consequences.

Other understandings of sacrifice have also been read back into the Hebrew Scriptures. James D. G. Dunn, for example, attributes to Paul an understanding of sacrifice revolving around ideas from the physical doctrine of redemption and the notion of participation. According to this view, as "the sinner's sin was transferred to the spotless sacrifice, so the spotless life of the sacrifice was transferred (or reckoned) to the sinner."[27] Behind this interpretation of sacrifice is an understanding of Christ's work according to which he takes on the fallen humanity common to all, in which sin has inhered as a type of "malignant, poisonous organism" or "cancer." Christ then delivers that humanity from its fallen condition by destroying the "cancer" of sin in it through his death and then raising it to new life, so that all may participate in it. This involves a type of "exchange" between Christ and human beings.[28] Others have argued for what is in effect a "moral influence" understanding of sacrifice, in which the objective of presenting sacrificial offerings was to bring people to recognize their sin, repent, and lead a new life; Christ's sacrificial death is then understood in the same way.[29] Of course, many other interpretations of the meaning and purpose of sacrificial offerings have been proposed as well, by both Jewish and Christian scholars,[30] but the interest of the latter in the subject has generally been to identify ideas that can then be used to interpret Jesus' death in sacrificial terms.

Views of sacrifice such as these are problematic for several reasons. First, they are based on a great deal of speculation concerning certain passages from the Hebrew Scriptures that are quite ambiguous and therefore are susceptible to having all sorts of ideas read back into them. Thus, even Dunn must admit that his explanation of how sacrifice "works" is "speculative" and "cannot be traced back firmly to a Hebrew theology of sacrifice."[31] In fact, Dunn readily acknowledges that he is proceeding in reverse order, looking first to Paul's epistles to argue that Paul "had a fairly well-defined theory of sacrifice" so as then to "read back Paul's understanding of sacrifice" into the Old Testament texts regarding sacrificial rites.[32]

This appears to be precisely what has happened with the idea of substitution. Considerable evidence has been adduced against the claim that the Jews of antiquity understood sacrifice in terms of an animal's vicariously suffering the penalty or consequences of the sin of those who offered the sacrifice.[33] Such an idea is not only absent from the Old Testament texts but also runs counter to them. According to the Mosaic law, a person who had committed a sin for which the penalty was death could not avert the death penalty by offering an animal substitute in his or her place. Conversely, those sins for which expiatory sacrifices were offered were generally inadvertent sins, not sins deserving of death. While a person who had not offered the proper sacrifice for sin might be regarded as impure and be barred from participation in Israel's worship, he or she was certainly not subject to a death sentence. Thus, expiatory sacrifices did not involve substitutionary killing. This is further demonstrated by the fact that, according to Lev 5:11–13, those who could not afford an animal could offer up instead "one-tenth of an ephah of choice flour for a sin offering"; according to the text, the result of this was that atonement was made and the sin forgiven. Obviously, this did not involve putting the flour to death or transferring sins to it, so it can hardly be claimed that "a death was necessary to compensate for even an inadvertent sin."[34] Other sacrifices in which animals were put to death, such as the peace offering, were not for expiation and atonement, nor were they believed to procure forgiveness; thus, it can hardly be claimed that those animal victims were also thought to be killed as substitutes.

Likewise, there is no clear evidence that the Jews believed that sins were literally transferred to the animal victim, as, for example, Dunn has claimed.[35] The only text that comes close to such an idea is Lev 16:20–22, which describes the scapegoat ritual of the annual Day of Atonement. There it is prescribed that the high priest is to lay both hands on the head of the live goat (rather than only one hand, as in all the other sacrifices), confess the sins of the people, and then send the goat out to the wilderness so as to bear away the people's iniquities. This goat, however, was not sacrificed; nor is it ever said in the biblical texts that the other goat (or any other animal) bore the sins and iniquities of the people when it was sacrificed. Moreover, following the expiatory sacrifices, which generally involved rituals with the animal victim's blood, the remains of the animal were not believed to become impure; instead, the animal's remains continued to be regarded as "most holy" (Lev 6:29), and its flesh was eaten by the priests.[36] This means that the victim was not believed to have been contaminated by having the sinner's sin or guilt transferred to it.

Perhaps the most serious problem with views such as these, however, is that they ultimately conceive of sacrifice in mechanical fashion, as if killing an animal victim automatically produced some "effect," such as divine forgiveness, atonement, or the eradication of sin as a power. Thus, proponents of such views commonly speak of the "mechanism" by which sin is dealt with and for-giveness obtained, or discuss how sacrifice "works."[37] When sin is understood in terms of guilt, liability to punishment, or subjection to certain inevitable consequences, then its removal is said to be brought about merely by having a substitute assume the guilt and endure the punishment or consequences in the place of the guilty. Similarly, to speak of sin as a "malignant, poisonous organism" or a "cancer" that can be transferred from a person to an animal so as to be eliminated, or as some type of impure substance that can be washed off or absorbed by blood, is to ascribe to sin an objective existence of its own, as if it could be dealt with in the same way that cancerous tumors are treated by surgery or chemotherapy, or that dirt is washed away by water and deter-gent. Likewise, to say that "the death caused by sin and uncleanness is annulled by substitutionary death" is in effect to posit a mechanical, cause-and-effect understanding of sacrifice.[38]

Often it is argued that such views of sacrifice are neither mechanical nor magical, first, because something such as faith or repentance was believed to be necessary for the rite to be efficacious and, second, because the rite was thought to be efficacious only because God had chosen to grant it such efficacy.[39] Once it is said that faith or repentance is necessary, however, then divine forgiveness ultimately is made to depend not on the rite but on the presence of faith or repentance in the one offering the sacrifice, since this is the determining fac-tor: if a sacrifice was offered without faith or repentance, then supposedly the mechanics would not "work" and the sacrifice actually effected nothing. In this way, faith and repentance are viewed as part of a "formula" that, together with the sacrificial offerings and rites, would automatically or unfailingly have the "effect" of obtaining forgiveness of sins. This conveys once again the idea that God had set up a system by which people could save themselves by obtain-ing or even purchasing his favor, or by carrying out quasi-magical rites that in themselves would eliminate sin or guilt, as long as they were carried out in the proper spirit. This involves a loss of sovereignty on God's part, since God must now respect the system he established, or merely stand back and let that system "work" to eliminate sin and guilt without intervening. It also implies that God is no longer willing or able to forgive sins without a proper sacrificial rite being carried out, and that God has granted some "power" to sacrificial offerings or sacrificial blood, so that in themselves sacrifices can achieve their objective.

In both biblical and Jewish thought, Israel's God did not *need* sacrifices or sacrificial blood in order to forgive; nor had he bound himself irreversibly to a system that he was now obliged to respect. It was always up to God to judge whether the proper repentance was present in the hearts of his people when they presented him their offerings, and to grant or deny forgiveness as appropriate, according to his purposes. Once again, there could be no objective criteria independent of God that might determine whether there was the proper spirit of repentance in the hearts of those who offered sacrifices. Thus, not even faith, repentance, and obedience could automatically or unfailingly have the "effect" of obtaining forgiveness of sins through the sacrificial rites. The fact that the Jews were able to replace the sacrificial means of atonement by other means when it was not possible to present sacrifices is further evidence that it was not the sacrificial offerings themselves that were believed to obtain divine forgiveness but the spirit of repentance and obedience of which they were an expression. The Essenes, for example, substituted prayer and good deeds for sacrifices of atonement when they believed that the Temple system had become corrupt, while the Rabbis later also came to stress other means of repentance following the destruction of the Temple, "substituting study for sacrifice."[40] Conversely, there were times when Israel apparently *was* carrying out properly the sacrificial rites prescribed by the Torah, yet nevertheless came under God's judgment, such as when Jerusalem and the Temple were destroyed by the Babylonian army. Obviously, merely carrying out those rites neither ensured forgiveness nor effected atonement for or purification from the sins of God's people. This point is repeatedly stressed by the prophets, who insist that what truly pleases and appeases God are not sacrificial offerings in themselves but the practice of justice, mercy, and righteousness in accordance with God's will (e.g., Isa 1:10–17; Hos 6:6; Mic 6:6–8).

As to the "inner rationale" of sacrifices, it has often been noted that the ancient Jews themselves recognized that it was not possible to understand the logic behind all of the sacrificial laws.[41] While there was obviously much symbolism in the sacrificial system that was comprehensible to all, in the end what mattered was that God had chosen to command sacrifices, and the people were simply to obey, whether or not they understood.

It is also important to stress that the central idea regarding sacrifices was not "the killing of animals and birds," as N. T. Wright affirms.[42] Animals and birds were slaughtered only in order to be presented as *offerings* to God, and these offerings were seen as accompanying and representing *acts of prayer*. The Temple was a "house of prayer" (Isa 56:7) where prayers were raised up to God together with incense and sacrificial offerings (Ps 141:2). In 1 Kings 8:22–53, which relates the dedication of the Temple by Solomon and his prayer to God, the idea is repeatedly stressed that the function of the Temple was to be a place where the Israelites might present their supplications before God, who had graciously chosen to make his name and presence dwell there (cf. 2 Chron 7:15). This is precisely the understanding of sacrifice that we find in Josephus, who attributes to Solomon the following prayer on the occasion of the Temple's dedication:

> But I have built this temple to Thy name so that from it we may, when sacrificing and seeking good omens, send up our prayers into the air to Thee, and may ever be persuaded that Thou art present and not far removed. . . . We cannot but praise Thy greatness and give thanks for Thy kindnesses to our house and the Hebrew people, for with what other thing is it more fitting for us to appease Thee when wrathful, and, when ill disposed, to make Thee gracious than with our voice, which we have from the air, and know to ascend again through this element?[43]

Thus, according to Josephus, what actually pleased Israel's God were the prayers of thanksgiving and praise offered up to him; likewise, what appeased God's anger and obtained God's favor were not the offerings themselves but the people's "voice," that is, the prayer of confession and repentance that ascended to God together with the offerings. Certainly the offerings were also believed to please God, but this was because they were material expressions of the sincerity of the people's prayers and signs of their submission and obedience in carrying out the sacrifices God had commanded in the way he had ordained. The fact that sacrificial offerings were in essence acts of prayer accompanied by gifts to God means that it is inappropriate to ask how sacrifice "works," just as it would be inappropriate to ask how prayer "works." In Jewish thought, God cannot be manipulated through prayer or sacrifice, nor can God's favor be bought. God merely promised to accept offerings presented to him with the right spirit and to grant forgiveness to those making such offerings, just as he promised to hear and answer petitions made to him with a pure heart.[44]

The priests who approached God in representation of the people as a whole or of individuals in particular, presenting sacrifices on their behalf, were also believed to be offering up petitions and prayers to God. As Roland de Vaux observes regarding ancient Israel, when the priest "took the blood and flesh of victims to the altar, or burned incense upon the altar, he was presenting to God the prayers and petitions of the faithful."[45] He further notes that it is "quite certain" that "in Israel cultic actions were accompanied by words," including the hymns that were sung while offerings were being made to God.[46]

This was undoubtedly the case in the first century as well. The Jewish people offered up their prayers every morning and evening at the same hours in which the daily offerings were being presented to God, so that those prayers might rise up to God together with the smoke and incense from the sacrificial offerings (Ps 141:2; cf. Rev 8:4). As Sanders has indicated, in describing the Day of Atonement rite, the Mishnah mentions the petitions that accompanied each part of the rite, including the prayer of confession made by the priest and prayers "for the Law, for the Temple-Service, for the Thanksgiving, for the Forgiveness of Sin, and for the Temple separately, and for the Israelites separately, and for the priests separately; and for the rest a [general] prayer."[47] Sanders also refers to other Rabbinic sources, as well as the writings of Philo, Ben Sira, and Josephus, which give evidence of the centrality of prayer in the sacrificial rites.[48] Stanislas Lyonnet and Royden Keith Yerkes both note that in Greek and Latin, from at least the time of the translation of the Septuagint to the time of the church fathers, "expiation" was regularly understood in terms of intercession.[49] Similarly, Adolf Büchler observes that "the sprinkling of the blood of the daily burnt-offering was accompanied by prayers for forgiveness," and in this regard quotes Jubilees 6:14: "They shall observe it throughout their generations, so that they may continue supplicating on your behalf with blood before the altar; every day and at the time of morning and evening they shall seek forgiveness on your behalf perpetually before the Lord."[50]

Of course, many other rituals were involved in the presentation of sacrificial offerings in the Jerusalem Temple. All of them, however, should be understood in *symbolic* terms. They symbolized such things as the identification of the worshipers with the offerings presented on their behalf; the sincerity of the persons presenting sacrifices and petitions; the purification of certain people, places, and objects; and also repentance, obedience, and divine forgiveness. The scapegoat rite, for example, must be understood as merely symbolizing the manner in which Israel's God graciously removed the people's sins from his sight for good. However, it was recognized that if God considered that his people were not sufficiently repentant and were not committed to living according to his will, even though they performed the rite, he would not remove their sins from his sight. This makes it clear that this rite in itself was not believed to accomplish or effect remission of sins. What took away guilt and sin was not some mechanical or magical transfer of these things to a goat but the spirit of obedience and repentance that was expressed through the rite, as well as in other ways. In the case of the sin offerings, the sacrifice was seen as an expression of the sincerity of the repentance of the people or person offering it; the sprinkling, smearing, and pouring out of blood no doubt symbolized at least in part the gravity of the offense, since the price paid by the offerers was very high. The fact that in this case the offerers received nothing of the remains after the sacrificial rite also served to underscore the cost involved, since they derived no material benefit from the rite.

Similar observations must be made with regard to the blood used in sacrificial rites. While sacrificial blood was certainly considered holy, in first-century Judaism it was not believed to have "atoning efficacy" or "power" to obtain divine forgiveness.[51] God was not obligated to forgive just because blood had been shed or offered to him, nor had God granted sacrificial blood such "power" over himself. There is no reason to see in the application of blood to people, places, or objects anything more than a symbolic act, representing, among other things, the manner in which sins were washed away by God.

Those supporting the idea that blood itself was believed to bring about the "effect" of forgiveness have often cited Lev 17:11 in support of their view: "For the life of the flesh is in the blood; and I have given it to you for making atonement for your lives on the altar; for, as life, it is the blood that makes atonement." In reality, however, all this passage affirms is that the blood belongs to God, as life itself does, but that God allows it to be used in a sacrificial context.[52] It "makes atonement" only in the sense that it is used in the atonement rites prescribed by God, to which the divine promises of forgiveness are attached; because it is the "life" of the victim, it is the most precious of all substances, and thus it is fitting that it be used in these rites. Yet, strictly speaking, what atoned in biblical and Jewish thought was the spirit of repentance and submission to God's will that was expressed through the performance of the *whole rite*. If that spirit was not being manifested in the people's behavior, then no matter how much blood was shed, there was no forgiveness, because it was not the blood itself that procured remission of sins or atonement.

Suffering, Death, Atonement, and Redemption

In addition to the sacrificial means of atonement God had provided, in ancient Jewish thought there were other ways to atone for sin. Sanders, for example, mentions that suffering and death were believed to be atoning. Yet this idea has also been frequently misunderstood. In support of the view that the death of a righteous man could make atonement for others, scholars often cite the examples of the deaths of Eleazar and his sons in 2 Maccabees and 4 Maccabees.[53] In 4 Macc 6:27–29, as he was about to die, Eleazar prayed, "You know, O God, that though I might have saved myself, I am dying in burning torments for the sake of the law. Be merciful to your people, and let our punishment suffice for them. Make my blood their purification [*hilastērion*], and take my life in exchange for theirs." Later on, the author of the book concludes, "Because of them our enemies did not rule over our nation, the tyrant was punished, and the homeland purified—they having become, as it were, a ransom [*antipsychon*] for the sin of our nation. And through the blood of those devout ones and their death as an atoning sacrifice [*hilastērion*], divine Providence preserved Israel that previously had been mistreated" (17:20–22). Some have regarded these passages as supporting a penal substitution view of atonement, as if Eleazar and his sons were believed to have undergone the divine punishment of death for the sins of the people in their place, so as to procure their salvation or deliverance.

As Sanders stresses, however, both suffering and death were atoning only when accompanied by repentance and a commitment to obey God's laws.[54] What was atoning about the suffering and death of the Maccabean martyrs, therefore, was the fact that in the midst of persecution and torments, they remained committed to God's laws until the end and inspired others to repentance and obedience as well.[55] According to the author of 2 Maccabees, those who were suffering believed that this was a chastisement sent from God: "These punishments were designed not to destroy but to discipline our people. In fact, it is a sign of great kindness not to let the impious alone for long, but to punish them immediately. . . . Although [the Lord] disciplines us with calamities, he does not forsake his own people" (2 Macc 6:12–13, 16). "For we are suffering because of our own sins. And if our living Lord is angry for a little while, to rebuke and discipline us, he will again be reconciled with his own servants" (2 Macc 7:32–33; cf. 4:16–17; 5:17, 20; 7:18). Just as in

Rabbinic thought "chastisements lead one to repent and seek God,"[56] so the sufferings experienced by the Jewish people were understood as having the purpose of testing their commitment to God's will and bringing them back to God. According to both 2 and 4 Maccabees, this is what the deaths of Eleazar and his sons helped accomplish: they inspired others to obey by leaving "a noble example of how to die a good death willingly and nobly for the revered and holy laws" (2 Macc 6:28) and "strengthened [the people's] loyalty to the law through [their] glorious endurance" (4 Macc 7:9).

It is important to note that the words attributed to Eleazar in the passages quoted above are presented as *a prayer on behalf of others*.[57] Basically, Eleazar was asking God to put away his wrath at the people's sins because of his faithfulness to God's will to the point of suffering torments and death; this demonstrated that the punishments sent by God had accomplished their end of bringing about the obedience God desired. Because of Eleazar's obedience and his prayer on behalf of the nation, God put an end to the chastisements and delivered the people from their oppression under Antiochus. In this way God was "wholly reconciled with his servants" (2 Macc 8:29). The basis for Eleazar's petition and God's favorable response to it was therefore the commitment to obedience shown first by Eleazar and then by others as a result of his unbending faithfulness to God's law. In Jewish thought *this was the only thing that could satisfy and please God and turn away God's wrath*. Eleazar's death was thus an "atonement" or "propitiation" (*hilastērion*) and a "ransom," because it was the expression and cause of repentance and a renewed commitment to God's will on the part of God's people, as well as a petition on their behalf. It was this that pleased God and moved God to be reconciled to them, putting away his anger at their sins and redeeming them from their afflictions. When the author of 4 Maccabees ascribes Israel's purification and preservation to the martyrs' "blood," it is clear that he has in mind their faithfulness unto death in keeping God's law, and not merely their death per se, as if this in itself had fulfilled some condition necessary for God to save the people. There is no hint here of the idea that Eleazar's life or the punishment he endured was equivalent to what the people owed for their sins, or that it was not possible for God to forgive and redeem the people until his wrath had been exhausted by being poured out on Eleazar as their substitute. God had been punishing the people, not for *his own* sake, but for *theirs*.

Of course, this story also illustrates the Jewish belief that the righteousness of one might in some sense avail for others; but behind this belief was the conviction that God listens to the prayers of the righteous and grants them what they ask for others, especially those who are less worthy of having their petitions heard. A similar idea is that at times God mercifully "suspends his judgment against the world for the sake of a few,"[58] just as God suspended the chastisement of Israel for the sake of a few in the story of the Maccabean martyrs. Neither one of these ideas, however, contradicts the notion that in the end repentance and a commitment to doing God's will are necessary in order for one to enjoy God's favor and have a share in Israel's redemption.

Some have argued that according to ancient Jewish sources, before Israel could be redeemed, a period of intense tribulation would need to come upon Israel and the world, namely, the "messianic travail" or "messianic woes" that would precede the end of the present age.[59] While there is undoubtedly a basis for such a belief in ancient Judaism, this must be properly understood. The purpose of this tribulation was to purif and test God's people, separating those truly committed to God's will from those who were not; only those who remained obedient and faithful would be saved. Thus, the condition for salvation was still a commitment on the part of the people to do God's will. Furthermore, it should be stressed that this commitment had to be *their own* and not that of some representative or substitute. For a substitute to endure this tribulation in the place of others would defeat its purpose entirely, since then it would not serve to separate the righteous from the unrighteous. God wanted *all* of his people to be obedient and practice righteousness, not merely one person to do this in their place.

There is thus no convincing basis for arguing that something besides repentance and obedience was necessary for God to bring about Israel's salvation. Even if the need for some type of atonement for past sins is posited, it must be remembered that *what atoned for sins were precisely repentance and a commitment to obedience on the part of the people*. These were the only things that could please and satisfy God and take away God's anger at the people's sins. As Sanders emphasizes, "For those in the covenant, repentance was the sovereign means of atonement. . . . It is virtually impossible to find any exceptions to the rule that repentance atones."[60]

Once again, all of this must be seen against the background of the Jewish belief in the absolute sovereignty of God: in Jewish thought, *there is no type of necessity to which Israel's God is subject.* In contrast, the arguments for necessity in later Christian thought are based on foundational assumptions regarding the nature of God or the created order. These assumptions are used to argue that God is subject to various limitations that make it impossible for him to bring about human salvation unless certain conditions are met. For example, as mentioned in chapter 1, it is often said that God *by nature* must be just, and therefore his justice prohibits him from forgiving human sins freely without requiring satisfaction or punishment, or from overpowering Satan without treating him fairly. Arguments based on the nature of the created order similarly maintain that fallen human nature could be restored only from within, or that the only way for human beings to die to sin and death and rise to the life of the new age was for a particular death and resurrection to occur in which they might participate. In both cases, foundational arguments are used to claim that God is subject to certain natural laws or to the laws of the divine nature (as defined by human beings), so as to limit what God *can* do or determine what he *must* do in order to save human beings. These foundational arguments then provide the basis for Christian theologians to argue for the necessity of God's sending his Son in order to save sinful humanity, and to claim that in no other way could the conditions necessary for salvation be fulfilled. Such arguments for necessity are then read back into ancient Jewish thought so as to affirm that without bloody sacrifices it was impossible to attain divine forgiveness, or that without the death of a righteous martyr or the suffering of the great tribulation, no redemption could come.

Discussions such as these concerning what God can and cannot do are for the most part foreign to both biblical and Jewish thought, in which Israel's God is consistently viewed as almighty and capable of doing whatever he wills. According to this view, God is subject to nothing (including God's own nature) that might prevent him from redeeming Israel or the world at any time and in any way he chooses.[61] There was no reason why God might not forgive sins freely without demanding sacrifice, satisfaction, or punishment for sin, or overthrow the powers of evil by a mere fiat, or renew sinful human nature by pouring out the Holy Spirit on human beings so as to transform their hearts. Nothing prevented God from raising the dead at any moment and bestowing immortality on those raised, making the corruptible incorruptible with the same power he employed when creating the universe. To accomplish this it was not necessary first for God to infuse some "resurrection-principle" into the bodies of those to be raised to life, introduce some mysterious divine power into human flesh, or unite the "divine" with the "human" (an idea particularly foreign to Jewish thought). Israel's God was capable of bringing about the promises of salvation he had made at any moment he wished; the reason *why* he had not done so ultimately remained a mystery. Certainly, God's behavior in relation to his people was believed to be consistent, loving, just, and fair rather than arbitrary or capricious; however, to say that he *is* loving, just, and fair is not the same as arguing that he *must* be so. To affirm the latter would once again involve positing certain foundational philosophical assumptions so as to argue that *by necessity* God must behave a certain way, either because God is subject to the laws of his own nature or because by means of the covenant God has irreversibly bound himself to certain laws regarding the way he will relate to others, so that he is no longer free to act in any way he desires. All of this runs counter to Jewish beliefs, in which nothing limits what God can do. The only condition necessary for salvation to occur is that God will it to occur.

To affirm this does not contradict the claim that the condition for Israel's redemption in Jewish thought was that the people manifest the proper spirit of repentance and obedience. While it was believed that Israel's God desired to see this occur and had delayed Israel's redemption because he was not yet satisfied with his people's response to all of his gracious activity, there was still nothing above or superior to God that could prevent him from redeeming Israel at any time. God alone could determine what response was sufficient for him to act to redeem, and he could graciously accept any degree of obedience as satisfactory, since all human obedience was ultimately imperfect. Furthermore, as noted above, even Israel's response of obedience ultimately depended on God and would be the result of God's activity of purifying his people and graciously giving them new hearts and spirits, rather than something the Jewish people would bring about entirely on their own. Thus, in the ancient Jewish worldview we simply do not find the type of foundational arguments for necessity characteristic of later Christian thought, which are ultimately attempts to demonstrate that without the incarnation, life, death, and resurrection of God's Son, human salvation would have been impossible.

CHAPTER 3
The Early Christian Story of Redemption

For a number of years prior to Paul's experience on the road to Damascus, the community of those who had believed in Jesus of Nazareth as the promised Messiah had been telling a story of redemption that revolved around Jesus, yet was in close continuity with the Jewish story of redemption considered in chapter 2. Because of our sources, however, any attempt to reconstruct the early Christian story encounters certain difficulties. The earliest Christian writings we have, of course, are the Pauline epistles, but there we find only scattered bits and pieces of that story—brief allusions to it, but no orderly, comprehensive, or systematic presentation of it. Most of the other New Testament writings present the same problem, and they were probably written at least a couple of decades after Paul's letters.

The only first-century works that *do* contain all of the basic elements of a story of redemption revolving around Jesus of Nazareth in a somewhat orderly fashion are the Gospels and Acts. In spite of their later date, however, these writings unquestionably make use of much traditional material that goes back to the first Christian communities and even to Jesus himself, although there is much disagreement and uncertainty as to how much of that material reflects later developments in the theology of the evangelists or of the Christian communities to which they belonged. Most problematic in this regard is the Fourth Gospel, probably the last to be written, which clearly contains many ideas that are the product of later theological reflection on the part of the author and the community to which he belonged.

All of this means that if we want to reconstruct in broad terms the early Christian story of redemption that preceded Paul, outside of Paul's epistles themselves our best sources will be the Synoptic Gospels and the Acts of the Apostles (particularly the passages that purport to describe the early Christian proclamation), in spite of the problems they present. Undoubtedly, we must employ them with caution and discernment so as to avoid ascribing to the early tradition elements that are evidently later developments. Here we will look primarily at the most common and general elements of the story presented in these writings as well as those that appear most frequently and are found in more than one of these sources. It seems logical to assume that the elements most strongly attested in the Synoptics and Acts are more likely to have formed part of the early Christian story of redemption. In this chapter, we will examine this story in the light of the Jewish story outlined in the previous chapter, attempting to discern similarities and differences between the two, and then draw some comparisons between the early Christian story as reconstructed here and the stories of redemption outlined in chapter 1.

Jesus and the Mosaic Law

According to the Synoptic Gospels, Jesus' ministry developed in some way out of that of John the Baptist.[1] There John is presented as directing a renewal movement among the Jewish people, calling on them to confess their sins and "bear fruits that befit repentance" (Matt 3:6, 8; Mark 1:4–5; Luke 3:8). Luke's portrayal of John's preaching, in which John tells people to share with those in need and to be honest in their dealings with others (Luke 3:10–14), suggests that John called people not only to a stricter obedience to the commandments of the Mosaic law but also to the principles underlying them. The fact that John retired to the desert and apparently did not enjoy good relationships with the Pharisees and teachers of the law also indicates that John's understanding of the repentance and obedience required was distinct from theirs. The repentance or conversion (*teshubah*) John preached was symbolized by a rite of baptism, which no doubt was understood in terms of purification as well as incorporation into a separate, special group of people distinct from other practicing Jews. This new group would constitute the "true Israel."[2] John's baptism of forgiveness may also have been understood as taking the place of sacrificial offerings for sin and "as an alternative to the Temple ritual."[3]

Matthew and Luke state that John told his listeners not to put any confidence in their descent from Abraham according to the flesh, implying that God's people were to be defined not in terms of physical ancestry but on the basis of obedience to God's will as defined by John. John's work, therefore, seems to have laid the groundwork both for Jesus' proclamation and that of Jesus' disciples following his death, in that membership in God's people was being defined in terms of a reinterpretation of what constituted true obedience to God's will.

Like John and other Jewish teachers of his day, Jesus is also said to have proclaimed the need for repentance.[4] With regard to the need to obey the commandments of the Mosaic law, however, we find a certain ambiguity that, according to the Gospels, dates back to the ministry of Jesus himself. On the one hand, the Synoptics never present Jesus as questioning the validity of the Torah as a whole or declaring it abolished. Matthew in particular insists that Jesus taught that he had not come to *abolish* the law in any one of its most minute points, but that the law and the commandments still had to be fulfilled (Matt 5:17–20; cf. Luke 16:17). On the other hand, according to the Gospels, Jesus' teaching and practice in relation to the law aroused a great deal of controversy and led many to accuse him of not respecting the law.[5]

A review of passages in the Synoptics that present conflicts over the law reveals that while Jesus' opponents are often presented as insisting on strict obedience to the literal commandments of the law (usually as interpreted according to their oral tradition), Jesus is presented as interpreting the commandments on the basis of a concern for human wholeness and well-being.[6] In Mark 2:23—3:6, for example, Jesus permits his disciples to pluck grain on the Sabbath in order to satisfy their hunger, and he heals a man with a withered hand on the Sabbath. When the Pharisees object, Jesus argues that "the sabbath was made for humankind, not humankind for the sabbath," and that what is lawful on the Sabbath is to "do good" and "save life." The idea here is that the law was given for the benefit of "humankind," in order to promote "life" and what is "good" for human beings. This same idea is found in other passages of the Synoptics. Jesus rebukes the Pharisees for using the law to oppress others or to justify failing to provide them with what they need, insisting that they have forgotten "the weightier matters of the law," such as justice, mercy, faith, and love (Matt 23:23; Mark 7:9–13; 12:40; Luke 6:32–36; 11:42). His teaching concerning what defiles a person is based on the same principle of avoiding any word or deed that injures others; it is this that matters more than mere observance of the Jewish dietary laws (Mark 7:14–23). He reinterprets the commandments that forbid killing, committing adultery, swearing falsely, and demanding an "eye for an eye," insisting that true fulfillment of these commandments involves much more than a literal observance (Matt 5:21–30, 33–42). Thus, for Jesus the law can be summed up by the commands to love God and to love others as oneself (Matt 7:12; 22:34–40; Luke 10:25–28).

Of course, as numerous scholars have pointed out, in Judaism there has always been a strong emphasis on the need to practice mercy, kindness, and love; in insisting on these things, Jesus was not going *against* Jewish tradition but was being *faithful* to it. Nevertheless, it does appear that at times Jesus was more willing than others to set aside a literal observance of the law in order to observe certain principles underlying the law. This involved giving priority to those principles and in some sense placing them *above* the commandments so as, in effect, to redefine what true obedience to the law consists of. It may be that this is how the "greater righteousness" mentioned by Jesus in Matt 5:20 should be understood: what God truly desires and commands is the observance of the principles of justice, love, and mercy on which the law is based, and at times this requires the freedom to set aside a literal observance of the commandments.[7]

In any case, it seems clear that Jesus was in continuity with the "covenantal nomism" common to Judaism, and that he also advocated some type of "Torah-intensification," as other Jews of his day did. The difference was that Jesus claimed that the stricter obedience to the commandments that God required had to do with fulfilling more closely the *purpose* or *intention* behind the commandments, namely, the concern for human wholeness and well-being. This led to Jesus' practice of openness toward those who were thought by many to be violating the law or were regarded as impure and "sinners," as well as his concern for those who were in need of healing or were suffering in other ways. For Jesus, to fulfill the law as God desired meant showing compassion by reaching out to such people to help restore them to wholeness rather than shunning or avoiding them. Those who opposed Jesus, however, apparently believed that in having fellowship with so-called sinners, he was undermining the law rather than upholding and observing it.

This stress on fulfilling the principles behind the commandments, together with Jesus' openness toward the impure and "sinners," may have laid the foundation for the work among the Gentiles after Jesus' death. If what really mattered was fulfilling the "spirit" of the law, then the literal observance of commandments regarding such things as circumcision and dietary prescriptions might become secondary, and Gentile "sinners" might be accepted into the community of the "righteous" without submitting to those commandments, just as Jewish "sinners" had been accepted by Jesus during his lifetime.[8]

Of course, to teach that fulfillment of the law involves obeying the principles behind the commandments is not necessarily to affirm that literal observance of the commandments is no longer necessary. As Matthew's Gospel, Acts, and Paul's letters clearly attest, some Jewish Christians continued to insist that the commandments of the Torah still had to be observed literally, at least by believers of Jewish origin. Others, however, evidently interpreted Jesus' teaching regarding the law to mean that it was admissible to set aside the "letter" of the law, at least in the case of certain commandments, so as to focus on observing its "spirit." No doubt it was possible for Jesus' teaching and practice regarding the law to be interpreted in either way, especially because he had ministered almost exclusively to Jews and thus had not dealt with the question of whether obedience to the Mosaic law was necessary on the part of Gentiles. The result of this ambiguity regarding the need for literal observance of the commandments led to infighting and division both in the Jewish communities and in the earliest Christian communities.

Jesus' Authority

According to the Synoptics, Jesus did not merely call on others to observe the commandments as he interpreted them; he also called them to *follow him*. As E. P. Sanders argues, this involved the implicit claim to be *above* the law in some sense: Jesus saw himself as "God's spokesman, God's agent," and "regarded himself as having full authority to speak and act on behalf of God."[9] The idea that Jesus carried out his ministry with full divine authority is stressed repeatedly in the Synoptics: it is said that he taught with authority (Matt 7:29; Mark 1:22; Luke 4:32), forgave sins (Mark 2:5–11), and cast out demons with authority (Mark 1:27; Luke 4:36), and that even the winds and the sea obeyed him (Mark 4:41). For this reason, the evangelists insist that Jesus must be listened to and obeyed; to reject him is to reject God himself

(Matt 10:40; Mark 8:38; 9:37; 13:31; Luke 6:47; 10:16). Jesus' followers are to take *his* yoke upon themselves, rather than the "yoke of the commandments," as in Jewish thought (Matt 11:28–29).[10] As Jesus told the rich young man, it was not enough to keep all the commandments in order to inherit eternal life; this could be obtained only by following Jesus (Mark 10:17–22). Mark even presents Jesus as abolishing the dietary laws given through Moses (Mark 7:19), thus placing Jesus' word above the law. In Matthew's Gospel, Jesus is the one who will judge the world and determine who will and will not enter the coming kingdom (Matt 7:21–24; 25:31–46; cf. 10:32); in effect, this involves claiming that people will be judged on the basis of their faithfulness to Jesus rather than their faithfulness to the Torah.[11]

These claims made by the evangelists regarding Jesus' authority could be taken to imply not only that Jesus is *above* the law but that in some sense he *replaces* the law as God's instrument of salvation.[12] As Sanders has noted, while Jesus is not presented in the Gospels as abolishing the Mosaic law, it does appear that for Jesus it was inadequate;[13] it could not offer the salvation that he offered. In Jewish thought, blessings such as fullness of life, health, and abundance were to be obtained through obedience to the commandments; those who obeyed the law would be saved by God from the suffering and oppression to which they were subject, both in this world and in the world to come. According to the Gospels, however, all of this was to be obtained through Jesus, who "saved" others both through his teaching and through his ministry of healing and casting out demons (Matt 9:21–22; 27:42; Mark 6:56; 10:52; Luke 7:50; 8:36; 17:19).

Yet it was not only the Mosaic law that promised salvation to God's people but also the system of worship it prescribed, which revolved around the Jerusalem Temple. It was there that people, both individually and collectively, sought health, healing, and deliverance from various forms of suffering and evil through their prayers and sacrifices. They also sought forgiveness of sins; and when people suffered such things as personal ailments and difficulties or oppression by evil spirits or foreign powers, they apparently often believed that this was on account of their sins. Thus, they needed to approach God at the Temple, imploring God to forgive their sins so as to deliver them from the evils they suffered, which they believed were the consequence of their sins.

Therefore, the claim that Jesus had the authority to forgive sins and bring health, healing, and deliverance from evil spirits was essentially a claim that *what had been offered at the Temple was now offered through Jesus.* Whereas previously people had sought God's presence and blessings at the Temple, now it was being affirmed that God was present in Jesus to communicate those blessings through him. This idea may be behind Jesus' words in Matt 12:6, "Something greater than the temple is here." Sanders has noted that Jesus' action of forgiving sins personally would have been interpreted as a claim that forgiveness, purity, and access to God were to be found in him in a way that they were not to be found in the system of sacrificial worship associated with the Temple.[14] The affirmation in Matt 1:21 that Jesus would "save his people from their sins" must be understood against the same background. In the Jewish context of the time, Jesus' ministry of preaching, teaching, healing, and casting out demons would be understood as saving people from their sins, both in the sense of delivering them from the ailments and oppression that had come upon them because of their sins, and in the sense of enabling them to change their sinful lives so that they might no longer experience the sufferings that were believed to be the consequence of those sins. In this regard, Jesus would be seen as fulfilling the salvific role of both the Temple and the Mosaic law.

Jesus' Rejection and Death as the Foundation of Something New

As Jack Kingsbury has argued, in all three Synoptics "the matter of 'authority' lies at the heart of the conflict between Jesus and the religious authorities."[15] The scribes and Pharisees become upset when Jesus claims to have the authority to forgive sins and to violate the Sabbath commandment as they interpreted it, and they claim that Jesus' power comes from the devil rather than from God (Mark 2:1–12, 23–28; 3:1–6, 22–30). In Jerusalem the "chief priests, the scribes, and the elders" demand to know by what authority Jesus carries out his ministry (Mark 11:27–33). In general, they repeatedly reject the notion that Jesus had authority from God to teach, heal, and exorcise demons.

For the evangelists, this rejection of Jesus and his authority ultimately led to his death on the cross. All three Synoptics mention the desire of some to do away with Jesus almost from the start of his ministry because of his teaching and healing activity (Matt 12:14; Mark 3:6; Luke 4:28–31). The passion predictions in the Synoptics repeatedly speak not only of Jesus' *dying* but of his being *rejected and killed* (Matt 16:21–23; 17:22–23; 20:17–19; Mark

8:31–33; 9:30–32; 10:32–34; Luke 9:22, 43–45; 17:25; 18:31–34; 24:6–7, 44–46). The same ideas are found in the kerygmatic passages of Acts, where Jesus' death is ascribed to the Jewish authorities and the inhabitants of Jerusalem, who rejected Jesus (2:23; 3:13–15; 4:10–11; 5:30; 10:39; 13:27–29; cf. 7:52).[16] Other texts, such as the parable of the wicked tenants, compare Jesus' death with the deaths of the prophets, who were persecuted and rejected by Israel (Matt 21:33–46; 23:29–39; Mark 12:1–12; Luke 13:33–34; 20:9–19; Acts 7:51–53). Above all, the passion accounts stress the notion that Jesus was rejected, mocked, and scorned during his trial and crucifixion.

Two other ideas appear in several of the passages that speak of Jesus' rejection and death. First, it is said that following his crucifixion Jesus would rise from the dead (Matt 16:21; 17:23; 20:19; Mark 8:31; 9:31; 10:34; Luke 9:22; 18:33). This would make it possible for him to return in glory someday to judge the world and establish the kingdom of God that he had proclaimed (Matt 10:23; 13:41–43; 24:31; 25:31–46; Mark 8:38; 13:26–27; 14:62; Luke 12:40; 18:8; Acts 1:6–11). In this sense, strictly speaking, Jesus' full salvific activity would take place *in the future*, at his second coming.

A second idea found in the Gospels is that a new reality centered on Jesus would come about following his rejection. This is stated most clearly at the end of the parable of the wicked tenants, where Ps 118:22–23 is quoted to claim that Jesus' rejection would lead to his becoming the "head of the corner" of a new construction, evidently the church conceived of as a temple (Matt 21:42; Mark 12:10–11; Luke 20:17; cf. Acts 4:11). The conclusion drawn at the end of the parable, that the vineyard or kingdom would be taken away from those killing Jesus so as to be given to others, may imply that not only Jews but Gentiles would form part of this new people.[17]

The idea of Jesus' constructing a new temple appears in the passion accounts of both Matthew and Mark, which assert that Jesus was accused of claiming that he would (or could) destroy the Temple and rebuild it in three days (Matt 26:61; Mark 14:58; 15:29). In his account of Jesus' action at the Temple, the author of the Fourth Gospel comments that when Jesus spoke of destroying the Temple and then raising it up in three days, "he spoke of the temple of his body" (John 2:21). While it is not certain whether this idea is to be attributed to Matthew and Mark as well, the three days must surely be taken as referring to Jesus' resurrection, after which he himself would either become the new temple or bring a new temple into existence.[18] If the new temple is taken to refer to Jesus himself or his body, then the idea is that God would come to dwell in him or his body as God had dwelt in the Temple. From then on *Jesus would in some way fulfill the functions of the Temple*: people would come to Jesus for the things that they previously sought in the Temple, such as healing, forgiveness, and salvation from their sins. If Jesus' words are interpreted as referring to the church, then the idea would be that through his death a new, sanctified people would come into existence. These ideas may also be behind the accounts concerning Jesus' action of "cleansing" the Temple. While this action has been interpreted in many ways, it seems clear that in some sense Jesus was condemning what took place there and perhaps looking forward to a new, purified temple as well, either in a literal or in a figurative sense.[19]

Jesus' Death as Sacrificial

A number of passages from the Synoptics associate sacrificial ideas with Jesus' death. These appear to have developed out of the conviction that Jesus had not merely *died* but had voluntarily *given up his life* in sacrificial fashion. According to the Gospels, when faced with the threat of death, Jesus did not run or hide or attempt to defend himself but instead submitted to the cross. This is particularly evident in the arrest scenes, where Jesus does not resist or oppose those who have come to arrest him, as well as during his trial, where he makes no effort to escape judgment and condemnation.[20] His prayer in the Garden of Gethsemane as presented in the Synoptics conveys the same idea, but adds another as well: it was God's will that he give up his life, submitting to death on the cross (Matt 26:36–42; Mark 14:32–39; Luke 22:40–42). Thus, it is clear that, for the Synoptics, Jesus gave up his life voluntarily; and because it was his Father's will, it could also be said that the Father gave up his Son.

Yet all this must be seen against the background of Jesus' ministry. Jesus was put to death because of his insistence on continuing to carry out the work he believed God had given him. Significantly, the Synoptics present Jesus as teaching and even healing during his last days in Jerusalem (Matt 21:14, 23; 26:55; Mark 14:49; Luke 20:1; 21:37–38; 22:53). In fact, he may have left Galilee for Jerusalem to proclaim the gospel there, just as he had felt it necessary to leave Capernaum to proclaim the gospel in other cities at the outset of his ministry (Luke 4:43–44). Jesus' refusal to put an end to all of this activity, together with his prophetic action in the Temple, ultimately led to his being arrested and sentenced to death. Thus, what was sacrificial about Jesus' death was not just his willingness to *die* for others but his unbending commitment to *live* for others, doing his Father's will in seeking to bring God's blessings into the lives of others and save them from their sins through his teaching and healing activity.

The sacrificial language regarding Jesus' death is most explicit in the words over the bread and wine at the Last Supper attributed to him by the Synoptics. Jesus refers to the bread as his body ("given for you," according to Luke 22:19) and to the cup as the new covenant in his blood poured out for his followers (Luke 22:20), or as his blood of the covenant poured out for many; Matthew adds "for the forgiveness of sins" (Matt 26:28; Mark 14:24). Although there are numerous difficulties associated with these Synoptic passages (as well as Paul's account in 1 Cor 11),[21] there can be no doubt that Jesus' death is spoken of here in sacrificial terms.[22] In fact, the language clearly echoes that of Exod 24:3–8, which tells of the establishment of the covenant with Israel. There Moses took part of the sacrificial blood and "dashed it on the people, and said, 'See the blood of the covenant that the LORD has made with you in accordance with all these words'" (v. 8).[23] Thus, Jesus' words communicate the idea that through his sacrificial death a new covenant would be established.

As noted in the last chapter, however, sacrifice was understood in terms of presenting not only *offerings* to God but *prayers* as well. Thus, if sacrificial significance was being given to Jesus' death, there must have been some type of implicit petition associated with his death. Although the Synoptics present Jesus as offering up a number of different prayers during his last hours (Matt 26:39–44; 27:46; Mark 14:22–23; Luke 22:31–32; 23:34, 46; cf. John 17), they mention nothing similar to what is found in the prayer of Eleazar in 4 Macc 6:27–29, where he asks God to make his death an expiation or propitiation for others. If we see Jesus' death against the background of his ministry, however, it would be natural to conclude that Jesus was seeking in his death precisely what he had sought in life, namely, the redemption and salvation of others. It was his activity on behalf of others that had led to opposition, persecution, and the threat of a violent death; and in the face of that, Jesus remained faithful to his mission as he understood it, "drinking the cup" set before him.

According to the story told by the Synoptics, of course, Jesus expected to be raised on the third day after his death. This is most likely an idea attributed to Jesus only after his death and the disciples' subsequent conviction that he had risen from the dead.[24] If so, then Jesus probably would have understood his death as sacrificial in the sense that, similar to Eleazar, he was asking God that the redemption and salvation of others that he had sought throughout his ministry might come to pass, perhaps even through Jesus himself at some future time. In that case, if Jesus did pronounce some version of the words ascribed to him at the Last Supper, he may have been calling on his disciples to remember his dedication and service to them and others ("Do this in remembrance of me"). This also would involve the hope or expectation that some good or something new would come about as a result of his death, such as a new covenant or the redemption of Israel involving the arrival of the kingdom in which Jesus would drink with his disciples once again (Matt 26:29; Luke 22:18).[25] This is similar to what we find in the parable of the wicked tenants: perhaps God would respond to the evil done to Jesus so as to act to bring in the awaited kingdom to which Jesus had dedicated his life. On this, of course, there can be no certainty. But if Jesus was aware that he was about to suffer a violent death and did not attempt to avoid it but instead "gave himself up," his death would be understood in a sacrificial sense, as an offering of himself to God. And viewed in the light of his life of service to others, his death would also be seen as an implicit petition to God that what he had lived and worked for might become a reality in spite of his death or *through* his death. In that sense his death would be an offering on behalf of others, seeking their deliverance from the plight in which they found themselves on account of their sins.

This idea may be behind the saying attributed to Jesus regarding his death in Matt 20:27–28 and Mark 10:44–45. There, after rebuking his disciples for seeking positions of power and authority, he says, "For the Son of man came not to be served, but to serve, and to give his life a ransom for many." It is important that the idea of a ransom (*lytron*) here does not necessarily imply that his death would be a price paid *to* someone—in this case either God or the devil. Rather, the giving up of his life would be a ransom in that, as a result of his faithfulness unto death in seeking the redemption of others, God would grant that redemption by acting to bring it about. The idea once again would be similar to what we find in the story of Eleazar, where God responded to Eleazar's faithfulness and obedience unto death by delivering the people of Israel from the oppression they were experiencing.

Important here, however, is not so much what Jesus thought about his own death but the interpretation later given to his death by his followers. Even if the ransom saying and the words attributed to Jesus at the Last Supper were actually spoken by him, after his death they were undoubtedly interpreted in light of the belief that he had been raised from the dead and taken up into heaven, from where he would return in power and glory to bring in the kingdom that he had proclaimed, thereby bringing to fulfillment the divine promises.

When Jesus' death is viewed in connection with his resurrection, ascension, and return in glory, another element is added to the sacrificial interpretation of his death, namely, that through his death Jesus had attained the salvation and redemption he had sought for others in his life and death in obedience to God's will. In effect, by raising and exalting him, God had accepted Jesus' sacrifice, responding favorably to Jesus' petition on behalf of others by granting Jesus the power and authority to bring about what he had sought someday in the future.

When we view Jesus' words at the Last Supper against the background of these ideas, as well as those noted previously, then his death and resurrection may be seen as establishing a new or alternative system of relating to God revolving around Jesus himself, that is, a new covenant. This would involve the existence of a new covenant *people*, a chosen people who, like the Israelites of old, would live according to God's word, now as known through Jesus. Whereas previously God had made himself present to heal and save others at the Jerusalem Temple, God would now make himself present through the risen Jesus and the community under him. In contrast to the sacrifices offered to God according to the stipulations of the previous covenant, in this new covenant the sacrifice would be that of Jesus himself. Instead of being cleansed by the blood of the sacrificial offerings presented at the Jerusalem Temple, this new covenant people would now be cleansed by Jesus' own blood, through which they would receive remission of sins (Matt 26:28). What would distinguish this new covenant people would no longer be their participation in the sacrificial worship at the Jerusalem Temple but their communion with Jesus' own sacrifice.[26] In fact, if Jesus' allusion to his body in the Last Supper accounts is viewed in combination with the idea that he would construct a new temple, the idea might be that, in offering himself up, Jesus was constituting himself or his body as the new temple for others.

In this way Jesus' death would be "for the many," according to Matthew's and Mark's account, or "for you," as in Luke's account, referring probably not only to the twelve disciples gathered there with him but to the community into which they would develop.[27] By giving up his body and shedding his blood so that a new covenant might be established through him and then proclaimed throughout the world, many who previously did not have access to God's blessings of salvation and forgiveness of sins would attain these things through him, the mediator of this new covenant. The *lytron* saying would be interpreted in similar fashion: in exchange for being faithful to the end to the ministry given him and offering up his life rather than seeking to escape death, he would obtain the redemption not only of those with whom he came into contact during his earthly life but also of the "many" who would come to believe in him and form part of the church after his death, since his resurrection would enable him to return to bring about that redemption for them. Once again, it is important to stress the intimate relation between Jesus' ministry and his death that is reflected in this saying: just as Jesus had dedicated his life to serving others (*diakonēsai*) in obedience to God's will so as to seek their redemption and salvation, by dying (and consequently rising) he would obtain what he had sought for them throughout his life of service on their behalf. His death, therefore, must not be seen in isolation from his ministry.

Finally, one other text that has sacrificial implications should be noted, namely, the rending of the Temple veil mentioned in Matt 27:51 and Mark 5:38. This passage has been interpreted in various ways, as symbolizing the destruction of the Jerusalem Temple, the end of the sacrificial system carried out there, Jesus' entrance into God's presence, or the access of all people (including Gentiles) to God.[28] All of these interpretations fit well with the ideas presented here. As a result of Jesus' death (and resurrection), the old Temple is surpassed by a new temple through Jesus or his body, and the old sacrifices are fulfilled in Jesus' own sacrifice so that access to God's blessings and forgiveness is now open to all people through him. Once again, this was something Jesus had sought not just in his death but also in his ministry: that others—particularly those who did not have access to the blessings and forgiveness promised in the covenant by God to those participating in the Temple worship—might come to share in the promised salvation through him. Thus, a new system or covenant revolving around Jesus was said to have come into existence through his death.

The Scriptures and the Divine Plan

When speaking of Jesus' death, the Gospels and Acts repeatedly stress another point, namely, that all that occurred took place in fulfillment of the Scriptures. While this claim is made regarding a number of the things that took place during Jesus' passion and death, such as his betrayal at the hands of Judas for the price of thirty pieces of silver, the scattering of his disciples, Jesus' being reckoned with the transgressors, the casting of lots over his tunic, and his bones not being broken, in general it is made concerning his passion and death as a whole.[29] In the arrest scene in Matthew's Gospel, Jesus tells his disciples, "Do you think that I cannot appeal to my Father, and he will at once send me more than twelve legions of angels? But how then would the scriptures be fulfilled, which say it must happen in this way?" He then adds, "But all this has taken place, so that the scriptures of the prophets may be fulfilled" (Matt 26:53–54, 56). Similarly, in Mark's account, Jesus tells those arresting him, "Let the scriptures be fulfilled" (Mark 14:49).

It is Luke, however, who particularly stresses this idea both in his Gospel and in Acts. On his way to Jerusalem, Jesus tells his disciples that "everything that is written about the Son of Man by the prophets will be accomplished," alluding to the events surrounding his passion, death, and resurrection (Luke 18:31). Then, once risen, Jesus tells the disciples on the road to Emmaus, "Was it not necessary that the Messiah should suffer these things and then enter into his glory?" Luke then adds that "beginning with Moses and all the prophets, he interpreted to them the things about himself in all the scriptures" (24:26–27). Several verses later, Luke presents Jesus' appearance to the rest of his disciples on the same day: "Then he said to them, 'These are my words that I spoke to you while I was still with you—that everything written about me in the law of Moses, the prophets, and the psalms must be fulfilled.' Then he opened their minds to understand the scriptures, and he said to them, 'Thus it is written, that the Messiah is to suffer and to rise from the dead on the third day, and that repentance and forgiveness of sins is to be proclaimed in his name to all nations, beginning from Jerusalem" (24:44–47).

In Acts, we find the same claims. On the day of Pentecost, after affirming that several passages from the Hebrew Scriptures foretold Jesus' resurrection and exaltation as well as the outpouring of the Holy Spirit, Peter proclaims that Jesus was "handed over according to the definite plan and foreknowledge of God" (2:23). In the next chapter, Peter tells the crowd at the temple, "God fulfilled what he had foretold through all the prophets, that his Messiah would suffer" (3:18). The community of Jesus' disciples later rejoices, saying to God, "For in this city, in fact, both Herod and Pontius Pilate, with the Gentiles and the peoples of Israel, gathered together against your holy servant Jesus, whom you anointed, to do whatever your hand and your plan had predestined to take place" (4:27–28). In a number of other passages, Luke attributes to Philip and Paul the idea that Jesus' passion and death were necessary and were foreseen by the prophets (8:32–35; 17:2–3; 26:22–23; cf. 7:52; 28:23).

The idea behind all of these passages is not merely that Jesus' passion, death, and resurrection were foretold by the Scriptures but that *they formed part of a divine plan.* This plan had been "hidden" previously, and constituted a "mystery" unknown to all except Jesus himself; only after his death did his disciples come to discern this plan in the Scriptures. The divine plan embraced not only the events surrounding Jesus' death but also certain things that preceded and followed those events. The ministry of John as well as Jesus' birth and his ministry also took place in fulfillment of Scripture and thus formed part of this divine plan. However, this plan also looked forward to what would happen *after* Jesus' resurrection: Luke stresses not only that the outpouring of the Holy Spirit was prophesied but that the proclamation of the gospel to all peoples was at the heart of this plan. As noted above, according to Luke 24:46–48, what was "written" was not only that Jesus would die and rise but that repentance and forgiveness of sins would be preached in Jesus' name to all the nations, that is, the Gentiles. The same point is made at the outset of Acts, where Jesus says that before the restoration of the kingdom to Israel, the disciples will receive the Holy Spirit and will be his witnesses in Jerusalem, Judea, Samaria, and to the ends of the earth (1:6–8). In Mark 13:10 Jesus tells his disciples that before the Son of Man returns in glory, "the good news must first be proclaimed to all the nations." Likewise, Matthew has Jesus foretell that "this good news of the kingdom will be proclaimed throughout the world, as a testimony to all nations; and then the end will come" (24:14), and at the conclusion of his Gospel, he presents Jesus sending out his disciples to "make disciples of all nations" (28:19). According to these texts, therefore, *the proclamation of the gospel to the ends of the earth was just as much an integral part of the divine plan foreordained in the Scriptures as was Jesus' death.*

Yet in addition to foretelling the proclamation of the gospel to the Gentiles, Jesus tells his disciples that before the end comes they will be hated and face persecution and death at the hands of the nations, as well as be beaten in the Jewish synagogues. In this way, however, they will bear testimony (Matt 10:17–23; 24:9; Mark 13:9–13; Luke 21:12–17). In Acts, Luke develops these ideas further, insisting that the Scriptures foretold the rejection of the gospel on the part of many Jews and also its subsequent proclamation to the nations (13:40–51; 18:5–6; 28:23–29). In fact, Luke even relates these two ideas by seeing the persecution of the disciples and the rejection of the gospel on the part of many Jews as leading to the spread of the gospel and the work among Gentiles.[30] Just as what happened to Jesus is spoken of as "necessary," so also the sufferings of Paul and his going to Jerusalem and then to Rome to appear before Caesar are said to be "necessary," since these events also form part of the divine plan for the proclamation of the gospel throughout the world.[31]

Of course, the idea that the rejection of the gospel by many Jews would have as its consequence the mission to the Gentiles is found in passages from the first two Gospels as well.[32] The parable of the wicked tenants, as noted above, conveys the idea of the kingdom of God being given to another people or nation as a result of the rejection of Jesus on the part of the Jewish authorities, at least in Matthew's version (Matt 21:33–43; cf. Mark 12:9; Luke 20:16). This new people would now include Gentiles as well as Jews. This idea may also be present in the parable of the wedding feast (Matt 22:1–10; Luke 14:16–24), in which those who are invited refuse to come, and others take their place, as well as in the account of Jesus' cursing of the fig tree (Matt 21:18–19; Mark 11:12–14, 20–21).[33] When Jesus insists that both his ministry and that of the disciples be carried out initially only among Jews (Matt 10:5–6; 15:24), the idea apparently is that God's covenant people Israel are given the first opportunity to accept the gospel; only when it has been preached throughout Israel and rejected by many will its proclamation to the Gentile nations be justified. According to Matthew, the acceptance of the gospel among Gentiles and their inclusion in the coming kingdom were foretold not only by Jesus but by Isaiah (Matt 8:11–12; 12:17–21), who also prophesied the rejection of the gospel by many of God's people (Matt 13:14–15; cf. Acts 28:26–27).

The Early Christian Story

On the basis of what has been presented above, it is now possible to reconstruct in general terms the story of salvation told by the first Christians and to understand the role Jesus' death played in that story. According to this story, a divine plan had been conceived from of old involving the election of Israel and the establishment of the Mosaic covenant, as well as divine promises of salvation. It was also God's intention, however, to send his own Son, which he did in Jesus, to bring those promises to fulfillment. In obedience to God and with God's authority, Jesus dedicated himself to a ministry of healing and teaching so as to bring God's blessings to Israel and to call Israel to repentance and conversion, as had been prophesied. He also prepared disciples to continue his ministry on behalf of the gospel of God's kingdom, apparently in anticipation of the work they would do as his apostles following his death and resurrection. The response of many in Israel, however, including particularly the majority of the Jewish leaders, was to reject Jesus and his message. In spite of this, Jesus went to Jerusalem, knowing that he would be delivered over to the authorities and die a violent death, but placing his life and his work in God's hands, and thus remained faithful and obedient to his mission. In fulfillment of the divine plan, the Jewish leaders had Jesus arrested and crucified at the hands of the Gentiles. Nevertheless, God raised him from the dead, so that he might one day return in power and glory to establish God's kingdom and bring to fulfillment all of the promises God had made of old. Through the risen Jesus, God poured out the Holy Spirit on Jesus' disciples, and Jesus sent them out to proclaim the gospel, not only to Israel but to the Gentiles, whose ignorance and sin God had previously overlooked, but who were now commanded to repent (Acts 17:30). While some Jews accepted the message proclaimed by the apostles, many rejected it and persecuted the apostles; as a result, they turned in even greater measure to the Gentiles, many of whom were receptive to the gospel. All those who believed and committed themselves to following Jesus were baptized so as to become part of the community of Jesus' followers, that is, the church. In this way, they received the Holy Spirit and came to live under a new covenant revolving around Jesus, a covenant that fulfilled and surpassed the one previously made with Israel. This had been the objective of the divine plan from the start, namely, that people from all nations might come to participate in the promises of blessing God had given, becoming part of the people God had chosen from before creation.

Seen in the context of this story, Jesus' death is salvific *not in itself* but *because of what preceded and followed it.* All that he did previous to his death, including his ministry on behalf of others, his teaching in word and deed, and his preparation of disciples, laid the foundation necessary for what came later, and revealed God's will to people in a new way so that they might live according to that will under a new covenant. His death was the consequence of his unbending dedication to this work. However, what follows upon Jesus' death is also salvific. His resurrection and exaltation led to the outpouring of the Holy Spirit and the establishment of the church; enabled him to carry out his present, ongoing work in relation to believers; and in relation to God on their behalf, and made it possible for him to return someday in glory to establish the awaited kingdom. All of this was what Jesus had sought in life and in death: that God might save and forgive others, in particular his followers. And this implicit petition was granted when God raised him from the dead so as to ensure that he might return someday to bring about that salvation definitively. In this sense, all who now come to form part of his community of followers can be certain of their salvation and forgiveness.

According to this story, Jesus' death was necessary in that it formed part of the divine plan foretold in the Scriptures. Nevertheless, the question remains as to *why* it was a necessary part of this plan. For many Jews, it was extremely difficult to accept the claim that a man who had been condemned by the Jewish leaders and had suffered the most humiliating of deaths on a cross was the promised Messiah. Such a claim seems to have had no basis in Jewish beliefs concerning the Messiah or the redemption of Israel, and it went against everything the Jewish people expected. How could God have allowed such a thing to happen to the Messiah? And if Jesus really was the Messiah, why had he not yet redeemed Israel? The Synoptics present Jews asking these same questions: all three mention the crowd of bystanders at the foot of the cross, waiting to see if God would intervene to save Jesus (Matt 27:39–44; Mark 15:29–32; Luke 23:35–41). As noted above, as if to address such questions, Matthew's Gospel portrays Jesus in the arrest scene contemplating the possibility that God could send twelve legions of angels to deliver him. Luke mentions the expectation of some of Jesus' followers as they drew near to Jerusalem that "the kingdom of God was to appear immediately" (19:11), as well as their disappointment after Jesus' death that the kingdom had not arrived: "We had hoped that he was the one to redeem Israel" (24:21). According to Acts, even after Jesus' resurrection, his disciples at first still expected the restoration of Israel to come immediately (1:6). If we take these as representing Jewish expectations regarding the Messiah, we may imagine the sort of questions that the proclamation of Jesus' messiahship after his death had to address. Why was

Jesus' death a necessary part of the divine plan? What purpose did it fulfill? Why could God not merely have taken Jesus up into heaven without his suffering and dying, as he had done with Enoch, Elijah, and perhaps even Moses (according to Jewish tradition)?

One possible answer to these questions would have been that, had Jesus restored the kingdom immediately, there would have been no opportunity for the gospel to be proclaimed throughout the world so that a greater number of people might repent and be converted and thus share in that kingdom. At the same time, because of the increasing opposition he faced, Jesus could not continue his ministry indefinitely. Thus, if there was to be time for more people to be brought into the kingdom according to the divine plan, Jesus had to die.

While such a response might have seemed plausible, it still does not resolve the question of why God did not intervene at the last moment to spare Jesus the suffering of the cross. In theory, God might have glorified Jesus before his passion and death without ushering in the kingdom immediately, since he might still have allowed for a period of time between Jesus' glorification and the end, so that the gospel might be proclaimed to the nations. There seems to be no answer in the Gospels and Acts to questions such as this, other than that there was a divine plan foretold in the Scriptures that had to be carried out.

Of course, it might be argued that the first Christians believed that there was something in God's nature or the nature of the created order that left God no alternative but to let his Son be crucified if the world was to be saved. This is the claim made by most of the later stories of redemption considered in chapter 1, particularly those that revolve around the notions of satisfaction and penal substitution: it was impossible for God to forgive sins without Jesus' death. Yet no such claim is found in the Gospels or Acts, either explicitly or implicitly; instead, the Jewish view that nothing is impossible for God is consistently upheld.[34]

Rather than claim that God *had* to give his Son over to death in order to fulfill his promises of salvation, what the evangelists maintain is that God *willed* to do so. It could be argued that God's will was not so much that his Son *die* but that he be faithful to the end to the ministry given him and suffer the consequences of that ministry. Seen from that perspective, Jesus' death would be an expression of the love of both God and Jesus. Nevertheless, if God could have saved the world without having his Son die such a cruel death, it remains unclear as to why a God of love would allow his Son to suffer such things.

Once again, there is no clear evidence from the Gospels and Acts that this question was answered—or even raised. On the basis of what has been argued above, however, it is possible to speculate on how the first Christians might have answered it. First, they might have responded that, given Jesus' total commitment to others and his love for them, it would hardly have been appropriate for him to be spared death at the last moment, perhaps by being taken up into heaven suddenly by God. If he had not been willing to suffer such a death as the consequence of what he had done out of love for others and to be in full solidarity with others, enduring the same kinds of suffering and the same death that other people endure (including especially his own followers), his love for others could hardly have been said to be full and complete. The same observation might be made regarding God. For God to have sent his Son to dedicate his life to the salvation of others, and then to have intervened at the last moment to spare him the suffering and death of the cross because he considered the cost too high, would hardly have been seen as a sign of God's love for the people for whom he had sent his Son. Had God glorified and exalted Jesus before his suffering and death, taking him up into heaven directly like Elijah, it might have appeared as if God's love for his people had limits and was imperfect, and that God was not willing to give up everything or pay any cost to bring the people back to himself.

A second possible answer as to why God did not intervene to spare Jesus from the death of the cross might have had to do with the establishment of the new covenant. Up to that moment, the only covenant through which people could have access to God's blessings of forgiveness and salvation was the one established through Moses. Yet in spite of their efforts to obey that covenant, evidently the Jewish people had not done so sufficiently, since the promises made to them on the condition of their obedience had not been fulfilled. Furthermore, the Gentile peoples had not entered into that covenant, and most found it extremely difficult to do so. Thus, according to the Christians, a new covenant was necessary. Such a covenant could be established only by one having full divine authority. It might be expected that God would establish the new covenant in a way similar to the making of the previous covenant, that is, through a covenant sacrifice. This was how God had established his covenant with Israel both in Abraham's time (Gen 15:7–21) and under Moses (Exod 24:3–8). Even the covenant with Noah had been established following a sacrifice (Gen 8:20—9:17). Furthermore, it might have been argued that a new covenant could be justified only if the previous one had been invalidated in some way. Obviously, what might invalidate it would be the disobedience of many of those living under it and their rejection of God and those sent by him. In this case, proponents of such a view might have regarded Christ's death as necessary to "bring to a head the sum of their sins who had persecuted his prophets to the death," as the Epistle of Barnabas later came to state (5:42–43). For these reasons, Jesus' rejection and death could have been regarded as necessary in order for the new covenant to be established. In this regard, it is important to note that, while the evangelists may have seen Jesus' ministry (particularly his teaching) as laying the foundation for a new covenant, there is no explicit mention of the idea of a new covenant until the Last Supper scene, where Jesus ties its establishment to his death. The idea may therefore have been that Jesus first had to offer himself up sacrificially to God in order for the new covenant to become a reality.

According to Jewish belief, however, the Mosaic covenant also prescribed sacrifices of atonement. The first Christians, therefore, might have believed that in the new covenant, an atoning sacrifice was also required, not because God's righteous nature made it impossible for God to forgive sins without such a sacrifice, but simply because in Jewish thought forgiveness was always granted in the context of a covenant relationship in which sacrifices for sin were offered. Thus, the first Christians might have argued that Jesus' self-offering unto death fulfilled the need for an atoning sacrifice in the new covenant. It may have seemed ironic that those who had in effect "sacrificed" Jesus were the religious authorities, especially the Jewish high priest.[35] But Jesus' death would also be seen as a self-sacrifice, in that he went to his death imploring God to forgive and accept the people on whose behalf he offered up his life, just as the priests did when they approached God with sacrificial blood, offering up prayers on behalf of God's people. According to this line of thought, what had been prefigured in the sacrifices for sin associated with the old covenant had to be fulfilled in the new.

In any case, the first Christians saw the necessity of Jesus' death in the context of the divine plan established in the Scriptures. They regarded it as fulfilling not only the particular passages that foretold what would happen to Jesus but "all the scriptures," from beginning to end (Luke 24:27), since *everything found in the Mosaic covenant was now to be found in its fullness in the new covenant under Jesus.* Just as obedience to God would now be defined in terms of obedience to Jesus' words rather than to those of Moses alone, and a new temple where God would dwell would be raised up through Jesus (or his body), so also a new means of atonement would be provided through Jesus' death. All of this would make it possible for a new covenant people to come into existence. This people would now also have access to God and God's forgiveness through Jesus rather than through observance of the Mosaic law and participation in the sacrificial worship at the Temple. This could be proclaimed by the apostles only *after* Jesus' death and resurrection, since only after Jesus had been rejected and raised up would this new covenant come into effect.

Ideas such as these seem clearly to be present in the thought of the Epistle to the Hebrews. It has often been claimed that Hebrews in particular develops the argument that Christ's death was necessary for human sins to be forgiven, most notably in 9:22, where it is said that "under the law almost everything is purified with blood, and without the shedding of blood there is no forgiveness of sins." In reality, however, the only necessity mentioned by the author in the immediate context appears in the following verse: "It was necessary for the copies [*hypodeigmata*] of the heavenly things to be purified with these rites, but the heavenly things themselves had to be purified with better sacrifices than these" (9:23*). In other words, the sacrificial rites carried out under the stipulations of the first covenant in the tabernacle, which for the author were merely "figures," "shadows," or "copies" of the heavenly things (8:5; 9:9, 23–24), have been surpassed or rendered "obsolete" (8:13) as a result of Christ's coming. This is because Christ fulfills and perfects what the Old Testament sacrificial rituals imperfectly symbolized. Therefore, because in the purification rites as prescribed in the Mosaic law it was generally necessary for blood to be used to make expiation and obtain divine forgiveness, in order for Christ to fulfill, perfect, and surpass the old rites and obtain the expiation and forgiveness they promised but could not actually give, he also had to shed his blood. Yet this necessity is *not rooted in the divine nature*, as if it were impossible for God to forgive without blood, or in some natural law inherent in the cosmos, but *in the Scriptures*, which Christ had to fulfill. In Heb 9:22, therefore, the author is simply making an observation concerning how purification and forgiveness of sins were obtained according to the stipulations of the old covenant, rather than arguing about what was possible or impossible for God to do. He does not write that under the law everything *must* be purified with blood, nor that without the shedding of blood there *cannot* be forgiveness of sins, but that under the law (that is, according to the commandments regarding sacrifices) *almost* everything is purified with blood (but not *everything*),[36] and the rites stipulated there aimed at procuring atonement or forgiveness prescribe the shedding of blood as part of the expiatory rite.

Similarly, Heb 9:15–17 argues that where a covenant or testament (*diathēkē*) is involved, "the death of the one who made it must [*anagkē*] be established." The idea, however, is that a new covenant had to be founded so that God's people might now receive the forgiveness and redemption that they could not attain under the first covenant. Once more, Christ's death was necessary for this to come about, not because God's righteous nature made forgiveness impossible without a substitutionary death, but because every testament or covenant (*diathēkē*) is established through a death. The idea in both this passage and Heb 9:22, therefore, is essentially the same one we find in the Synoptics and Acts: *Christ died so that the Scriptures might be fulfilled.* In this case, everything that the old covenant pointed to and imperfectly foreshadowed needed to be accomplished in Christ.

It must also be stressed, however, that according to the story told by the first Christians, salvation and forgiveness do not result *directly* from Jesus' death. Rather, Jesus' death is the *means* by which a new situation is brought into place, so that many can now obtain salvation and forgiveness through him as members of his community of followers. It was still necessary for people to repent, believe, and be baptized in order to have access to that salvation and forgiveness.[37] Through baptism, they were "cleansed" and "purified" by being incorporated into the community of God's new people, and following this they had to live faithfully as members of that people. In this regard, Christian thought was in close continuity with Jewish thought; in both it was necessary to repent and live in obedience to God's will in order to be forgiven. The *basis* for their forgiveness, therefore, was not Jesus' death per se but their incorporation through faith and baptism into the community whose forgiveness and salvation he had obtained from God at the price of his death. For this reason, in Acts, forgiveness of sins is tied not explicitly to Jesus' death but to repentance, faith, and baptism, as well as to Jesus' new status as risen Lord and Savior (Acts 2:38; 3:19; 5:31; 10:43; 22:16; 26:18).[38] As in Judaism, it is as one lives as a member of the covenant community that one obtains the promises of salvation and forgiveness of sins.

Of course, the book of Acts also stresses that God not only *requires* repentance but actually *gives* it, not only to Jews but also to Gentiles (Acts 5:31; 11:18). God also is said to give the gift of the Holy Spirit, which is a sign that one forms part of God's people and thus shares in the promises of salvation and forgiveness. The idea appears to be that in this new covenant, God graciously gives what he requires, enabling believers to live according to his will through Jesus and the Spirit. In this regard, the new covenant would be seen as superior to the old. As Paul proclaims to the Jews in Acts 13:38–39*, "Through this man forgiveness of sins is proclaimed to you; by him everyone who believes is set free from everything from which you could not be freed by the law of Moses." According to the Christian proclamation, those who could not obtain salvation and forgiveness under the Mosaic covenant could now receive these things as members of God's new covenant people, since through Jesus they received a new ability to live according to God's will in addition to the divine forgiveness Jesus had obtained for them.

The Early Christian Story and the Later Stories

How does the early Christian story of redemption as we find it in the Synoptics and Acts compare to the other stories outlined in chapter 1 and to the Jewish story outlined in chapter 2? With regard to the latter, it is clear that the Christian story represents a continuation of the story told in the Hebrew Scriptures and in ancient Judaism. As N. T. Wright affirms, the Christians (like the Jews) "continued to regard the story of Israel as the earlier chapters of their own story."[39] Certain ideas remain the same: the Christian story still speaks of the raising and judging of the dead, the redemption of Israel, the gathering in of the "elect," and the arrival of a glorious new age. The idea that this redemption would be accomplished through a Messiah or king descended from David was also a common element of the Jewish hope adopted by the Christians. Many also took up a Jewish belief that the prophet Elijah would return before the arrival of the Messiah, and they interpreted this as fulfilled in the work of John the Baptist (Matt 11:13–14; 17:10–13).

Nevertheless, there are also important differences. In the Christian story, at least as we find it in the New Testament texts composed several decades after Jesus' death, Gentiles play a more prominent role than in the Jewish story. While the New Testament texts still speak of the redemption of God's chosen people Israel, they also regard uncircumcised Gentiles who come to faith as members of God's people. The specific promises regarding the restoration of the land, the Temple, and the city of Jerusalem do not play a prominent role in the Christian story,[40] and the "elect" to be gathered in at the end are not so much the Jews of the diaspora but Christian believers throughout the world. These alterations of the Jewish story may have been due precisely to the incorporation of Gentiles into the Christian community, since the Jewish hopes just mentioned would be less important for them and might even be seen as excluding them. Similarly, the Christian concept of "Messiah" appears to have been less nationalistic than it was in Jewish thought.

More important, however, the idea that the expected Messiah might come, die, and be raised from the dead so as to have to come *again* in order to bring about Israel's redemption was totally foreign to the Jewish story. The belief in what are essentially *two* comings of Jesus as Messiah, with an interim period between the two, raised problems. If the redemption of Israel and the inauguration of the new age were linked to Jesus' *second* coming, what had been accomplished by his *first* coming, and in particular by his ministry, death, and resurrection?

In order to address this difficulty, it appears that the Christians began to use language that implied some type of "realized eschatology," according to which either the members of God's people or the world in general had *already* been redeemed or saved in some sense. While we find this type of language somewhat frequently in Paul's epistles, as will be noted later, there are nevertheless a few instances of it in the Third Gospel and in Acts. Two of these appear in the hymns of the infancy narratives at the outset of Luke.[41] In the hymn attributed to Mary, she says:

> He has shown strength with his arm;
>   he has scattered the proud in the thoughts of their hearts.
> He has brought down the powerful from their thrones,
>   and lifted up the lowly;
> he has filled the hungry with good things,
>   and sent the rich away empty.
> He has helped his servant Israel,
>   in remembrance of his mercy,
> according to the promise he made to our ancestors,
>   to Abraham and to his descendants forever. (Luke 1:51–55)

Similar language appears at the outset of the hymn of Zechariah:

> Blessed be the Lord God of Israel,
>> for he has looked favorably on his people and redeemed them.
> He has raised up a mighty savior for us
>> in the house of his servant David,
> as he spoke through the mouth of his holy prophets from of old,
>> that we would be saved from our enemies and from the hand
>> of all who hate us. (1:68-71)

In both of these passages the idea behind the use of the past tense of the verbs that speak of salvation cannot be that these things have already taken place: God had not yet *actually* brought down the powerful from their thrones, filled the hungry, and sent the rich away empty. All that God had done was bring a savior to Israel in Jesus, as yet unborn. Nevertheless, because God's action ensured that the promises made to Abraham and his descendants would be fulfilled through Jesus, the past tense is used: *all of these things were now certain to occur through Jesus.* In the events surrounding Jesus, God had finally begun to act so as to bring about all that he had promised.

We find the same type of realized eschatology in Acts 13:32–33, where Paul proclaims that "what God promised to our ancestors he has fulfilled [*ekpeplērōken*] for us, their children, by raising Jesus." The idea here is not that all the promises made to the fathers have already been fulfilled; it was obvious to all that Israel's glorious redemption had not arrived and that things on earth in general remained the same.[42] Rather, the idea is that by raising Jesus God has in effect declared and given assurance that all the promises he had made will indeed be fulfilled through Jesus. This is precisely what Paul proclaims in Acts 17:31: God "has fixed a day on which he will have the world judged in righteousness by a man whom he has appointed, and of this *he has given assurance* to all by raising him from the dead" (emphasis added). What was believed, therefore, was not that the redemption of Israel had already become a reality with Jesus' coming or his resurrection but that the promised redemption was now certain to come through Jesus.

This kind of realized eschatology is different from what we find in many of the stories of redemption considered in chapter 1. In those stories, it is often claimed that some type of actual change in the condition of the world or humanity has taken place as a result of Jesus' coming, ministry, death, and resurrection: the divine wrath at human sin has been exhausted, the punishment or consequences of that sin are done away with, the forces of evil have been defeated, and human nature or the world in general has undergone some mysterious or invisible transformation. There is no clear evidence in either the Synoptics or Acts, however, that the first Christians believed that Jesus' death had "effected" some such change. Undoubtedly, Jesus' death and resurrection were followed by several new developments, such as the pouring out of the Holy Spirit and the establishment of the church, whereby the members of the Christian community experienced a new kind of joy, peace, and communion with God. Yet while in this sense they could be said to have come to participate in blessings that were associated with the age to come, it was clear that they, along with the rest of the world, were still living in the same age as previous to Jesus' coming. According to the Christian story, therefore, what had changed was that by sending his Son and raising him from the dead, God had given assurance that all the promises he had made of old would come to pass through Jesus.

As noted above, the claims regarding the *necessity* of Jesus' death found in the early Christian story are different from those of the later Christian stories. According to the evangelists, Jesus' death was necessary in order for the divine plan conceived of old and foretold in the Scriptures to come to pass. As part of that plan, Jesus' death was no more and no less necessary than everything else that took place, including Jesus' coming, his ministry, his rejection and passion, his resurrection and exaltation, the coming of the Holy Spirit, the sending out of the apostles, and the spread of the gospel throughout the world. This understanding of the necessity of Jesus' death stands in contrast to the understandings found in the later Christian stories, which make use of foundational arguments regarding the nature of God, humanity, or the world to claim that human salvation was impossible without God's Son becoming man, dying, and rising. There is nothing even remotely resembling such claims in the Synoptics or Acts. Not even the idea of an eternal divine plan was understood according to such an idea, as if the nature of God or the world made it impossible for God to save the world without that plan. The God of Israel always remained free to act as he wished, and nothing impeded him from saving people without Jesus' passion, death, and resurrection.

In the later Christian stories of redemption, the notion that Jesus' death has some salvific "effect" is combined with the claim that it satisfies the condition necessary for human salvation so as to speak of an objective salvation affecting *all people*, at least in principle. Jesus' suffering and death are regarded as "sufficient" for the sins of all humanity to be remitted, since these events satisfy God's just requirement for satisfaction or punishment. In other views, Jesus' incarnation, death, and resurrection are said to have had some effect on the one human nature in which all persons share so that that nature is now delivered from corruption and mortality. Needless to say, such ideas are nowhere to be found in the Synoptics or Acts. The only condition that Jesus' death satisfies in these writings is that the Scriptures be fulfilled so that the divine plan of salvation might be carried out. According to this idea, while Jesus was certainly seeking the salvation of the world in general when he offered up his life, only those who would come to form part of the new covenant community would benefit from what he had done. This idea, however, differs from the doctrine of "limited atonement" associated with some Calvinist theology in that, while Jesus was in a sense dying only for the "elect," that is, the new chosen people who would live under him, his hope and objective were that people throughout the world might come to form part of this chosen people; in this sense, he died *for all* or *for the whole world*, since he was ultimately seeking the salvation of *all*, not just of *some*. The idea that Jesus' death was necessary, valid, or sufficient for the salvation of those who lived previous to his coming, as well as of people throughout the world who would have no opportunity to hear the gospel, must also be rejected as foreign to the thought of the Synoptic evangelists. As noted in chapter 2, in Jewish thought God is able, ultimately, to save whomever he wills, even those living outside of the covenant, such as the "righteous Gentiles." Thus, we find no claims in the Synoptics or Acts that God will eternally condemn those who do not live under the new covenant, either because they lived prior to its establishment or because they never heard the gospel. Even Peter's affirmation in Acts 4:12, "There is salvation in no one else, for there is no other name under heaven given among mortals by which we must be saved," must be viewed in the light of the other words attributed to him in Acts 10:34–35, "God shows no partiality, but in every nation anyone who fears him and does what is right is acceptable to him." While salvation would be through Jesus alone, who would come again to judge all people, those who had never heard the gospel might still be saved, just as in some Jewish thought many righteous Gentiles would be saved at the eschatological ingathering of God's people. The blessings that those never hearing the gospel would miss out on would not necessarily be the ones having to do with the life of the age to come but the gifts of peace, hope, life, and wholeness that Jesus' followers receive in the present age.

A final difference between the understanding of Jesus' death in the Synoptic Gospels and Acts and many of those noted in chapter 1 is that the former does not regard Jesus' death as being of a different nature than the death of any other person. Undoubtedly, the Synoptics claim that several extraordinary events took place during Jesus' crucifixion and immediately afterwards, such as darkness covering the earth, the parting of the Temple veil, an earthquake, and the raising of some dead persons (Matt 27:45, 51–53; Mark 15:33, 38; Luke 23:44–45). However, these must be seen as signs brought about by God and not by Jesus' death itself, as if it had produced some type of mysterious effects on earth. Similarly, it must be remembered that Jesus' cry of dereliction, "My God, my God, why have you forsaken me?" (Matt 27:46; Mark 15:34) is actually the cry of a psalmist (22:1) from many centuries before Jesus, and that two others were crucified and died together with Jesus. Several passages in the Synoptics show that Jesus' death was seen as comparable to the deaths of other persons, including the Old Testament prophets, John the Baptist, and especially Jesus' disciples. Jesus uses the same terms and expressions regarding their being delivered up and killed as he applies to himself, and he tells his followers that they must take up a cross, as he would do.[43] In particular, he tells James and John that they will drink *the same cup* that he is to drink, and be baptized with *the same baptism*, obviously referring to his death (Mark 10:39); this is not regarded as some sort of mysterious or mystical participation in Jesus' passion and death, but rather is the consequence of following Jesus. While the Gospels do speak of Jesus' being troubled prior to his betrayal (Matt 26:38; Mark 14:33–34; cf. John 12:27), none of them particularly emphasizes the physical or emotional pain he experienced during his trial and crucifixion, as if this had some type of salvific significance. There is thus no clear evidence that the first Christians maintained that Jesus had suffered something unparalleled in human history, as if he had taken on himself the dreadful consequences of human sin, exhausted God's wrath, or experienced something such as the pangs of hell. Instead, they clearly communicate the idea that *others suffered and suffer the very same things Jesus did.*

From this it is clear that although a number of ideas from the stories mentioned in chapter 1 can be read back into certain passages from the Gospel narratives, such as those that relate Jesus' cry of Godforsakenness and the supernatural events surrounding his death, in reality these passages provide no clear support for such ideas. What the narratives *do* stress strongly and repeatedly are the fulfillment of the Scriptures by the events surrounding Jesus' passion and death, the rejection of Jesus by the authorities in the same way that the prophets before him had been rejected, and the injustices of the procedure against Jesus. These ideas are relatively unimportant for the stories outlined in chapter 1, since the *historical* reasons for Jesus' death in those stories are secondary. Ultimately, Jesus died not because what he had said or done generated opposition among the authorities who had him killed, but because his death was necessary in order for human sin to be forgiven, fallen human nature to be restored, Satan to be overcome, or human beings to be transferred into the new age through some type of participation in his death. According to most of the stories in chapter 1, therefore, Jesus' death is separated from his life and ministry: in the end Jesus dies not because of the life he lived but because for some theological reason there was no other possible way for God to save humanity. To be sure, the Synoptics and Acts also posit theological reasons for Jesus' death as well as the necessity that he die. But *the theological reasons in the Synoptics and Acts are precisely the historical reasons*, in that what was necessary was that the Scriptures be fulfilled and that the divine plan of which Jesus' death formed a part be carried out.

CHAPTER 4

The Story of Redemption according to Paul

Ever since the rise of biblical scholarship, the general consensus among New Testament and Pauline scholars has been that Paul was somewhat of a theological innovator, and that in many regards his teaching concerning salvation was at odds not only with the Judaism of his day but also with the faith of many of his fellow Christians. Although E. P. Sanders in *Paul and Palestinian Judaism* successfully challenges the idea that Paul was an ardent opponent of Judaism because it denied God's grace and proclaimed a legalistic works-righteousness, he still ends up maintaining that Paul's soteriology was fundamentally different from that of the Judaism of his day. In Sanders's view, rather than moving from "plight to solution," as was common in Jewish thought, Paul began with the conviction that Christ provided the "solution" to the human predicament and then defined humanity's "plight" on that basis.[1] Thus, Paul's "pattern of religion" was not the covenantal nomism that characterized the Jewish faith. Instead, according to Sanders, "Paul presents an essentially different type of religiousness from any found in Palestinian Jewish literature" and ends up "consciously denying the basis of Judaism."[2]

Equally widespread has been the idea that Paul's soteriology was fundamentally distinct from that of Jesus and the first believers. In part, this view is based on Paul's claim to have received his gospel through a direct revelation and on the evidence in his letters of differences and conflicts with other leaders in the early church.[3] The primary basis for this view, however, is the fact that Paul uses many terms and images that are unique to him. Some of the key soteriological concepts for Paul, such as justification by faith, reconciliation with God through Christ's death, the new creation, the church as the body of Christ, and the idea that believers are "in Christ," are scarcely to be found outside of the Pauline and deuteropauline epistles.[4] In addition, in his letters Paul rarely makes reference to the tradition regarding Jesus' life, passion, and death as we find it in the Gospels. All of this together leads to the conclusion that Paul looked outside of the early Christian tradition for the ideas necessary to develop a story of redemption in Christ that was in important ways distinct from the one outlined in chapter 3.

Ideas such as these have been associated particularly with Rudolf Bultmann. Bultmann claimed that Paul had little interest in the historical Jesus. In essence, all that Paul cared about was the "bare fact" of Jesus' earthly life. Jesus' death and resurrection constituted "the sole thing of importance" for Paul, because he abstracted Jesus' death and resurrection from the context of the story in which these events originally appeared and fit them into a story that was quite different from anything told by Jesus' original followers, a story constructed from ideas supposedly taken from Gnosticism and the mystery religions.[5] The use of the term "Christ-event" serves the same purpose: to speak of Jesus' coming, passion, death, and resurrection as an "event" can make an abstraction of these occurrences, detaching them from their original historical context. For Bultmann, Paul did not start from scratch in developing his story, because the Hellenistic church had already begun to alter the kerygma of the oldest church. Paul, who was introduced to the Christian faith in the context of the Hellenistic church, merely took this process further.[6] As noted at the end of chapter 1, while Pauline scholars have departed from Bultmann's views on many points, in general they continue to maintain his claim that the story of redemption told by Paul is in important respects distinct from the fairly simple story outlined in chapter 3.

It is also generally assumed that Paul took Jesus' death and resurrection as the starting point for his doctrine of redemption and placed these events at the center of his soteriology. Here, the "proof texts" generally cited are 1 Cor 1:23 and 2:2, in which Paul insists that he proclaims nothing except Christ crucified, as well as Gal 3:1.[7] Sanders, for example, claims that "the content of Paul's preaching and his hearers' faith was the death and resurrection of Christ."[8] The logical conclusion of this assumption is precisely the one Sanders draws: Paul began with the "solution" and then defined the "plight" on that basis. If Paul's soteriology revolved around the notion of participation in Christ's death and resurrection, as Sanders affirms, then the human plight must be defined in terms of the need for a means of transfer from the lordship of sin to the lordship of Christ; it is this that Christ's death and resurrection provide by enabling believers to die and rise together with him.[9] Each of the other understandings of redemption outlined in chapter 1 proceeds in the same way. If Christ's death and resurrection destroy the powers of sin and death in human nature or deliver human beings from their bondage to Satan and the forces of evil, then the human "plight" is defined in these terms: it was impossible for mortal human beings to accomplish this deliverance by themselves or for God to accomplish it for them without Christ's death and resurrection. If Jesus died to endure the punishment or consequences of human sin for others as their substitute, then the "plight" is defined in terms of the inability of human beings to deliver themselves from that punishment or those consequences on their own.

In any case, when it is assumed from the start that Jesus' death and resurrection provide the "solution" for the human "plight," fulfilling a necessary condition for human salvation that could be fulfilled by no one else and in no other way, the story of redemption ends up being quite different from the relatively simple story we find in the Synoptics and Acts. Paul is then not interested in the details we find in the Gospels concerning Jesus' life and ministry or the historical reasons they give for Jesus' crucifixion, because he is telling another story in which those details are for the most part irrelevant. Instead, Paul attributes Jesus' death to some "theological" necessity that the sin of humanity be expiated, a means of transfer from one lordship to another be provided, or our fallen human nature be transformed and delivered from its subjection to evil. Here the assumption is that the story we find in the early Christian proclamation does not provide the elements necessary to understand what Paul says about being redeemed, justified, and reconciled to God through Christ's death. Therefore, to understand what Paul means, we must look elsewhere.

In developing these interpretations of Paul's soteriology and his understanding of the salvific significance of Jesus' death, Pauline scholars have generally taken as a starting point the "creedal or kerygmatic formulae" and "brief allusions" that Paul uses to refer to Jesus' death,[10] so as then to read back into them one or more of the kinds of stories of redemption considered in chapter 1, with all of the assumptions inherent in those stories. Among these assumptions is the notion that Jesus' death "effects" human salvation in some way. Most scholars continue to adhere as well to the notion that Paul taught that Christ effected an "objective" redemption or reconciliation affecting all of humanity "potentially" or "in principle," which nevertheless must be appropriated by individuals subjectively through faith in order to become "actual." This objective redemption or reconciliation is often said to involve some type of actual change or transformation in the created order or the human situation. Richard Hays, for example, writes that for Paul "Jesus' death/resurrection has put an end to the world as it was and has adumbrated the 'new creation,'" and that "Jesus' death terminates the old age and ushers in a new one, in such a way that the very structure of reality is transformed."[11] For John Ziesler, what Paul taught is that "Christ's death consequently not only represents but brings about the end of the Old Age, the old world, and his resurrection not only represents but brings about the beginning of the New Age, the new world"; this is because "in his death Christ ended the grip of sin on human beings generally."[12] Thus, when Paul speaks of a "new creation," he has in mind some mysterious alteration in the world or human nature or the culmination of one period of history and the initiation of a new age. And when he speaks of believers' having already been justified, he is claiming that God's wrath against human sin has been put away or that the consequences of that sin have been endured by Christ on the cross as humankind's substitute so that human beings are no longer subject to them.

All of these assumptions have led Pauline scholars to the conclusion that the story of salvation and the cross told by Paul is very different from that which we find in the early Christian proclamation. What will be argued here, however, is that this approach to Paul's soteriology is fundamentally flawed. It involves taking stories of redemption such as those found in chapter 1 as a starting point and reading them back into Paul, and particularly into the brief formulae and allusions that Paul uses to refer to Jesus' death, which readily lend themselves to all kinds of interpretations. Because of their ambiguous nature, we cannot reconstruct the story Paul told regarding salvation in Christ by looking first to those formulae and allusions.

Instead, the approach adopted here will be to take as a starting point the ancient Jewish and early Christian stories of redemption outlined in the previous chapters so as to explore whether there is evidence that the story told by Paul was essentially the same as that of the early church. One reason for adopting this approach is that throughout his letters, Paul expects that his readers will understand the brief formulae he uses to allude to Jesus' death and its redemptive significance because he believes they are well acquainted either with those formulae themselves or with the story underlying them. While one might argue that the basis for such an expectation on the part of Paul was that he himself had taught them his own story of redemption, in the case of at least one of his letters, this is not the case. In his letter to the Romans, we find many of the formulaic or allusive references to Jesus' death or blood that are characteristic of Paul (e.g., Rom 3:24–25; 4:24–25; 5:6–10; 6:2–11; 8:32; 14:15). Yet because Paul had not founded the church in Rome, and in fact had never even visited it, he could not assume that the believers there would be familiar with his own particular teaching regarding the cross. He nonetheless evidently expected the Romans to understand perfectly well his allusions to Jesus' death or blood, because he believed that the story of redemption in Christ told in Rome was the same one that he himself was accustomed to telling and proclaiming—and probably the same one told by Christians everywhere.

Therefore, it seems logical to begin by examining Paul's letters to see if we can discern there the same story of redemption outlined in the last chapter, looking at the same time for evidence that Paul may be telling a different story. Once this has been done, the passages in which Paul speaks of the redemptive significance of Jesus' death may be considered in the following chapters in order to examine whether this narrative framework is sufficient to explain Paul's thought in those passages.

Evidence of the Early Christian Story of Redemption in Paul's Letters

Throughout Paul's letters, there is ample evidence that the story of redemption told by Paul was thoroughly grounded in the ancient Jewish story drawn from the Hebrew Scriptures. Paul often alludes to the main parts of that story, such as the creation, the sin of Adam, God's election of Abraham and his descendants, the lives of the patriarchs, the crossing of the Red Sea, the giving of the law under Moses, and Israel's wandering in the wilderness.[13] Of particular importance to Paul are the promises made to Abraham and his descendants, which he mentions on several occasions (Rom 4:13, 17–18; 9:4–5; 15:8; Gal 3:8, 16). Paul also makes the Jewish distinction between the two ages, a present one characterized by suffering, sin, and evil, and an age to come in which God's promises will be fulfilled. In Gal 1:4 he speaks of "the present evil age [*aiōn*]," and elsewhere he expresses the belief that this age is subject to forces hostile to God (1 Cor 2:6–8; 2 Cor 4:4). While Paul never mentions explicitly the "age to come," he does employ repeatedly the phrase *zoē aiōnios*, which is probably best translated as "life of the age to come" rather than simply "eternal life."[14] This suggests that Paul is in general agreement with the basic Jewish understanding of the present "plight" of Israel and the world: what is needed is deliverance or redemption from the present situation marked by sin and evil and the inauguration of the new age of glory in fulfillment of the divine promises.

According to Paul, in order to bring about this redemption, God sent his Son Jesus Christ, who was "descended from David according to the flesh" (Rom 1:3) and "born under the law" (Gal 4:4). As Don Garlington comments with regard to the former passage, "Paul underscores to his readers that the subject of his gospel is a *thoroughly Jewish* Messiah, the Son of David prophesied, . . . and, therefore, the fulfillment of Israel's eschatological expectations."[15] While Paul never mentions Jesus' baptism by John or the signs and wonders he performed during his ministry, Paul does allude on at least two occasions to Jesus' teaching as we have it in the Gospels (1 Cor 7:10; 9:14). In addition, there are numerous implicit allusions to Jesus' teaching throughout Paul's epistles, as several recent works have demonstrated. In particular, David Wenham has shown that "there is massive evidence of Pauline knowledge of Jesus-traditions."[16] Others have argued convincingly that Paul also knew other details regarding Jesus' ministry, particularly the fact that Jesus lived in celibacy, was meek and gentle, endured persecution, and led a life of poverty and deprivation in his dedication to serving others.[17] All of this justifies James Dunn's conclusion: "It can be demonstrated with a fair degree of probability, then, that Paul both knew and cared about the ministry of Jesus prior to his passion and death . . . [and] that he recalled, alluded to, and was himself influenced in his own theology and conduct by important features of the Jesus tradition."[18]

A number of other passages indicate that Paul knew the historical circumstances surrounding the cross and expected his readers to know them as well. In 1 Cor 2:8 Paul mentions that "the rulers of this age" crucified Christ out of ignorance, and in 1 Thess 2:14–15 he states that the Jews "killed both the

Lord Jesus and the prophets." Although, for different reasons, both of these passages are problematic,[19] we can hardly doubt that Paul knew that both Jewish and Roman authorities had played a role in Jesus' crucifixion. Other passages also give clear indication that Paul was acquainted with the passion narratives. In 1 Cor 11:23–24 Paul recites the tradition regarding Jesus' words and actions over the bread and cup at the Last Supper and mentions Jesus' betrayal. In Rom 15:3, quoting Ps 69:9, he refers to the abuse Christ endured during his trial and crucifixion.[20] And in 1 Cor 15:3–7 Paul mentions Jesus' burial and the testimonies of many of Jesus' first disciples concerning Jesus' postresurrection appearances. Paul's affirmations that Jesus "gave himself up" (Gal 1:4) and was "crucified in weakness" (2 Cor 13:4) demonstrate that he was aware that Jesus went to his death passively rather than trying to defend himself or flee. These and other passages suggest that Paul was acquainted with the same traditions regarding Jesus' passion, death, and resurrection that we find in the Gospels and Acts.[21]

When speaking of Jesus' resurrection and exaltation (which are generally regarded as a single event),[22] Paul never says or implies that Jesus raised *himself* from the grave. Rather, as the kerygma in Acts consistently stresses, it was *God* who "raised Jesus our Lord from the dead" (Rom 4:24; cf. 8:11; 10:9; 1 Cor 6:14; 15:15; 2 Cor 4:14; Gal 1:1; 1 Thess 1:10). Even in the passages in which Paul does not mention God explicitly as the one who raised Christ from the dead, his use of the passive voice of the verb *egeirō* in relation to Christ should be understood in the same fashion: Christ "was raised" by God. Paul mentions the sending out of apostles, echoing an idea found at the end of Matthew and Luke, and he includes himself as one of those commissioned. He also speaks of the gospel's being proclaimed throughout the world to the nations, in accordance with the early Christian proclamation.[23] Through these apostles, God (or Christ) establishes the "church of God," the community of the righteous or "saints," which is defined on the basis of faith in God and his Son, Jesus Christ.[24] Believers are incorporated into the church through baptism (1 Cor 12:13; Gal 3:27) and receive the Holy Spirit, who guides them and enables them to live in love and obedience to God's will (Rom 5:5; 8:14; 16:19; 2 Cor 2:9; 6:6; Gal 3:5; 5:18; 1 Thess 4:8). This involves living under the "new covenant" founded by Jesus through his death and now proclaimed by the apostles (1 Cor 11:25; 2 Cor 3:6). Ultimately, Jesus will come again in glory to raise the dead and judge the world, subject all things under his feet

(1 Cor 15:24–28), and bring to fulfillment "all the promises of God," which find their "Yes" in him (2 Cor 1:20; cf. Rom 1:2; Gal 3:16, 22).

For Paul, as for the early Christian tradition, all of these things form part of an eternal divine plan announced in the Scriptures. This plan provides the framework against which history as a whole is interpreted. From of old God intended to form for himself a chosen people, composed not only of Jews but of Gentiles, and promised to bless them (Rom 4:1–25; 8:29–30; Gal 3:7–9, 16–19). These blessings would eventually be accomplished by means of God's Son; however, before that, God chose the people of Israel descended from Abraham "according to the flesh" for a special role in this plan (Rom 1:16; 3:1–2; 9:3–5). God gave them the law through Moses, letting the other nations go their own ways in the meantime (Rom 1:24; 3:25). That law, added because of trespasses and serving to increase those trespasses, served as the "pedagogue" or "custodian" of God's people until God would send his Son (Rom 7:13; Gal 3:19, 24*). This God did "when the time had fully come," in order to redeem those under the law (Gal 4:4). Christ's death also formed part of this plan: it occurred "according to the Scriptures" (1 Cor 15:3) and "at the right time" (Rom 5:6). The powers who crucified him were ignorant of this eternal plan (1 Cor 2:7–8). Likewise, his resurrection and exaltation were foretold in the Scriptures (Rom 1:1–4; 1 Cor 15:3). All of this constitutes the "gospel," which God "promised beforehand through his prophets in the holy scriptures" (Rom 1:2).

At the heart of this plan, however, was the salvation of Gentile peoples through the proclamation of the gospel to them. What has been revealed is "the mystery that was kept secret for long ages but is now disclosed, and through the prophetic writings is made known to all the Gentiles, according to the command of the eternal God, to bring about the obedience of faith" (Rom 16:25–26). In his mind, Paul's own ministry as apostle to the Gentiles forms an integral part of this eternal plan found in the Scriptures (Rom 1:1–6; cf. Rom 8:36; 15:15–21; 2 Cor 5:18–20; 6:1–13; Gal 1:1, 11–16; 2:7–9; 1 Thess 2:4); he is one of the "stewards of God's mysteries" (1 Cor 4:1). Paul repeatedly quotes the Hebrew Scriptures in order to argue that from the beginning God intended for the gospel to be proclaimed among the Gentiles in order to bring salvation to them. In Gal 3:7–8, for example, he writes that "the scripture, foreseeing that God would justify the Gentiles by faith, declared the gospel beforehand to Abraham, saying, 'All the Gentiles shall be blessed in you.'"

Paul's most elaborate discussion of his understanding of this plan occurs in Romans, particularly in chapters 9–11. Briefly stated, Paul's argument there is that the rejection of Jesus (the "stumbling stone," 9:32–33) and the gospel by many of the Jews was foreseen in the Scriptures, and that from the beginning not only Jews but Gentiles had been elected to belong to God's people. This rejection led to the proclamation of the gospel among the Gentiles. Paul almost certainly had in mind the same chain of events we find in Acts, where the persecution on the part of some Jews leads to the work among the Gentiles. According to this "mystery," however, the "hardening" that has "come upon part of Israel" is only to last "until the full number of the Gentiles has come in"; then "all Israel will be saved" (Rom 11:25–26). For Paul, then, all that had occurred through Christ as well as what was taking place in his own ministry formed part of the divine plan decreed from eternity and foretold in the Scriptures.[25] These ideas are developed even further in the deuteropaulines, which repeatedly allude to God's eternal plan or purpose in Christ, and the "mystery hidden for ages" (Eph 3:9, 11) involving the inclusion of the Gentiles, all of which is revealed in part through Paul's ministry (see Eph 1:4–11; 2:10; 3:1–12; Col 1:24–27; 2:2; 4:3; 2 Tim 1:9; Titus 1:1–3).

Paul's repeated references to God's mercy, kindness, patience, wisdom, and grace must be viewed against the same background. The ultimate objective of God's plan from the start was that his salvation extend to people from all over the world, who are also objects of God's love.[26] In particular, God's love was revealed in his willingness to give his Son over to death, "delivering him up" so that this plan might be accomplished (Rom 4:24–25; 5:8; 8:31–39). The idea is not that God had his Son killed or crucified but that God "gave him over" or "delivered him up" in the sense of not intervening to save him from suffering at the hands of evildoers, and letting them put him to death on a cross.

At the same time Jesus' willingness to give up his life so that this plan might be accomplished is a sign of his own love. Although Paul mentions Christ's love in giving up his life explicitly in only two passages (2 Cor 5:14; Gal 2:20), he alludes to it through the phrases he employs when speaking of Christ's death and in the contexts in which he discusses the cross. Perhaps the most important of these phrases are those in which Paul employs the Greek preposition *hyper.* Paul makes use of this preposition to speak of Christ's death "for" or "on behalf of" others at least ten times in his letters, thereby alluding to Christ's love for them.[27] When Paul says that Christ "gave himself up" (Gal 1:4; 2:20), it must be remembered that to give up one's life is not merely to *die* but to die *for some cause or objective*, seeking the benefit of others out of love for them. When Paul refers to Jesus' "obedience" (Rom 5:19; Phil 2:8), he no doubt has in mind both the love of God, who willed that his Son give up his life on behalf of others, and that of Christ, who obeyed God's will and was willing to become a "servant" or "slave" (*doulos*) for the benefit of others (Phil 2:7). These passages also make it clear that whenever Paul refers to Jesus' death or blood or the cross, he has in mind not merely Jesus' "bare death" or the fact that Jesus physically expired, but the immense love Jesus showed for others by giving up his life so that they might attain salvation.

Paul viewed and interpreted Jesus' death not only against the background of the divine plan foretold in the Scriptures but against the background of Jesus' life and ministry as well. From 1 Thess 2:14–16 it is clear that Paul knew that Jesus was persecuted and killed as a prophet, that is, put to death because of the activity he carried out during his life. Elsewhere Paul also mentions Jesus' death in the context of allusions to enduring persecutions and suffering for a cause, thereby relating the cross to the ministry of which it was the result.[28] As noted above, Paul was aware that Jesus had carried out a ministry of teaching. There can thus be little doubt that Paul knew that Jesus had been crucified for what he had said and done: what had ultimately led to Jesus' death was the activity of service in which Jesus had been involved as well as Jesus' refusal to desist from that activity when it led to conflict, opposition, and persecution. To carry out a ministry of service and teaching, of course, is to do something *on behalf of others*. Such a ministry by definition must have some objective or goal; in Paul's mind, Jesus must have been seeking something for others, not only in his life but also in his death. But what?

A close look at Paul's letters reveals that in several places he offers answers to this question through the use of purpose clauses. In Rom 15:8–9 he writes, "For I tell you that Christ has become a servant of the circumcised on behalf of the truth of God in order that he might confirm the promises given to the patriarchs, and in order that the Gentiles might glorify God for his mercy." Paul's mention of God's "truth" here should be taken as an allusion to God's *emeth*, his faithfulness to his promises, or his reliability. For Paul, what Jesus was seeking through his service to the circumcised was that the promises God had made of old might come to fulfillment. Among these promises, according to Paul, was the salvation of Gentiles. It is significant that here Paul apparently recognizes that Jesus carried out a ministry primarily to the circumcised (as the Synoptics also affirm), yet also sees as the objective of this ministry the work among Gentiles that would follow upon Jesus' death and resurrection.

Although this is the only instance in which Paul seems to allude to Jesus' ministry with a purpose clause, on a number of occasions he does so when referring to Jesus' death. Ideas closely parallel to those in Rom 15:8–9 are found in Gal 3:13–14*, where Paul writes of Christ's "having become a curse for us—for it is written, 'Cursed is everyone who hangs on a tree'—in order that [*hina*] in Christ Jesus the blessing of Abraham might come to the Gentiles, so that [*hina*] we might receive the promise of the Spirit through faith." According to this passage, the objective of Christ's submitting to the accursed death of the cross was that the promises of blessing made to Abraham concerning the Gentiles might be fulfilled, as well as that believers might receive the promise of God's Spirit. Earlier in the same letter, Paul uses another purpose clause to affirm that Christ "gave himself for our sins to deliver us from the present evil age" (Gal 1:4*). Here, Christ's objective in giving himself up was that believers be delivered from the present age so as to attain the life of the new age. In Rom 14:9, the objective of both Christ's death and resurrection is said to be his current status as Lord: "For to this end Christ died and lived again, so that he might be Lord of both the dead and the living." The context of this passage makes clear that, for Paul, Jesus sought to be Lord not for his own sake but for that of others. As believers are to do, Jesus lived and died to others rather than to himself (14:7). A similar idea is found in 1 Thess 5:10, where Paul uses a purpose clause to state that Christ "died for us, so that whether we are awake or asleep we may live with him." This passage combines ideas from the two just considered: Christ sought to be in a position in which he might save both the living and the dead (as in Rom 14:9) and bring believers to "live with him," that is, participate with him in the life of the coming age. The idea that believers might "live no longer for themselves" but for Christ is stated as the objective of Christ's death "for all" in 2 Cor 5:15. There it seems that, for Paul, the objective Christ had in death was not only that of giving life to others but also that of bringing about in believers a new manner of living.

For Paul, because in all of this Jesus was doing not only his own will but that of his Father (Gal 1:4), what he sought for others was also what God sought for them. For this reason, Paul can use a purpose clause in 2 Cor 5:21: "For our sake [God] made him to be sin who knew no sin, so that in him we might become the righteousness of God." Although this verse presents a number of difficulties, in some sense the idea is that God made his Son sin (either by sending him in "sinful flesh" or by delivering him up to the cross), so that others might become righteous with the righteousness of God. This should probably be understood in terms of practicing the righteousness of God, although Paul may also have some type of forensic righteousness in mind. In Rom 8:3–4*, Paul uses a purpose clause as well: "For God has done what the law, weakened by the flesh, could not do: by sending his own Son in the likeness of sinful flesh and for sin, he condemned sin in the flesh, *so that* the just requirement of the law might be fulfilled in us, who walk not according to the flesh but according to the Spirit" (emphasis added). Here, the objective of Jesus' coming, as well as perhaps his death, is that believers might fulfill the law's just requirement; this is possible as they receive the Holy Spirit. A similar idea appears in Gal 4:4–5, where Paul states that "God sent his Son, born of a woman, born under the law, in order to redeem those who were under the law, so that we might receive adoption as children." Here God's objective in sending his Son is to bring about the redemption of those under the law. Whether or not Paul considered the Gentiles to be under the law, he clearly contemplates their redemption (and adoption) as one of the goals of Christ's coming. In the following verse he also alludes to the outpouring of the Holy Spirit.

Taken together, these passages indicate that *for Paul the ultimate goal or purpose for which Christ gave up his life in obedience to God was the redemption of God's people*, of whom Jewish and Gentile believers (both Jew and Gentile) now form part. Yet it was also that Christ might be Lord of both the living and the dead, and that those belonging to God's people might practice the righteousness God desired and demanded, fulfilling the just requirement of the law with the aid of the Holy Spirit. It must be stressed, however, that all of this was not only the goal of Christ's *death*; it was also the goal of Christ's *coming*, as well as the goal of his *ministry*. In other words, for Paul, what Christ was seeking for others in his *death* was the same thing he had been seeking for others in his *life of service*: the fulfillment of God's promises. According to Paul, Jesus had been sent by God as his agent to bring about the promised redemption, and it was to this that he had dedicated himself in life and death.

For Paul, Jesus' resurrection had the same objective as his life and ministry and was also accomplished on behalf of others. This latter idea appears in 2 Cor 5:15*, where Paul speaks of Christ as the one "who for their sake died and was raised [*hyper autōn*]," and Rom 4:25*, where Paul writes that Christ "was delivered up for our transgressions and was raised for our justification." The idea that God raised his Son so that he might accomplish something for others is also present in Rom 7:4, where Paul teaches that believers now "belong to another, to him who has been raised from the dead in order that we may bear fruit for God." In a number of other passages, while Paul does not explicitly mention God's purpose in raising Christ, he sees an intimate relationship between Christ's resurrection and his ongoing and future activity on behalf of believers. In 1 Thess 1:9–10, Paul mentions how the Thessalonian Christians turned to God from idols to serve him and "to wait for his Son from heaven, whom he raised from the dead—Jesus, who rescues us from the wrath that is coming." In this way, Paul ties Jesus' resurrection to his second coming, when he will deliver believers from the day of wrath, effecting their redemption. The same basic idea is found later on in the same letter: "For since we believe that Jesus died and rose again, even so, through Jesus, God will bring with him those who have died" (4:14); he then refers to the Lord's coming from heaven and the eschatological salvation of believers (4:15–17). Obviously, Christ can come to bring about their salvation only because he has been raised from the dead; his resurrection is thus "for others" in that it enables him to make the promised redemption a reality for them someday. Because he was "designated Son of God in power according to the Spirit of holiness by his resurrection from the dead" (Rom 1:4), he can now bring about the fulfillment of the divine promises, subjecting all things, and finally raising the dead so as to destroy death; as Paul insists elsewhere, this was the purpose for which he was raised from the dead (Phil 3:20–21; cf. 1 Cor 15:24–28; 2 Cor 13:4). Elsewhere, Paul claims that because Christ has been "raised from the dead by the glory of the Father," believers can be certain that they will be raised like him and will live with him (Rom 6:4–8). This is because God has designated him as his chosen instrument to bring about redemption and has given him the power and authority to do so. Not only has he been designated God's Son by virtue of his resurrection; he has also become "Lord of both the dead and the living" (Rom 14:9). According to Paul, Christ, now risen, also intercedes for believers at God's right hand (Rom 8:34, RSV).

All of this makes it clear that, for Paul, God raised his Son so that he might bring about the life of the new age for God's people, and also do what is necessary in the present for God's people to be able to attain that life some-day. Although Paul regards Christ's past activity (including his death) and his ongoing activity in the present as salvific, he repeatedly stresses the saving work that Christ will carry out *in the future*. What matters for Paul is not merely that Christ died, or even that he rose, but that as a result of his death and resurrection he is alive as Lord and has been given the power to bring about the promised redemption. For this reason, Paul employs not only the aorist "*was* raised" but the perfect tense: Christ "*has been* raised" (*egēgertai*) and thus now remains alive as the Risen One (1 Cor 15:4, 12–20). Even when he uses the aorist, however, the context often indicates that he has in mind the fact that, as a result of his resurrection, Christ is alive (Rom 6:9; 8:34; 10:9; 14:9; 2 Cor 5:15; 1 Thess 4:14). Thus, for Paul, *Christ's resurrection had as its purpose his present and future activity: God raised his Son so that through him all that God had promised of old might now come to pass.*

This means that, for Paul, Jesus' coming, ministry, death, and resurrection are a unified whole and had a single objective: the redemption of God's people. Strictly speaking, this redemption still lies in the future: the way Jesus will save God's people is by coming in glory and power to raise the dead and bring in the life of the new age. However, his past activity also contributes to their redemption, since his ministry of teaching, his commissioning of apostles (both before and after his death), his faithfulness to his mission unto death, and the outpouring of the Holy Spirit through him laid the foundation necessary for many now to be brought into conformity with God's will and come to live as God's obedient children in a new covenant as members of the church, where they await their inheritance in hope.

This understanding of the manner in which people are saved through Christ differs on several accounts from the understandings considered in chapter 1. In virtually all of those stories, Christ's death and resurrection are taken out of the context of the story of which they originally formed part and fit into a different story that has to do with things such as deliverance from the power of the devil, the renewal of fallen human nature, the satisfaction of divine justice, and participation in the event of Christ's death and resurrection. In the story outlined here, however, it is not *Jesus' death* that redeems believers, as if they were saved by an *event*, but *Jesus himself*, or rather, God through his Son, Jesus. Here Jesus' death does not "effect" anything or produce some type of change in the situation of believers or humanity as a whole. God does not send Jesus *to die*, as if the cross were the objective. In fact, Jesus' death is salvific not in itself but *only because of what precedes and follows it*, that is, the activity God carried out through Jesus prior to his death, together with that which follows his resurrection and will continue until the end: *it is all this activity that is redemptive*. What Jesus *died* for is the same thing he had *lived* for. His life and death thus form a unity, together with his resurrection, and all of these events occurred "at the right time" so as to form part of a divine plan that continues to be carried out in the world. While Jesus' death is no doubt of great significance for Paul, he does not regard it in isolation from the story of which it forms a part, which is in broad terms the same story we find in the Gospels. Paul does not *abstract* it from its original historical context in order to fit it into the context of a different story of redemption. Paul repeatedly alludes to the cross not because in itself it is salvific but because it epitomizes everything Jesus had lived and died for and because it is the ultimate expression of the grace and love of God manifested in *all* that God has done and continues to do through Jesus. At the same time, it is the ultimate expression of the love of Jesus himself, who was willing to endure the cross out of faithfulness to his mission and in order that the promises made by God to his people might come to pass through him, as they now certainly will.

Righteousness, Christ, and the Law

Was Paul in agreement with the idea—common to both the ancient Jewish and the early Christian stories of redemption—that one had to obey God's commandments and practice righteousness in order to be included among those to be redeemed as members of God's covenant people? According to many traditional interpretations of Paul's thought, he was not; instead, he rejected outright the notion that one could attain salvation through one's own obedience, because "even the one who tries his utmost is powerless to obey the law."[29] C. K. Barrett summarizes well this traditional view: "As a Jew, Paul had believed that man's status of righteousness before God was to be achieved by himself, through obedience to the law. As a Christian, he had come to believe that God, gracious as Jesus had shown him to be, justified men freely on the basis not of works done in obedience to the law but of faith."[30] Thus, according to views such as this, the new condition for salvation for Paul was no longer obedience to God's commandments, but simply faith, usually understood as "trust that Christ's ransom and expiatory sacrifice has been effective, and trust in Jesus himself."[31]

A close look at Paul's letters, however, reveals considerable evidence that he continued to maintain that salvation was conditional upon obedience to God's will and fulfillment of the divine commandments, as some scholars have argued.[32] In a number of passages, he defines his objective as bringing about obedience in others, especially the Gentiles (Rom 1:5; 6:16–17; 10:16; 16:26; 2 Cor 2:9; 9:13; 10:5–6; Gal 5:7). Particularly noteworthy in this regard is 1 Cor 7:19, where Paul writes, "Circumcision is nothing, and uncircumcision is nothing; but obeying the commandments of God is everything."

Furthermore, in accordance with Jewish belief, Paul consistently teaches that the final judgment will be according to one's works or deeds.[33] It is those who "do good" who will be saved, while those who "obey not the truth, but wickedness" and "do evil" will face God's wrath and fury; "it is not the hearers of the law who are righteous in God's sight, but the doers of the law who will be justified" (Rom 2:7–10, 13; cf. 2 Cor 5:10). Nowhere does Paul affirm that the basis upon which people will be judged is whether they had faith or not. Nor is it Paul's teaching that the final judgment will be made on the basis of works merely because "works are indispensable as the demonstration of the true nature of faith."[34] Such an attempt to maintain the notion that salvation is by "faith alone" in reality ends up being no different than the view that salvation is by works, since it raises the question of how many good works are sufficient to demonstrate the presence of true faith. In the end, one is still being judged and saved not on account of one's faith but on account of the works one does. Thus, Paul seems to be in line with the Jewish views regarding salvation, judgment, and righteousness: the condition for being included among the "righteous" who will be saved is that one obeys God and does God's will.

Nevertheless, the idea that all will be judged on the basis of their works does appear to contradict other Pauline passages, where Paul insists that a person "is justified by faith apart from works of the law" and that God will justify both the circumcised and the uncircumcised through (or on the basis of) their faith (Rom 3:28, 30; cf. Gal 2:16). There is "no one who is righteous" since all are sinners (Rom 3:9–10); "'No human being will be justified in [God's] sight' by deeds prescribed by the law" (Rom 3:20). "For all who rely on works of the law are under a curse" (Gal 3:10). Thus, Paul seems to contradict himself, saying that obedience to the commandments is possible and impossible at the same time, and that one *can* be righteous according to the law, yet *cannot*. Likewise, at times the law seems to have been *abolished* for Paul, so that believers are under no obligation to obey it, while at other times it appears to have a "permanently normative character."[35]

Yet rather than maintaining that Paul contradicts himself and is logically inconsistent,[36] we can understand Paul's words by considering once more the teaching on the law ascribed to Jesus by the evangelists, which presents the same ambiguity as that found in Paul. On the one hand, Jesus claims to uphold or "fulfill" the law in its totality rather than abolishing it, and demands from his followers a righteousness greater than that of the scribes and Pharisees (Matt 5:17–20). On the other, however, he is consistently viewed by his opponents as one who violates the law's commandments and teaches others to do the same. The basic difference between Jesus and those who oppose him thus lies in the manner in which each defines what constitutes fulfillment or observance of the law. For Jesus, fulfillment of the law consists of obedience not simply to the "letter" of the commandments but to the intent, purpose, or "spirit" behind them, which in general has to do with concern for human wholeness. Paul makes this distinction explicit in Rom 2:25–29*:

> Circumcision indeed is of value if you obey the law; but if you break the law, your circumcision has become uncircumcision. So, if those who are uncircumcised keep the requirements [*ta dikaiōmata*] of the law, will not their uncircumcision be regarded as circumcision? Then those who are physically uncircumcised but keep the law will condemn you who have the letter and circumcision but break the law. For a person is not a Jew who is one outwardly, nor is true circumcision something external and physical. Rather, a person is a Jew who is one inwardly, and real circumcision is that which is of the heart, in spirit and not in letter.

As Heikki Räisänen notes, in Jewish thought, to disregard the commandments of the Torah concerning things such as circumcision, Sabbath observance, diet, and purity would be deemed an "annulment of the Torah": "To be selective about the Torah meant to disobey it, indeed to reject it."[37] The same problem lies behind 1 Cor 7:19, since "obeying the commandments of God" would necessarily include obeying the commandment regarding circumcision. For faithful Jews, therefore, it would be a contradiction in terms to say that circumcision does not matter but only keeping the commandments, or that an uncircumcised person might keep the law, as Paul does in Rom 2:27. Such an argument makes sense only if lying behind it is the distinction between a literal and a spiritual fulfillment of the commandments that Paul alludes to in the last verse. Thus, the fulfillment of the commandment to be circumcised is a matter of the heart and not a question of the flesh.

The distinction between the letter and the spirit of the law also appears in 2 Cor 3:6, where Paul speaks of himself and others as "ministers of a new covenant, not of letter but of spirit; for the letter kills, but the Spirit gives life." The language in the last phrase is strikingly similar to the affirmation made by Jesus in the dispute over healing on the Sabbath, when he asks whether the Sabbath law was given "to save life or to kill" (Mark 3:4) and then proceeds to break the "letter" of the Sabbath law in order to fulfill its "spirit." Thus, to obey the spirit of the law leads to life, but to adhere to the letter alone kills. The reference to the letter of recommendation written "not on tablets of stone but on tablets of human hearts" in the context of Paul's discussion of the new covenant in 2 Cor 3:1–6 seems to recall Jeremiah's promise that God's law would be written on the people's hearts (Jer 31:33–34). Paul may have had this passage in mind as well when speaking of the circumcision of the heart in Rom 2:29.[38]

Several verses later in 2 Corinthians 3, Paul insists that many of the Jewish people do not understand the law, whose true meaning is revealed only through Christ (vv. 14–16). He also mentions "freedom," associating this with the Spirit (v. 17). This freedom should be understood not so much in terms of freedom from sin, the law, and death,[39] or even "freedom to obey the Gospel,"[40] but in relation to the letter of the law. According to Paul, believers are free to disobey the *letter* of the law in order to fulfill its *spirit*. Elsewhere, Paul says that although believers are "not under law," they are still under obligation to do God's will, as "slaves of righteousness" and "slaves of God" (Rom 6:13–22). In other words, they must still do the righteousness that the law commands, even though in a sense they are not under the law. The same idea is found in Rom 7:2–6*, where Paul ends by arguing that "we are discharged from the law, dead to that which held us captive, so that we serve in the newness of the spirit and not the oldness of the letter." Likewise, in Gal 2:4 and 5:1, Paul speaks of the freedom believers have in Christ in the context of the main argument of the epistle, that Gentiles are not obligated to fulfill the literal commandments of the law such as circumcision and observance of the Jewish festivals (Gal 4:10; 5:2–3; 6:12–13). In Gal 5:14 Paul insists that "the whole law is summed up in a single commandment, 'You shall love your neighbor as yourself,'" an idea paralleled in Rom 13:8–10, where he sums up the law in terms of loving one's neighbors and claims that "the one who loves another has fulfilled the law. . . . Love is the fulfilling of the law." Here Paul clearly seems to be drawing on the Jesus tradition.[41] He also seems to be drawing on that tradition in Rom 14:13–21, where he claims that nothing one eats is unclean in itself (cf. Mark 7:14–23)[42] and that what really matters is avoiding anything that might result in harm to one's fellow Christians. Literal fulfillment of the biblical commandments regarding food here has become unimportant, although the principle of doing good to others remains. The same principle appears in 1 Cor 10:23–31, where Paul discusses what foods may be eaten: while all things are lawful, not all edify others.

These same ideas may be behind his allusion in Gal 6:2 to fulfilling the "law of Christ" by bearing one another's burdens, as well as his affirmation in 1 Cor 9:20–21* that he is both under the law and *not* under the law, though "not free from the law of God but under the law of Christ." Paul's use of this phrase is probably a reference to the teaching and example of Jesus himself, as John Barclay has argued.[43] If the law of Christ is understood in terms of Christ's interpretation of the Mosaic law, then Paul is saying in this last passage that he is obligated to keep the spirit of the law, as Christ taught, but has freedom with regard to its letter. All of this points to the same idea: true observance of the law involves practicing the righteousness it commands, keeping its spirit or intention. This does not involve "abolishing" the law, an idea that appears nowhere in Paul's letters; on the contrary, like Jesus, Paul insists that he is *upholding* the law (Rom 3:31; cf. Matt 5:17).[44] All of this is reason to conclude that Paul advocates the same type of "Torah-intensification" that the Synoptics attribute to Jesus.

These ideas may also be behind the traditionally difficult passage Rom 2:21–24*, which immediately precedes Paul's discussion regarding circumcision and the literal and spiritual fulfillment of the law. There Paul, addressing himself to the Jew, asks, "You, then, that teach others, will you not teach yourself? While you preach against stealing, do you steal? You that forbid adultery, do you commit adultery? You that abhor idols, are you a temple robber? You that boast in the law, do you dishonor God by breaking the law?" One of the main difficulties of this passage is that most observant Jews probably would have answered the questions regarding stealing, committing adultery, and especially being a temple robber in the negative, just as the rich young man in the Synoptics insisted he had kept all the commandments of the Decalogue from childhood (Mark 10:19–20). Thus, Paul's argument would not be very convincing to most.

However, if the same principles used by Jesus in the Sermon on the Mount to interpret several of the commandments in the Decalogue (including the one regarding adultery referred to here by Paul) are applied to the commandments mentioned by Paul, the answer would have to be that even if one has kept the letter of the law, one has *not* kept the commandments fully. This may have been a common Christian criticism of the Jewish understanding of the law.[45] Though the Jewish readers might not admit to stealing literally, they might rightly be accused of stealing in other ways, such as not paying just wages or not giving to others what they deserve or need. This would be similar to the criticism of the scribes and Pharisees attributed to Jesus in passages such as Matt 23:25 and Mark 7:11–13; 12:40, where he says that they are full of extortion and rapacity, accuses them of devouring the houses of widows, and rebukes them for using the law regarding things dedicated to God so as not to fulfill their obligations toward their parents. These criticisms were directed at devout Jews who apparently were extremely careful to keep the letter of the law but who, according to Jesus' teaching, were transgressing its spirit. Rather than actual stealing from pagan temples, the use by Jews of articles stolen from idol shrines, or simply idolatrous practices in general,[46] behind Paul's accusation of "temple robbing" (*hierosulein*) may be an idea such as that found in Mal 3:8–10, where the prophet accuses the people of stealing from God and the Temple by not paying properly their offerings and tithes. No doubt many would have had to recognize that they had not always given God what was due him.[47] Likewise, most Jewish males would have had to admit committing adultery in their heart, as Jesus mentions in Matt 5:28, even if they had never done so literally. This would all fit well with Paul's argument in the immediate context regarding what fulfillment of the law really involves.

The conclusion Paul draws from his discussion in Rom 1:1—3:8 is that "all, both Jews and Greeks, are under sin" and that "no one is righteous" (3:9–10*). He then goes on to state that "no human being will be justified in [God's] sight by works of the law" (3:20*). Dunn has argued that by "works of the law" Paul is referring to commandments regarding things such as circumcision, diet, purity, and Sabbath observance,[48] an argument that seems to have a fairly strong basis, since the discussion (particularly in Galatians) concerns precisely those things. Yet rather than claiming, as Dunn does, that the problem with such commandments is that they are "too narrowly nationalistic" and thus exclude non-Jews,[49] the reasoning behind Paul's statement would be that fulfillment of such "works of the law" does not make one righteous, because true righteousness has to do with fulfilling the spirit of the law, or its *dikaiōmata*. Thus, the problem has to do with the fulfillment of not only the commandments regarding circumcision, diet, and purity, but other commandments as well. According to Paul, while there is a type of righteousness that is based on literal observance of the law's commandments, this is not the righteousness that leads to salvation. Paul himself claims in Phil 3:6 to have been "blameless" according to the righteousness of the law, yet he distinguishes this righteousness "based on the law" from the righteousness coming from God in Christ (3:9). For the same reason, he can say in Gal 6:13 that "even the circumcised do not themselves obey the law," in spite of the fact that the opponents in Galatia to whom he is referring were extremely zealous regarding the literal observance of the commandments. His idea there cannot merely be that his opponents at times failed to keep certain commandments, since as noted previously, keeping the law in Jewish thought did not mean being absolutely perfect but making atonement when one broke a commandment, as no doubt Paul's opponents were careful to do. For Paul, in spite of this, they were not keeping the law, because like many other Jews they did not understand or obey the principles behind the law or admit that in Christ there is freedom with regard to its letter (2 Cor 3:14–17).

All of this leads to the conclusion that while Paul is in basic agreement with ancient Jewish thought in claiming that a life of righteousness and obedience to God's commandments is necessary in order to be counted among the "righteous" to be saved, he understands this righteousness and obedience in the same terms that the first Christians did: true observance of the law involves keeping its "spirit," or *dikaiōmata*, and fulfilling the principles underlying the commandments. This enabled Paul to redefine God's (new) covenant people in the same way that other Christians did so as to include uncircumcised Gentiles. It was this that led to conflict with many Jews and Jewish Christians, since to them it appeared that Paul was affirming that being Jewish was irrelevant, teaching "against the [Jewish] people and the law," as his accusers claim in Acts 21:28 (cf. Rom 3:1–2). While many Jews probably could accept the idea that Gentiles might be among those to participate in some way in the new age when Israel's redemption came, what was unacceptable for them was that uncircumcised Gentiles were being accepted into the community so as to share equal status before God as full members of "Israel" (Rom 9:6–8; Gal 3:7–9, 29; 6:16; Phil 3:3). Similarly, while they most likely agreed with Paul that true observance of the law involved keeping its spirit, they were not ready to follow Paul in regarding the literal observance of many of the commandments as unnecessary.

Plight and Solution in Paul

If Paul agreed that observing the law was necessary for redemption, did he also maintain the Jewish belief that the lack of redemption (i.e., the "plight") was due to the "sins" of God's people, that is, their failure to fulfill the law? And if so, how did he understand the "solution"? In several passages, as we have just seen, Paul does argue that the Jewish people have not kept the law or practiced the righteousness God commands. For Paul, however, the problem is not so much that they *do* not keep the law, but that they *cannot*, because they are "under sin" and "in the flesh." Here once more, Paul is expressing an idea found in the Hebrew Scriptures and Judaism, according to which God's people needed to receive from God new hearts and new spirits so that they might become obedient. This idea is repeated both in the Rabbinic writings and in the Dead Sea Scrolls, where it is said that without divine aid the evil impulse in human beings makes it impossible for them to attain the righteousness demanded by God.[50] Paul speaks of this condition in terms of being "in the flesh" and calls the result of this condition "death" (Rom 6:16, 21; 7:5, 10, 13; 8:6). Those who are "in the flesh" live subject to "sinful passions" and desires that work in their members, bearing "fruit for death" (Rom 7:5; cf. 13:14; Gal 5:16–17, 24). The sin dwelling in human beings, or in their flesh, leads them to do evil instead of good, even when they desire not to do evil (Rom 7:14–23). Those who live according to the flesh "set their minds on the things of the flesh," and "the mind that is set on the flesh is hostile to God; it does not submit to God's law—indeed it cannot, and those who are in the flesh cannot please God" (Rom 8:5, 7–8).

What is important for Paul is that this predicament is common to Jews and Gentiles; both are subject to the flesh. For this reason, the figure of Adam is important for Paul: because both Jews and Gentiles are descended from

Adam, they share the same problem, namely, that of being subject to sin and death (Rom 5:12–21). All need to be renewed equally, since neither group can live in accordance with God's will as long as they have not received what they need from God to overcome their condition. Although this would appear to put Jews and Gentiles in the same boat, Paul continues to claim a special status for Jews. They enjoy the privilege or "advantage" of having been "entrusted with the oracles of God" (Rom 3:2) and possess "the adoption, the glory, the covenants, the giving of the law, the worship," the promises, the patriarchs, and the Messiah (Rom 9:4–5). In spite of all of this, however, they still remain under sin's power and are subject to sin, death, and the flesh, just like the Gentiles, and in this sense are "no better off" (Rom 3:9). In other words, together with the Gentiles, they live in the "present evil age" (Gal 1:4) where sin and death reign and all are subject to the flesh. This makes it impossible for them to attain the true righteousness demanded by God through his law.

For Paul, the "solution" to this plight is not to strive harder to obey the law and call on others to do the same, as other forms of "Torah-intensification" maintained. The law simply cannot produce the life of righteousness it demands or overcome the flesh; it cannot give one the power to do good and obey God's will.[51] In Rom 8:3–4, Paul claims that it was "impossible" for the law to condemn sin in the flesh and to bring about the fulfillment of the "just requirement [*dikaiōma*] of the law" in God's people. Similarly, in Gal 3:21 he argues that no law "had been given that could make alive." For this reason, it is both senseless and wrong to insist that Gentiles submit to the Jewish law, since it cannot resolve the problem of sin and the flesh, that is, human existence in the present evil age.

After insisting that no one will be justified before God by works of the law, Paul states that "apart from law, the righteousness of God has been disclosed, and is attested by the law and the prophets, the righteousness of God through faith in Jesus Christ for all who believe" (Rom 3:21–22). If the "righteousness of God" is understood here and elsewhere not merely forensically but as the righteous way of life commanded by God and in accordance with his will,[52] then Paul is saying that the righteousness necessary for salvation is brought about not by obedience to the law but through faith in Christ. As he argues in the following verses and chapter, this righteousness is freely given by God, not something produced by human beings themselves. This is essentially the Jewish and early Christian teaching, in which God is said to *give* his people *by pure grace* the new life of obedience commanded in the law, that is, his "righteousness," at the same time that he graciously forgives them their sins, accepting them as righteous.

For Paul, then, everything depends on God's grace, mercy, and kindness (Rom 2:4; 3:24; 4:16; 5:15; 9:15–16; 11:6, 22–23, 30–32). Those to be saved are "those who receive the abundance of grace and the free gift of righteousness" (Rom 5:17); "They are now justified by his grace as a gift" (Rom 3:24). This grace should not be understood as referring to a single "deed," namely, "the fact that God gave Christ up to die on the cross";[53] this is to suppose once more that what was required for human salvation was simply that Christ die. Instead, God's grace is shown in *all* that God has done and will do in and for believers; while this includes sending his Son, it involves much more. If God sent his Son to bring to fulfillment the promises he had made to Abraham and his descendants as recorded in the law and the prophets, and gave the law to Moses to make known his will and to be a "pedagogue until Christ came" (Gal 3:24*), then what God did in the centuries previous to Christ also contributes to bringing about the new condition of righteousness in believers and thus plays a role in their justification. If believers are righteous because they "have become obedient from the heart to the form of teaching" committed to them (Rom 6:17) and because they live according to the "law of Christ," then the teaching ministry Christ carried out before his death also contributes in an important way to their being accepted by God as righteous. Likewise, not only Christ's death but also his resurrection to power and the pouring out of the Holy Spirit on believers make their justification possible. So also does the fact that apostles such as Paul spread the gospel according to God's will, bringing others into the community of believers where they live "in Christ," practicing his righteousness through faith and obedience. In other words, their righteousness is the consequence not only of Christ's death but of *all* of God's gracious activity, stretching throughout human history all the way from God's election of the people before creation to the *eschaton*.

The idea that God graciously gives to believers the righteousness commanded in the law seems to be particularly behind Paul's repeated references to the outpouring of the Holy Spirit on believers in passages such as Rom 8:1–17; Gal 3:1–5; and Gal 5:16–25.[54] For Paul, the Holy Spirit is a free gift of God's grace given to believers through faith (Rom 8:15–16; Gal 3:14; 4:6; 1 Thess 4:8). The Spirit enables believers to fulfill the just requirement of the law (Rom 8:4), guides them and gives them wisdom and new life (Rom 7:6; 8:14; Gal 5:18), pours God's love into their hearts (Rom 5:5), transforms them (2 Cor 3:18), and produces good fruits in them (Gal 5:22). Above all, the Holy Spirit is associated with power, since that Spirit empowers believers to live a new life according to God's will (Rom 1:4; 15:13, 19; 1 Cor 2:4, 12; 1 Thess 1:5). At the same time, because they are "led by the Spirit," they are "not under the law" (Gal 5:18), since they fulfill the just requirement of the law by living according to its spirit, and because the Spirit gives them the power and wisdom necessary to live according to God's will, which the law alone cannot give. In this new condition, sin no longer has dominion over them; they are "set free from sin and have become slaves of God," having the power to do his will and practice righteousness (Rom 6:13–22). Those who were disobedient become obedient (Rom 11:30; 16:25). Paul stresses that this new life of obedience and righteousness is from start to finish a work of God, who begins the "good work" in believers and will bring it to completion (Phil 1:6). Everything therefore depends on the grace of God, rather than being the fruit of human efforts.

The gift of righteousness given by God involves not only a new life of obedience to God on the part of believers; as in Jewish thought, divine forgiveness is also involved. The "righteous" were not totally innocent of sin so as to have nothing for God to forgive but were "those who obeyed the commandments and atoned for transgression."[55] Yet while there is undoubtedly a forensic aspect to righteousness, it must not be reduced to this, as if it merely involved a "right standing before God" independent of and prior to a life of obedience to God. As Garlington observes, "Neither the OT nor Paul know of a righteousness which is merely forensic."[56] The fact that righteousness for Paul is not simply forensic is evident from the fact that in a passage such as Rom 6:13–19, he contrasts righteousness with "sin," tells the Roman Christians to yield their members to God as "instruments of righteousness," and calls them "slaves of righteousness." Righteousness here obviously involves something more than a right standing before God; it is something one *does*. Similarly, justification must not be reduced to forgiveness or acquittal. The understanding of justification as "acquittal" has become popular among Pauline scholars because it implies that the basis for the justification of sinful human beings lies solely in God rather than in human beings. Instead of speaking of God's pronouncing sinners "not guilty," which would involve a "legal fiction" since they *are* guilty, it is said that God "acquits" them in spite of their guilt.[57] Justification, however, involves an acknowledgment or declaration on God's part, not of *innocence* or *guiltlessness* (an idea that reflects the false notion that one has to be perfectly sinless in order to be declared righteous by God), but of *righteousness*; these must be distinguished from each other. While in part justification depends on God's graciously accepting as righteous those who are *not* perfectly righteous, since they still sin, the basis for this acceptance is also something *in them*, namely, the life of righteousness brought about by God himself through his Son and Spirit by faith. Paul recognizes at one and the same time that believers can and do sin (1 Cor 6:1; 8:12; 2 Cor 2:7–11; 13:2; Phil 3:12), that they are no longer subject to sin (Rom 6:11, 14, 18, 22), and that they are "pure" and "blameless" before God (Phil 1:10; 2:15; 1 Thess 5:23). These ideas are not mutually contradictory for Paul because, as in passages such as Jer 31:31–34, God's forgiveness and his gift of a new life of righteousness go hand in hand. Thus, both the commitment to obedience to God's will in believers and the forgiveness of their sins depend entirely on God's grace, not their own efforts or achievements.

According to Paul, God's gift of righteousness as well as the justification that goes along with it are obtained through faith. This does not mean, however, that for Paul faith replaces obedience to God's commandments as the condition necessary for salvation. Rather, faith saves because through faith one receives the gracious gift of God, the life of righteousness, which comes *ek pisteōs* or *dia pisteōs* (Rom 1:17; 3:22, 26, 30; 4:13; 9:30; 10:6; 14:23; Gal 2:16; 3:7; Phil 3:9). The new life flows out of faith, just as love is produced by faith, according to Gal 5:6. The "obedience of faith" should be understood in the same way, as the obedience that is the result of faith.[58] The idea in these passages is not so much that faith itself produces love or obedience as an immediate consequence but that through faith one receives from God through Christ and the Holy Spirit the ability to love and obey.[59] Believers are truly "righteous," but this righteousness is not of their own, "based on the law"; instead, it is a "righteousness from God" that is theirs through faith (Phil 3:9).

As noted in chapter 2, virtually all Jews would have agreed with Paul that salvation was by faith. To be faithful to the law, believing in the promises it made and attempting to obey God's commandments, was to live by faith in God. To this extent, Paul was not introducing some teaching new to Judaism but merely reminding those acquainted with the Scriptures of what they already knew. At the same time, however, the faith Paul and his fellow believers called for was not merely a general faith in God like that in Judaism but a belief regarding God's Son, Jesus Christ: it was by accepting Jesus as Lord and Son of God that one received through him the promises of the Holy Spirit, forgiveness, righteousness, and new life.

This seems to be behind Paul's use of the genitive to speak of the "faith *of* [Jesus] Christ" (*pistis [Iēsou] Christou*) as that which leads to righteousness and justification for believers.[60] A number of Pauline scholars have argued that this phrase should not be translated as "faith *in* Christ," and there seem to be good reasons for rejecting such a translation. As an alternative, however, they have claimed that the phrase alludes to the personal faith or faithfulness of Jesus Christ himself; in this case, believers are justified when they share in Christ's own faith.[61] This idea clearly responds to a participatory understanding of redemption, according to which salvation involves participating not only in Christ's death and resurrection but in his own faith, which he manifested throughout his life and particularly in his passion and death. Nevertheless, this translation is also problematic, as others such as James Dunn have shown.[62] When this phrase is viewed against the background of what was just said regarding faith and obedience in Jewish thought, it appears that Paul uses it to distinguish between a general faith in God, common to all believing Jews, and the faith related to what God had now done and would do through Jesus Christ. It was "Jesus-Christ-faith" that led to justification rather than the faith in God alone that all practicing Jews had, because it was through Jesus Christ that the divine promises were to be fulfilled and that the righteousness required by God was now to be obtained. In this case, Paul is referring neither to Jesus' own faith nor to Jesus as the *object* of faith (faith *in* Jesus Christ) but is using the genitive as he does in phrases such as the "gospel of Christ," the "hope of Christ," the "witness of Christ," the "word of Christ," the "proclamation of Christ," the "revelation of Christ," the "knowledge of Christ," and others.[63] In these passages, he is not speaking of Christ's own personal gospel, hope, witness, word, proclamation, revelation, and knowledge, but about the gospel, hope, witness, word, proclamation, revelation, and knowledge *about* or *concerning* Christ, or of which Christ is the *content*. For Paul, the object of faith is still primarily God, as in Judaism (Rom 4:3, 17, 24; Gal 3:6; 1 Thess 1:8). Yet the faith Christians have, in contrast to Jewish non-Christians, is something more extensive, embracing everything related to the coming of Jesus Christ as God's Son and Messiah, including his life, death, and resurrection, the outpouring of the Spirit, Christ's future return, and the gospel as a whole (Rom 6:8; 10:9, 14–16; Phil 1:29; 1 Thess 4:14). For this same reason, faith cannot be reduced merely to believing that Christ died and rose, or "faith in Christ's death for us,"[64] as if this was all that mattered for Paul, or what he called others to believe. Like grace, faith for Paul is concerned with *all* that God has done and will do, especially through Jesus Christ and the Holy Spirit.

Paul's arguments regarding faith and works of the law should be understood against this same background. In rejecting the "works of the law" as a means to justification and salvation, Paul is arguing against the common Jewish idea that in order to be included among those belonging to the community of the "righteous," one needed to submit to all the commandments of the Torah, including circumcision. For Paul, the community of the righteous is defined not on the basis of literal observance of such commandments but on the basis of faith, since it is through faith that one receives the gift of righteousness and all of the promises made by God of old. Now that God has acted in Christ to give his people the righteousness he commanded and to enable them to fulfill the "just requirement of the law" (Rom 8:4), what is called for is simply to receive what God offers; to reject it is to reject God's grace. This is basically Paul's argument in Gal 2:21—3:5, where he insists that to attempt to be justified on the basis of the law is to "nullify the grace of God" (2:21). This is because in Christ God has freely and graciously poured out the Holy Spirit on those who receive God's promises through faith; Paul insists that the Galatian Gentiles received the Holy Spirit when they came to faith, and not by "works of the law" (3:2). As in the story of Peter and Cornelius in Acts 10:44–48, the reception of the Holy Spirit is a clear sign that one belongs to the community of the righteous. The fact that the Gentile believers in Galatia had already received the Holy Spirit when they came to faith, without having submitted to circumcision and other commandments of the Torah, was evidence that they had already been incorporated into the community of the righteous, and that God's promises came through faith, not through obedience to the works of the law. Therefore, it was obvious that submission to the Torah was not a condition for attaining the promises. To attempt to gain those promises by submitting to the literal commandments of the law was to nullify what God had done, rejecting the "new creation" and returning to the old situation of the "flesh" in which they found themselves previously (Gal 3:3; 6:15). Those who return to the law in order to be justified by it have "fallen away from grace" (Gal 5:4), because they are attempting to gain righteousness through obedience to the literal commandments of the law, instead of simply accepting the righteousness freely and graciously given by God.

Virtually the same argument appears in Rom 9:30—10:13. There Paul argues that the Gentiles, who did not seek righteousness, have attained it through faith, in contrast to "Israel," who pursued a righteousness based on the law but did not attain that righteousness or fulfill the law, because the people sought this "not through faith, but by works" (9:31–32*). In Christ, God had finally acted to make his righteousness possible, offering the repentance and obedience he desired and commanded. But those who rejected Christ, the "stumbling stone" (9:32–33), also rejected the "righteousness that comes from God," seeking to establish their own righteousness in their zeal for the law rather than submitting to that given by God (10:3). The "righteousness coming from faith" (*ek pisteōs*) merely accepts the gift given through Christ, whom God raised from the dead (10:5–10); God "bestows his riches upon all who call upon him" in faith (10:12), not upon those who zealously strive to keep the literal commandments of the law by their own power.

In both Romans and Galatians Paul looks to the story of Abraham to ground this same argument. Abraham had been pronounced righteous by God merely by accepting God's promises in faith, "fully convinced that God was able to do what he had promised" (Rom 4:21). This occurred "*before* he was circumcised" (Rom 4:10) and before the law had been given (Gal 3:17), which was proof that circumcision and obedience to the law were not required in order to be accepted by God as righteous and to be counted among the children of Abraham. Now through Christ God was graciously acting to fulfill his promises, and all that was necessary to receive them was to respond in faith, and live "out of" faith (*ek pisteōs*). In this sense, it can be said that faith itself *is* righteousness and obedience: those who believe in and trust God, as Abraham did, are graciously accepted by God as righteous, because they are doing what God wants them to do, merely receiving what he gives. For the same reason, it can also be said that salvation and justification are by faith *alone*, not because obedience is unnecessary, but because the life of righteousness is given by God to those who simply trust in him and receive what he offers. In that way, God himself enables them to do the works he commands, and on the basis of which he will judge human beings. What is called for, therefore, is simply to trust in God and put oneself entirely in God's hands, as Abraham did. Of course, the content of Abraham's faith was distinct from the content of the faith now found in believers, since in Abraham's day Christ had not yet come. Now that Christ had been revealed as God's instrument for fulfilling his promises, however, to reject Christ was to reject the promises regarding the new age, which was now to become a reality through him. Therefore, to return to the law and accept circumcision was to "turn back again to the weak and beggarly elemental spirits" of this age (Gal 4:9) and end up once more "with the flesh" (Gal 3:3), attempting to attain the righteousness necessary for redemption through the commandments of the Torah; this not only was futile but represented a return to the condition of slavery (Gal 2:4; 4:7–9; 5:1).

According to Paul, then, this kind of faith constitutes the "solution" to the "plight" of Israel as well as that of the rest of the world, in that it leads to the life of righteousness and obedience to God's will that God commands and desires, and to a life of trust in God's grace, mercy, and forgiveness. In this regard, Paul is once again in basic continuity with the Christian story of redemption considered in chapter 3, in which salvation depends on following Jesus Christ as Lord in faith and living according to God's will, fulfilling the law in the way Jesus taught, while at the same time looking to God's love and mercy for forgiveness.

Redemption as a Future Occurrence

As noted above, it has been common to attribute to Paul some type of realized eschatology, according to which some kind of change has taken place in the human situation or the world in general as a result of Christ's death and resurrection. This is due primarily to the fact that in a number of passages, Paul speaks of salvation, redemption, and reconciliation with God in the past tense, implying that in some sense it has already become a reality (e.g., Rom 5:10; 2 Cor 5:18–19; Gal 3:13). Elsewhere Paul writes that "if anyone is in Christ, that person is a new creation; the old things have passed away; see, they have become new" (2 Cor 5:17*). He also affirms that believers have been set free from sin and the flesh and have died and been crucified and buried with Christ (Rom 6:6–8, 18–22; 7:5–6, 9; 8:2; Gal 5:24). These passages seem to contradict others in Paul, often found in the same context, where he talks of redemption and liberation in the future tense, exhorts believers to be reconciled to God (as if they have not yet been reconciled), and insists that they are still under sin and in the flesh.[65]

While there are no doubt some passages that speak of salvation in the past tense, it is important to stress that the same type of futuristic eschatology found in ancient Jewish thought and the early Christian proclamation is much more common in Paul. According to the ancient Jewish story of salvation and the Christian story that grew out of it, the awaited redemption involving the restoration of Israel, the destruction of God's (and Israel's) enemies, the resurrection of the dead, and the final judgment still lies in the future. This is clearly the teaching of Paul as well, who repeatedly looks forward to Christ's *parousia*, the "day of the Lord" or of Jesus Christ.[66] James Dunn rightly observes that "the coming again of Christ was a firm part of Paul's theology, maintained consistently from first to last in our written sources."[67] Paul also affirms that on that day, the dead will be raised and all people judged, seeing these things as acts of both God and Christ, or of God *through* (*dia*) Christ (Rom 2:16; 1 Thess 4:14). Evildoers together with Satan and the rulers of this age will suffer wrath, tribulation, and destruction (Rom 2:5–10; 16:20; 1 Cor 2:6), while believers will receive eternal life and be "saved by [Christ] from the wrath to come" (Rom 5:9; cf. 1 Thess 1:10; 5:9). Here it is important to emphasize that, for Paul, this salvation from divine wrath is something that will occur *in the future*; nowhere does he write that believers have *already* been delivered from God's wrath, or that that wrath has already come to an end.

All of this means that, strictly speaking, for Paul salvation is *still to come*; it has *not yet actually taken place*. Paul repeatedly speaks of salvation as a "hope," something to be "awaited" (Rom 5:2; 15:12–13; 1 Cor 1:7; 2 Cor 4:17–18; Phil 3:20; 1 Thess 1:10; 5:8). This is true even in the one passage where he refers to salvation in the past tense:

> We ourselves . . . groan inwardly while we wait for adoption, the redemption of our bodies. For in this hope we were saved. Now hope that is seen is not hope. For who hopes for what is seen? But if we hope for what we do not see, we wait for it with patience. (Rom 8:23–25)

In this regard, then, Paul is fully in agreement with the early Christian proclamation and with ancient Jewish thought in seeing salvation as something still lying in the future, involving a visible and radical transformation of the present world or age.

Paul's use of the past tense in referring to certain aspects of salvation in Christ, therefore, must be seen against this background. A close look at Paul's epistles reveals that he never says that the new age has begun or that some type of cosmic transformation has occurred. On the contrary, as David Lull notes, in Gal 1:4 Paul "implies that the *present* age, even after the coming of Christ, is *still* 'evil,'" and that "the end of 'the present evil age' has not yet come."[68] Likewise, the fact that Paul speaks of the creation presently "groaning in travail" awaiting its liberation and redemption (Rom 8:21–22) means that for Paul the world has not undergone any type of mysterious transformation as a result of Christ's death and resurrection; it is still "subjected to futility." To be sure, Paul writes that the "appointed time has grown short," "the present form of this world is passing away," and the "last things [*ta telē*] of the ages have come" (1 Cor 7:29-31; 10:11*); yet such phrases only affirm that the *eschaton* is near, not that it has actually arrived in some sense.[69]

In order to understand the Pauline passages that appear to support some type of realized eschatology, we need merely consider once more several of the ideas presented in chapter 3. As noted there, what was proclaimed by Christians was that the fulfillment of the divine promises was now a certainty through Christ. This certainty was based, first, on Christ's resurrection: because he has been raised to power at God's right hand as Lord, Messiah, and Savior, there can be no question that he will make the promised redemption a reality. Therefore, those who belong to him, living "in" him or under his lordship, can be sure of their ultimate redemption. Second, the certainty of believers is also based on the fact that they have received the eschatological gift of the Holy Spirit; those who have received that Spirit and walk in the Spirit know that they belong to God and Christ and will be saved when Christ comes again.

The notion that Christ's resurrection to power provides certainty regarding salvation for believers is reflected in several passages in Paul's letters. In 1 Cor 15:12–17, for instance, Paul insists that if Christ has not been raised, the faith of the Corinthian Christians is "futile" and "in vain," and they are still in their sins. Here it is important to recall once more that in Jewish thought to speak of "forgiveness of sins" was to speak of the promised redemption. While in one sense both that redemption and the forgiveness of sins associated with it lay in the future, those who formed part of the community living under Christ as Lord could now be certain of their redemption, and hence the forgiveness of their sins as well. God would overlook their sins at the final judgment by virtue of their relationship to Christ, who would save them from God's wrath. For Paul, as in the rest of Scripture, this forgiveness is primarily an eschatological promise, as Rom 11:26–27 makes clear. However, their certainty of redemption and forgiveness through Christ depended on Christ's having been raised and exalted. If he had not been raised but remained dead in the grave, how could he return someday to bring in the new age and accomplish their redemption? In that case, they had no assurance of forgiveness of sins through him, and their faith was futile.

Paul's language concerning justification should be understood against the same background. Paul frequently speaks of justification in the *future* tense: those who are in Christ by virtue of their faith *will be* justified or pronounced righteous by God at the last judgment (Rom 2:13; 3:20, 30; Gal 2:16). Nevertheless, because Christ was "raised for our justification" (Rom 4:25), Paul can also speak of justification in the present and past tenses: by virtue of Christ's resurrection and the fact that believers are "in him," they can now be certain that God will ultimately accept them among the righteous to be redeemed. Because Christ "was raised from the dead" and is "at the right hand of God," believers know that no one will be able to bring any charge against them and that they will not be condemned; instead, God will give them "all things with him" (Rom 8:31–39). In effect, by raising Christ as Lord, God has already pronounced his acceptance of all those who belong to Christ, since God raised Christ precisely so that Christ might return to bring about their salvation. Thus, even though the final judgment still awaits believers, they can be certain that they will not be condemned but accepted as righteous by God, because in reality they already have been.

For Paul, Christ's resurrection also ensures the resurrection of believers. This is not, however, because believers have somehow participated mysteriously in the event of Christ's resurrection through their incorporation into him, or because there is some cause-and-effect relationship between Christ's resurrection and their own, so that their resurrection follows automatically upon his. Rather, the assurance of believers in this regard rests on the fact that their Lord, who loves them so much that he was willing to give up his life on their behalf, has now been given the "power that also enables him to make all things subject to himself" (Phil 3:21). Therefore, they know that nothing can now prevent him from returning to raise them from the dead in order to give them the life promised to them.

The second ground for certainty regarding salvation for believers is their reception of God's Holy Spirit. This idea is found in a number of Pauline passages. In Rom 8:11, for example, Paul writes, "If the Spirit of him who raised Jesus from the dead dwells in you, he who raised Christ from the dead will give life to your mortal bodies also through his Spirit that dwells in you." The fact that believers have received God's Spirit and walk in that Spirit means that they are members of the people chosen by God in Christ; as part of that people, they can be sure that they will be raised to participate in the life of the coming age. For this same reason, Paul speaks of the Holy Spirit as the *arrabōn*, the "guarantee" or "first installment" given to believers by God (1 Cor 1:22; 5:5). Because they have received the promise of the Spirit, they can be sure that they will receive all the other promises as well.[70] This means that they are also "sons and daughters" of God and his "heirs" (Rom 8:16–17; Gal 3:29; 4:6–7; cf. Rom 4:13–14; 1 Cor 6:9–10; Gal 3:18; 5:21). Just as "heirs" can be certain that someday they will receive their inheritance even though they do not yet actually possess it, so believers can be certain that they will receive the life of the age to come, even though in reality it is not yet theirs.

All of this means that, for Paul, as in the early Christian tradition, what has changed is that believers can now have full assurance of their inclusion among those to be saved by God. It is on this basis that Paul can use the past tense: when God raised the Son for them and poured out the Spirit on those belonging to the Son's community of followers, they were redeemed, saved, justified, and forgiven in the sense that these things were ensured. On an individual level, their incorporation through baptism into the community of the "saints" or "holy ones" who are "without blemish" (Phil 2:15) means that they have now been "washed," "sanctified," and "justified in the name of the Lord Jesus Christ and in the Spirit of our God" (1 Cor 6:11). Through faith and baptism they have come to form part of the community whose sins are forgiven by God and whose future redemption and justification are certain. At the same time, their adoption as God's children and the redemption of their bodies involve a "hope" and require patient waiting (Rom 8:24–25).

Nevertheless, in Paul's thought, it is not just Christ's resurrection that results in these things but his death as well. The idea, however, is not that Jesus' death in some way has "effected" salvation, redemption, justification, and reconciliation with God for believers, but rather that Jesus' faithfulness unto death in seeking these things for others in obedience to God's will led to God's raising him from the dead so that they might be accomplished through him. As was argued above, these were things sought by Jesus not only in death but in the ministry that led to his death. The idea that God raised Jesus because of his faithfulness to the end to the task given him by God is most clearly affirmed by Paul in Phil 2:5–11, where, after recalling Jesus' service and obedience unto death on a cross, he writes, "*Therefore* [*dio*] God highly exalted him and also gave him the name that is above every name" (v. 9, emphasis added). Thus, through his obedience unto death in seeking salvation and redemption for others, Jesus attained that salvation and redemption for others when he was raised by God as a result of that obedience. Furthermore, Jesus' death can also be said to have been the means by which God accomplished the salvation of many because it led to the establishment of a new covenant and the incorporation of many more people, especially Gentiles, into the community of those to be saved.

Of course, this does not mean that in Paul's mind there is no transformation in the present. Those who are in Christ are certainly a "new creation" in that, having subjected themselves to Christ's lordship and having begun to walk in the Spirit, they have left behind their former way of life and now identify with the coming age rather than the present evil one. Through that Spirit they are being changed into Christ's likeness "from one degree of glory to another" (2 Cor 3:18). This means that they are "those who are being saved" (*hoi sōzomenoi*, 1 Cor 1:18; 2 Cor 2:15). While in one sense they are already righteous and "perfect" or "complete," in another they still "wait for the hope of righteousness" (Gal 5:5) as well as their perfection, which is not yet a reality.[71] As long as they remain in Christ, however, they will attain the goal of righteousness, and the work begun in them will be completed (Phil 1:6).

Nevertheless, it is important to note that Paul does not speak of this transformation as affecting anything or anyone but believers. As Paul affirms in 2 Cor 5:17, it is only the person who is "in Christ" who is a "new creation." Similarly, in Gal 6:15, he contrasts the "new creation" with circumcision and uncircumcision, both of which have to do with states in which *individuals* find themselves. By using that phrase, Paul is probably saying nothing more than that those who come to believe in Christ become new persons. Believing Jews no longer live merely as other Jews nor as pagan Gentiles, and believing Gentiles neither remain the pagans they were nor become Jews; rather, both are a "new creation." This same phrase appears in the Jewish work *Joseph and Aseneth*, where it is applied to Aseneth on the occasion of her adoption of

Judaism. She became a "new creation" in the sense that she began a new life very different from the one she had led before, and thereby became a new person.[72] Thus, there is no basis here for arguing that when Paul speaks of a new creation, he has in mind a "new created world," the inauguration of the "ontological transformation of the created order" through Christ's death and resurrection, or some type of cosmic redemption or alteration of human nature as a whole.[73] Rather, as believers offer themselves as a "living sacrifice, holy and acceptable to God," refusing to be "conformed to this age" but instead being transformed by the renewal of their mind (Rom 12:1–2), they become new persons. Only in this sense can it be said that, for them, "the old things have passed away; see, they have become new" (2 Cor 5:17*).

For Paul, then, as for the first Christians, what had come was not the awaited redemption itself but the long-awaited divine activity through which that redemption would be brought about. Through his Son and Spirit, God had now been at work to ensure that all the promises he had made would be fulfilled, and he would continue to be active until those promises were fulfilled entirely. In this regard, Paul's proclamation is in line with the Jewish expectations concerning redemption, according to which God, who had apparently been "silent" and inactive for centuries while his people languished in oppression, had to become active once more in order for his people to be delivered from their plight. At the same time, however, as Paul himself recognized, this divine activity had not occurred in precisely the way that the Jews (including Paul himself) had been expecting. While many were expecting a Messiah, they had not been expecting a Messiah who would be put to death on a cross; this idea was a *skandalon* for many (1 Cor 1:23). Nor were they expecting things in the world to remain essentially the same after the Messiah had come. Instead, they looked for concrete and visible signs of the arrival of the new age (1 Cor 1:22), which no doubt included things such as the overthrow of Israel's enemies, the return of God's people from the diaspora, and the full restoration of Israel. For Paul, such things are yet to come.

Paul's Story and the Jewish and Christian Stories

How, then, does Paul's story compare with the ancient Jewish and early Christian stories of redemption? Like the early Christian story, Paul agrees with the story common to many first-century Jews in conceiving of redemption in terms of the restoration of Israel and the gathering in of the "elect," the resurrection of the dead, and a final judgment, as well as the coming of a new world or age. All of this is to take place through God's Messiah, Jesus. In addition, Paul claims that repentance, obedience, and fulfillment of the law are necessary in order to attain these promises, in continuity with ancient Jewish beliefs.

However, we also find in Paul the same differences from the Jewish story of redemption that we identified in the early Christian story. The specific promises regarding the land, the city of Jerusalem, and the Temple are relatively unimportant. In fact, Paul interprets in spiritual or allegorical terms the promises regarding the Temple and Jerusalem (Gal 5:25–26), just as he interprets in spiritual terms the ideas of circumcision and descent from Abraham, as previously noted. The law receives basically the same treatment: its fulfillment is understood more in spiritual than in literal terms.

Paul's understanding of the "plight" is essentially the same as that found in ancient Judaism and early Christianity: because of human sinfulness, redemption has not yet arrived. However, whereas in the Jewish tradition the plight of Israel was tied to the specific sins of Israel, particularly its failure to observe the law, Paul's desire to include uncircumcised Gentiles in a redefined Israel results in a more universal presentation of the plight and the coming redemption. For Paul, the plight of Israel on account of the people's sins is not different from the plight of the Gentiles, as it is in Jewish thought, but instead is *the same plight*: *all* are under sin and subject to death. The possession of the law of Moses on the part of the Jewish people does not alter this fact, since the law cannot provide the solution to the plight.

As in the early Christian story, Paul proclaims that the solution to this plight is found in Christ. Through faith one receives the gifts of forgiveness and a new life of righteousness in which one can fulfill the righteous demands of the law in the way taught by Jesus, guided and empowered by the Holy Spirit. While such an idea is a development of Jewish beliefs, at the same time it is different, both because it was not necessarily thought that these things would occur through a Messiah such as Jesus, and because it was expected that these things would only occur in the new age. What Paul and other Christians were saying was that instead of waiting for the arrival of the new age to pour out the Holy Spirit and change the hearts of his people, God had done so in the present age, at least to a degree. This claim was evidently rejected by non-Christian Jews, yet Paul nevertheless expected that his audience would readily understand it, and even pointed to evidence of it. In a passage such as Gal 3:2–5, he assumes that it is obvious even to his opponents that believers have received the Holy Spirit, probably because the presence and activity of the Spirit was manifested visibly in some way among them.

It is very likely that these ideas are behind much of the language that is unique to Paul. If the Holy Spirit had already been poured out as an *arrabōn* on God's people so as to change their situation radically, then Paul had to find a term he might use to describe the situation of those who had *not* received the Holy Spirit. The term he chose was "flesh," which refers to the existence of those who live only the life of the present age.[74] Likewise, in order to refer to the general human tendency or inclination to disobey God's will and practice unrighteousness, he chose the word "sin" (in the singular). Although it may have been common in Judaism to speak of the two tendencies in human beings, the impulse for good and the impulse for evil, Paul could not employ this distinction because his teaching was different. For Paul, what enables one to do good is not an impulse for good that is naturally present in human beings but the gift of the Spirit. A life lived under sin's power, according to the flesh, is for Paul "death," since it does not lead to the life of the new age; this is the condition that came to reign as a result of Adam's sin (Rom 5:14, 17, 21). Contrary to what has often been affirmed, ideas such as these can be understood quite well without looking outside of the ancient Jewish and early Christian traditions.[75]

Thus, although there are developments in Paul's thought in relation to the Jewish story of redemption, it is clear that his story of redemption is in close continuity with Jewish beliefs on the subject. The same must be said regarding the early Christian story of redemption: Paul is telling essentially the same story that we find in the Gospels and Acts. Undoubtedly, there are differences. Yet to a large extent these differences must be attributed to the fact that Paul wrote letters, and not a Gospel or a book such as the Acts of the Apostles. These latter writings purport to relate historical events in an orderly fashion, and although they are undoubtedly also theological writings, the theological interpretation of those events is generally not provided. The Synoptic evangelists rarely comment on the events they narrate. While neither Matthew nor Mark interprets the saying attributed to Jesus about destroying the Temple and raising it up in three days, as John does when he affirms that Jesus "spoke of the temple of his body" (John 2:19–21), it can hardly be doubted that they understood that saying in somewhat similar terms. Nor can there be any doubt that the Synoptics ascribed similar theological significance to events such as the cursing of the fig tree, the rending of the Temple veil at Jesus' death, and the feedings of the five thousand and four thousand that were followed by the collection of twelve baskets and seven baskets of leftovers, respectively (which the disciples did "not yet understand," Mark 8:17–21). Nevertheless, the evangelists do not interpret these events for their audience and instead assume that their readers will be able to "fill in" the theological significance of these events, evidently on the basis of a theological interpretation of the story that they are already acquainted with.

In contrast, in Acts the theological interpretation of certain events is often provided, primarily in the speeches and sayings ascribed to the apostles and first believers. Thus, for example, while the Synoptics tell of Jesus' resurrection, they never explicitly refer to Jesus' being "exalted" or affirm that God was the one who raised Jesus, as Acts consistently does, even though it can hardly be doubted that they understood Jesus' resurrection in those terms and expected that their readers would do so as well. Similarly, while in Acts it is explicitly stated that God predestined the events surrounding Jesus' death to take place (2:23; 4:27–28), such an idea is only hinted at by the writers of the Gospels, who evidently expected that their repeated mention of the Scriptures' being fulfilled would be understood in this way.

In Paul's letters we find the exact opposite of what is in the Synoptics. Instead of providing a narration of events and assuming that his audience will be able to understand their theological significance, Paul alludes to the theological significance and interpretation of events and assumes that his readers are already acquainted with the narratives regarding those events. This makes it easy to conclude that Paul is telling a different story. Such a conclusion, however, is unjustified, just as it would be unjustified to conclude that the Synoptics did not interpret theologically the events they relate in the way Paul did, simply because they do not provide us with those interpretations explicitly.

Paul's letters, therefore, certainly do present us with a story that goes beyond that which we find in the Gospels. There is what we might call a "proto-history" concerning Adam, the spread of sin and death on account of Adam's disobedience, the giving of the law, and a divine plan regarding human salvation preordained in some sense even before the creation of the world.

This proto-history also concerns the figure of Jesus himself, to whom Paul apparently ascribes some type of preexistence; the divine plan revolved around Jesus from the beginning, since God intended for many to be "conformed to the image of his Son" (Rom 8:29). The belief in the preexistence of Christ probably developed out of Jewish beliefs regarding the preexistence of God's wisdom and the Torah. If Christ as God's Son is the wisdom of God (1 Cor 1:24, 30) and is superior to the Torah, which in Jewish thought existed before creation, then he must have existed before creation as well, and the divine plan must have revolved around him from the start, rather than around the Torah, as many Jews believed.[76] At any rate, none of this is explicitly found in the Gospels, yet it can scarcely be doubted that the early Christian story of redemption included some such type of proto-history.

While it is difficult to reconstruct fully that part of the story, from what we have seen we can conclude that the story of redemption told by Paul was essentially the same as that told by the other Christians of his day, and that it combined historical and theological elements. If this is the case, then Paul would have expected his readers to look to that story for the background necessary to interpret his formulaic allusions to Jesus' death. Thus, we may tentatively conclude that the assumptions considered at the outset of this chapter are for the most part foreign to Paul's thought. Paul does *not* regard Christ's death as the solution to the human plight, so as to build his soteriology around that belief or take it as his starting point. Nor does Paul maintain that Christ's death has *effected* human salvation or forgiveness, or brought about some actual change in the created order or the human situation. From what has been seen so far, there is no reason to claim that Paul looked *outside* of the tradition he received in order to understand the redemptive significance of Jesus' death, or that he invented a story of redemption of his own that was fundamentally different from the early Christian story. Instead, a proper understanding of the story regarding Jesus that we find in the Gospels and Acts is sufficient for comprehending Paul's soteriological language, as will be argued further in the following chapters.

CHAPTER 5

Jesus' Death "For Us"
in Paul's Letters

At least since the time of Rudolf Bultmann, it has been common among Pauline scholars to separate Paul's language concerning Jesus' death into two categories: the "cultic" or "juristic," and the "participatory" or "mystical."[1] Generally, the two categories are defined in terms similar to those employed by E. P. Sanders, who claims that it is a "distinction which will not go away": "In brief, it is the distinction between saying that Christ dies *for* Christians and that they die *with* Christ, between saying that Christians are sanctified and justified from their past transgressions and that they have died with Christ to the power of sin."[2] According to this view, Jesus' death on the cross serves *two* purposes, that of dealing with the *penalty* or *consequences* of human sin, and that of dealing with its *power*: "Christ's death was for acquittal and to provide participation in his death to the power of sin, and these are conceived not as two different things, but as one."[3]

Yet if Christ's death for Paul has two distinct purposes, and thus two distinct effects, it is not clear how it can be said that these are "conceived not as two different things, but as one." It would appear that Paul is telling not *one* but *two* stories concerning the cross. According to one story, human beings are saved from the penalty or consequences of their sin through Christ, whom God sent to take that penalty or those consequences upon himself in their stead. According to the other story, human beings are saved from their subjection to sin and death by participating in Christ's death to these powers and his resurrection to new life. The fact that Paul seems to have more than one understanding of the redemptive significance of Christ's death has often led to the conclusion made by Sanders: Paul was not a systematic theologian and thus felt no need to work his juristic and participatory thought "into a coherent and logical whole."[4] While there is "a basic coherence" in his thought, "it is not *systematically* worked out. The precise relation, for example, between acquittal and death to the power of sin did not appear to Paul as a problem which required resolution."[5]

Of course, as we saw in chapter 1, Paul's references to the cross have been interpreted against the framework of other stories as well. If in fact a variety of different stories are behind his thought, and if it is impossible to reconcile these different stories to one another fully, then Paul's teaching cannot be reduced to a single system. This would mean that for Paul there was more than one purpose behind Jesus' death, and that Paul believed it had various "effects" or, in the words of Richard Hays, "multifaceted consequences."[6]

As has been argued in chapter 3, however, these interpretations of Jesus' death are fundamentally different from those found in the Synoptic Gospels and Acts. The question to be addressed here, therefore, is whether the story behind Paul's language regarding Jesus' death is the same as that outlined in chapter 3 or whether it is instead some version of one or more of the other stories considered in chapter 1. In this chapter, we will consider Paul's "cultic-juristic" language, and in chapter 6, his "participatory" language.

Paul and the Early Christian Understanding of Jesus' Death

If the story of redemption told by Paul was essentially the same story found in the tradition reflected in the Synoptic Gospels and Acts, as was argued in the last chapter, then it would seem logical to assume that he understood the salvific significance of Jesus' death in the same terms they did. In addition to the fact that Paul uses creedal and kerygmatic formulae to refer to Jesus' death, even when writing to Christians he did not know, there are other reasons to assume that Paul's interpretation of the cross was the same as that found elsewhere in the early church. The most important of these is that, in two passages in particular, Paul alludes to the tradition regarding Jesus' death that he had not only received but also taught to others. In 1 Cor 11:23–25, he writes that he had passed on to the Corinthians what he had "received from the Lord" regarding Jesus' words over the bread and wine at the Last Supper.[7] Later in the same letter he tells the Corinthians, "For I handed on to you as of first importance what I in turn had received: that Christ died for our sins in accordance with the scriptures, and that he was buried, and that he was raised on the third day in accordance with the scriptures, and that he appeared to Cephas, then to the twelve" (1 Cor 15:3–5). Both of these passages clearly indicate that the tradition regarding Jesus' death that Paul had received included not merely the "bare events" related to the crucifixion but also a theological interpretation of those events, and it was this theological interpretation that he passed on to others. Many scholars, in fact, believe that some of the other formulae Paul uses to refer to Jesus' death are taken from tradition as well. This supports the claim that Paul's theology of the cross was in continuity with that of his contemporaries rather than being something he developed on his own.

Another reason for supposing that Paul understood the significance of the cross in essentially the same terms as the other Christians of his day is that some of the same ideas associated with Jesus' death in the Synoptics and Acts are also found in Paul's letters. It was already noted in the last chapter that Paul ties Jesus' death to his ministry for others, and that he is acquainted with important aspects of the passion narratives, including the idea that Jesus was rejected and gave himself up in accordance with God's will, thus fulfilling the Scriptures. However, Paul's allusion to Jesus' words over the bread and wine at the Last Supper also demonstrates that he is acquainted with the idea that Jesus' death led to the establishment of a new covenant revolving around Jesus.

Outside of 1 Cor 11:25, the idea of a new covenant appears in two passages in Paul's letters, 2 Cor 3:1–18 and Gal 4:21–31. In the second of these passages, Paul claims that Hagar and Sarah represent "two covenants" (v. 24): the first of these covenants is the one associated with Sinai, while the second has to do with the "children of promise" who live in freedom rather than under the law. Paul's citation of Isa 54:1 with regard to the number of children each woman had seems to be an allusion to the incorporation of Gentiles into the church under the new covenant.[8] In 2 Corinthians 3, after affirming that God "has made us competent to be ministers of a new covenant, not of letter but of spirit" (v. 6), Paul speaks of the Mosaic covenant as an "old covenant" and a "dispensation of death" and "of condemnation"; this stands in contrast to the "dispensation of the spirit" and "of righteousness," which far exceeds the former in splendor and "is permanent" (vv. 7–11, 14*). The idea is that in the new covenant believers are guided by the spirit (or Spirit) rather than the letter of the law (v. 6). Paul's contrast between what is written on "tablets of human hearts" and what is written on "tablets of stone" (v. 3) seems to be a reference to a new dispensation of the law coming through Christ and the Spirit, replacing or surpassing the dispensation under Moses at Sinai. As noted previously, the idea of writing on "tablets of human hearts" may be an allusion to Jer 31:31–34, where God promises to write his law on the hearts of his people and make a new covenant with them.[9] This same passage from Jeremiah ties the notion of forgiveness of sins to the new covenant; there God promises, "I will forgive their iniquity, and I will remember their sin no more." The same connection between the new covenant and the forgiveness of sins made by Matthew in his account of Jesus' words at the Last Supper (Matt 26:28) is made by Paul in Rom 11:26–27, where he quotes from Isa 59:20–21 and 27:9: "Out of Zion will come the Deliverer; he will banish ungodliness from Jacob. And this is my covenant with them, when I take away their sins." Thus, for Paul as well as the Synoptics, the ideas of the incorporation of Gentiles, a new dispensation of the Spirit and of righteousness, and the forgiveness of sins are associated with the concept of a new covenant. Consequently, when Paul alludes to Jesus' words regarding "the new covenant in my blood," there can be little doubt that he has these ideas in mind as well. Through Jesus' death a new covenant was established in which both Jews and non-Jews now live under a new dispensation led by the Spirit and receive the forgiveness of sins.

Paul also appears to be acquainted with the idea that a new temple comes into existence through Jesus' death, and perhaps even associates this new temple with Jesus' body. As noted in chapter 3, the idea that through Jesus' death a new temple or new reality would come into existence appears to be present both in the conclusion to the parable of the wicked tenants and in the words attributed to Jesus about destroying and rebuilding the Temple in three days. In 1 Cor 3:10–17, Paul affirms that "no one can lay any foundation other than the one that has been laid; that foundation is Jesus Christ" (v. 11), and then tells the Corinthians, "Do you not know that you are God's temple and that God's Spirit dwells in you? If anyone destroys God's temple, God will destroy that person. For God's temple is holy, and you are that temple" (vv. 16–17). Undoubtedly, here Jesus is presented as the "foundation" rather than the "cornerstone," as in the conclusion of the parable of the wicked tenants. The basic idea is the same, however: Jesus has become the cornerstone or foundation for a new temple, in contrast to the Jerusalem Temple; and this new temple, composed of believers, has become the place where God dwells through his Spirit.[10] These ideas appear explicitly in Eph 2:18–22.

With regard to the words ascribed to Jesus about destroying and rebuilding the Temple in three days, it was observed in chapter 3 that in light of John 2:19–21 it appears that there may have been a connection between the concepts of Jesus' body and the new temple among the first Christians.[11] If so, Jesus' words over the bread at the Last Supper (1 Cor 11:24) may have been understood as communicating the idea that, by giving over his body to death, Jesus or his body would become a new temple or else become the foundation of a new temple composed of God's new covenant people. In 1 Cor 6:19 Paul relates the concepts of body and temple, though he never speaks of Christ's body as a new temple; instead, it is the body of believers that is God's temple (1 Cor 3:16; 2 Cor 6:16).[12] However, it is significant that he does call the believers at Corinth both "the temple of God" and "the body of Christ" (1 Cor 12:27). Elsewhere, Paul speaks of Christ's body in a seemingly ambiguous sense. In 1 Cor 11:29 he speaks of eating and drinking without "discerning the body" while discussing the need for the Corinthians to remain united as a community in celebrating the Lord's Supper. And in Rom 7:4, he tells the Roman believers, "You have died to the law through the body of Christ." Scholars have long debated whether in these passages Paul has in mind Christ's own body or the church as the body of Christ.[13] It may be, however, that Paul intentionally uses the phrase to bring together both ideas: by giving up his body in death for others, Jesus has brought into existence a new body of his own composed of believers who live as members of a community that is no longer under the law.

A number of other Pauline passages reflect the idea that a new covenant has come to surpass the old Mosaic covenant. Believers constitute a new covenant people, the Israel of God, the true children of Abraham, and the true circumcision (Rom 4:11–18; Gal 3:29; 6:16; Phil 3:3). The circumcision that now matters is not the "literal" circumcision prescribed in the old covenant, but the "spiritual" circumcision of the heart (Rom 2:29). The "baptism" of God's people that occurred under Moses and the food and drink that they received in the desert, have been replaced by a new baptism and a new "spiritual" food and drink in Christ, the Rock from whom all drank (1 Cor 10:1–4). Rather than presenting sacrifices at the Jerusalem Temple, believers offer up to God their own bodies "as a living sacrifice, holy and acceptable to God," as their "spiritual worship" (Rom 12:1). Like the old covenant, the new covenant also has its "ministers" (2 Cor 3:6), among whom is Paul himself, whose "priestly service" is that of seeking that "the offering of the Gentiles may be acceptable, sanctified by the Holy Spirit" (Rom 15:16). In Christ, believers have their own Passover lamb who has been sacrificed, and they celebrate this new Passover by cleansing out the old "yeast of malice and evil" and partaking of the "unleavened bread of sincerity and truth" (1 Cor 5:7–9). All of these ideas indicate that Paul is in agreement with the conclusion drawn in chapter 3: *everything found in the Mosaic covenant was now to be found in its fullness in the new covenant under Jesus.*

All of this must have been in Paul's mind, therefore, when he recalled Jesus' words at the Last Supper: the giving up of his body and the shedding of his blood had led to the establishment of a new covenant in which people might attain all the blessings promised of old by God, including the forgiveness of sins, a new life of righteousness, the gift of the Holy Spirit, and the certainty of the life of the age to come. In this regard, Paul is in close continuity with the tradition we find in the Synoptic Gospels and Acts.

"For Us"

The idea that Christ died "for" others is found in some form or another about ten times in Paul's epistles; usually the phrase employed is "for us" (*hyper hēmōn*).[14] While most of these passages will be examined below, here it is important to make a couple of observations regarding this phrase and how it might have been understood according to the early Christian story of redemption. First, when Paul uses the phrase "for us," he is writing to fellow Christians, almost all of whom have joined the church at least several years after the events surrounding Jesus' death. Thus, when referring to "us," Paul generally has a very specific group of people in mind.

Second, contrary to what many New Testament scholars have claimed,[15] there is no reason to translate the phrase *hyper hēmōn* as "in our stead." Such a translation depends on a penal substitution understanding of Christ's death, in which he dies in the place of others so that they need no longer die. Paul never claims, however, that believers no longer die, either in the spiritual or in the physical sense. On the contrary, he repeatedly states that they will and must die, both spiritually (Rom 6:8) and physically (unless Christ returns before they die). Nor does Paul ever imply that Christ suffered the penalty or consequences of human sin, such as the wrath of God or the torments of the condemned, when he died. While death no longer has any "sting" and is overcome, this is because of the certainty believers have in the resurrection (1 Cor 15:51–57). The normal meaning of the phrase *hyper hēmōn* is "for our sake" or "on our behalf," and this is how it should be understood unless there are good reasons to reject such a translation as inadequate. The preposition *hyper* regularly appears in the Pauline letters and elsewhere in the New Testament in the context of prayers offered on behalf of others.[16] Particularly significant in this regard is Rom 8:34, where Paul speaks of "Christ Jesus, who died, yes, who was raised, who is at the right hand of God, who indeed intercedes for us [*hyper hēmōn*]."

How would Jesus' death be understood as being "for" others, according to the early Christian story? Undoubtedly, given the use of *hyper* just mentioned and the intimate link between prayer and sacrifice in ancient Jewish thought, it might be understood as a self-offering and petition on behalf of others, similar to the death of Eleazar. In that sense, his death would be "for" them in that he gave up his life seeking salvation and forgiveness of sins on their behalf. God's response in raising Jesus would then be understood as his acceptance of Jesus' self-offering on behalf of others; this would mean that God granted Jesus what he implicitly asked when he gave up his life, and thus also granted to those on behalf of whom Jesus offered himself up the salvation and forgiveness he sought for them in dying.

However, it is difficult to believe that this would exhaust the meaning of the phrase. First, there seems to be no reason why God would send his Son merely to offer himself up sacrificially with a petition on behalf of others, given the fact that from a Jewish perspective God could just as easily grant what Jesus sought without his Son's self-offering unto death. It would seem strange to claim that God willed the Son to die merely so that he might carry out a "Godward" activity of intercession, that is, an activity in relation to God himself on behalf of others. Second, to understand Jesus' death in that fashion would isolate it from his life. Generally, when it is said that someone has died or given up one's life "for" others, the meaning is that the person died as a *consequence* of the activity that that person was carrying out on behalf of others or in order to obtain some benefit for others. In this case, the idea would be that Jesus died *as a consequence* of his activity on behalf of others, in particular those who would come to be incorporated into the church *after* his death ("us"), or that his death would benefit them in some way. Both of these ideas can be brought together in considering Jesus' death: he dedicated his life to the kingdom of God and to laying the foundation for a new covenant to come about, and he refused to put an end to that activity when threatened with death, thus suffering the consequences of his activity for others; and by giving up his life in faithfulness to that mission, he obtained what he had sought for others when God raised him from the dead. Thanks to what he did in life and in death, as well as to God's response in raising him from the dead, there is now a new covenant in which people may live and in which they may find assurance of salvation and forgiveness of sins. This occurs as they hear and believe the gospel proclaimed by those sent out by Jesus, in accordance with the divine plan established of old. According to the early Christian story, it was *all* of this that Jesus had lived and died for. His activity on behalf of others included both his work on behalf of the kingdom and the new covenant in which many would come to share as a result of his work, as well as the implicit petition made when he gave up his life that what he had lived and died for might become a reality.

To be sure, Paul never explicitly refers to any prayer offered up by Jesus in his death. In Rom 8:34 he does mention Jesus' death and resurrection in the context of his allusion to Jesus' heavenly intercession on behalf of believers. Yet his use of purpose clauses in relation to Jesus' death in the passages considered in the last chapter provides evidence that he understood Jesus' death in the way just proposed. According to Rom 14:9; 15:8; Gal 1:4; 3:13–14; and 1 Thess 5:10, Jesus died seeking for others their deliverance from the present evil age, the fulfillment of God's promises, the life of the age to come, and his present lordship on their behalf. All of these were things which *God alone could grant*, and which Jesus obtained from God by giving up his life and consequently being raised to power so that he might bring all of God's promises to fulfillment. In this sense, Jesus' death would be understood as sacrificial, involving the offering of himself up to God together with a petition on behalf of others.

What is implicit in the undisputed Pauline epistles is made explicit in Ephesians and Colossians. In Eph 5:2, both the Godward aspect of Christ's death and its sacrificial nature are stressed: "Christ loved us and gave himself up for us, a fragrant offering and sacrifice to God." Later on in the same epistle, it is said that "Christ loved the church and gave himself up for her [*hyper autēs*], in order to make her holy by cleansing her with the washing of water by the word, so as to present the church to himself in splendor, without a spot or wrinkle or anything of the kind—yes, so that she may be holy and without blemish" (Eph 5:25–27). Here Christ's death is "for" the church that would come into existence following his death in the sense that he gave up his life in love in order that many might come to form part of this new covenant community so as to be sanctified through its new rite of purification (i.e., baptism) and the proclamation of his word. The implication is that Jesus had foreknowledge that, following his death and resurrection and before he returned in glory, there would be a period in which the church would be built up, and he died so that this might take place. Similarly, Col 1:24 speaks of Paul's completing in his flesh "what is lacking in Christ's afflictions for the sake of (*hyper*) his body, that is, the church." Here the idea is that Christ suffered as a result of his efforts to establish the church. In fact, the affirmation that Paul also suffers for the sake of [*hyper*] the Colossian believers so as to complete what is lacking in Christ's afflictions makes it clear that the author does not understand Christ's death as being "for" others in the sense that in itself it satisfied some necessary condition for human salvation. A. J. M. Wedderburn, for example, comments on the need to avoid "the possible implication that somehow Christ's sufferings had been deficient or insufficient,"[17] as if a certain amount of suffering had been necessary to atone sufficiently for human sin. Instead, Jesus suffered "for" others in the same way that Paul is said here to have been suffering "for" others: both were afflicted as a result of their efforts to establish and extend the community of believers now known as the church. Christ's sufferings had been "lacking" or insufficient in that the task of establishing the church throughout the world had not been completed when he died. Thus, Paul was now "completing" in his own body the same sufferings that Christ himself had endured in order that that task might be fulfilled. If these passages are in continuity with Paul's thought, then they provide further support for the conclusion that Paul understood Jesus' death as being "for us" in the sense that it was the consequence of Jesus' efforts to found a new, righteous community, and was a self-offering to God, seeking salvation and forgiveness for all who would come to form part of that community.

All of this stands in contrast to the mechanical interpretations of Jesus' death noted previously. According to those interpretations, what Jesus was

looking for as he died was not a response from God but to fulfill some requirement that such interpretations deem necessary for salvation: he was looking to
undergo the penalty or consequences of sin in the stead of others, effect the
cleansing and restoration of the human nature or flesh he had assumed, provide participation in his death, conquer Satan, or lay down some example for
believers to follow. With the exception of this last interpretation, the "effect"
Jesus was seeking to produce would follow *automatically* or *mechanically* from
his death, since the condition or requirement deemed necessary for salvation
would thereby be fulfilled. According to these views, virtually all that was
required was a "bare death" on his part. In that case, his death did not involve
a petition made to God and granted by him at the resurrection, or any type
of Godward act. In fact, these mechanical views take God out of the picture:
Jesus' death is not a self-offering *to God* but merely a giving of himself over *to
death* so that some condition necessary for salvation might be fulfilled. There
simply is no reason to attribute to Paul such ideas.

"For Our Sins"

The idea that Jesus died "for our sins" is found in three Pauline passages:
1 Cor 15:3 (cited above); Gal 1:4*, where it is said that Jesus "gave himself
for our sins to deliver us from the present evil age, according to the will of our
God and Father"; and Rom 4:25*, where Paul writes that Jesus "was delivered
up for our transgressions and raised for our justification." At least the first of
these is from a tradition handed down to Paul; the same may be true of Rom
4:25 and perhaps even Gal 1:4.

Among biblical scholars, the idea that "Christ died for our sins" has been
understood in a variety of ways. In fact, because of the brevity of the phrase,
virtually any of the different doctrines of redemption outlined in chapter 1
can provide the necessary narrative framework. Christ can be said to have died
"for our sins" in the sense that, by overcoming the power of sin in our human
flesh, providing participation in his death to sin, ransoming humanity from the
dominion of Satan, or laying down an example that believers can now imitate,
he made it possible for believers to be delivered from their slavery to sin and
on that basis have their sins forgiven.[18] More frequently, however, interpreters
have looked to the notion of penal substitution to understand Paul's words:
he "died for our sins" in that he "died on behalf of others to satisfy the penalty
and to overcome the alienation."[19]

In support of this interpretation of 1 Cor 15:3, scholars have generally looked to Isaiah 53 as the Scripture passage Paul has in mind. There it is said that the servant "was wounded for our transgressions" and "crushed for our iniquities" (v. 5), that he bore the people's sins and iniquities (vv. 11–12; cf. v. 6), and that he made himself "an offering for sin" (v. 10). The Septuagint version differs somewhat, in that it speaks not only of his "bearing" sins and iniquities (vv. 4, 11), but of his suffering and being delivered up "on account of" our sins and iniquities, using either *dia* with the accusative case (vv. 5, 12) or the dative (v. 6).[20] Furthermore, in the Septuagint the last part of v. 12 reads, "And he bore the sins of many and on account of their sins was delivered up," in contrast to the Hebrew, which affirms that he "bore the sin of many, and made intercession for the transgressors." The explicit mention in v. 10 in the Hebrew of the servant's being an *asham* or sin offering is also absent from the Septuagint, which instead has, "If you give for sins . . ." Nevertheless, the allusion is still probably to a sin offering, since the phrase *peri hamartias* occurs regularly in the Septuagint in the passages in which the *asham* or sin offering is mentioned. In contrast, the Greek phrase *hyper tōn hamartiōn* that Paul uses in 1 Cor 15:3 is extremely rare in the Septuagint and does not appear in Isaiah 53. Thus, while Paul may have Isaiah 53 in mind in 1 Cor 15:3, this cannot be concluded with certainty.

Even if Paul is alluding to Isaiah 53, however, it does not follow that he is looking to some idea of penal substitution to interpret Christ's death. To say that the servant was "wounded on account of our transgressions" and "bruised on account of our iniquities," and that "with his stripes we are healed" (vv. 4–5), is simply to establish a relationship between his sufferings and the sins of the people, as well as their being healed; precisely what this relationship consists of is not made explicit. While the phrase "to bear iniquities" does appear in the description of the scapegoat ritual in Lev 16:20–22, the idea there is simply that the scapegoat symbolically carries the sins of the people off into the desert (as noted previously), and it is highly unlikely that such an idea is present here. More frequently, the phrase "to bear sins" is used in connection with those who have sinned or become impure and are thus required either to present an offering aimed at their purification or to be separated from the community (Lev 5:1, 17; 7:18; 17:16; 19:8; 20:17–20; 22:9, 16; 24:15). In this case, while they are subject to some type of penalty or required to present an offering, the idea of substitution does not play any role. Either they are cut off from the community, a penalty that no person or animal victim is allowed to undergo in their stead, or they must present a sin offering, in which case the offering is made "on their behalf" rather than "in their stead."²¹ In several cases, the priests are said to "bear iniquities" on behalf of the people; however, this means that they have the responsibility of presenting sin offerings on behalf of others (Lev 10:17; Num 18:1, 22–23, 32), not that they suffer the penalty or consequences of the sin of others in their place.²²

Of course, the thought that God is behind the suffering of the servant is present in Isa 53:10 and perhaps also v. 4. However, even if the idea is that God had his servant suffer the punishment that the people's iniquities deserved, this still need not be understood in terms of penal substitution, as if merely by suffering the punishment deserved by the people's sins, the servant effects their deliverance. In fact, if Isaiah 53 is applied directly to Christ, it can be interpreted on the basis of virtually any of the other interpretations considered in chapter 1. By suffering the punishment due the people, the servant may be said to have moved the people who observed this spectacle to acknowledge their sin and repent of it, as in a moral influence view, so that in this way their sins might be forgiven and they might be "healed"; in fact, the passage seems to stress the impression the servant's sufferings leave on the people.²³ According to a participatory understanding, the servant's undergoing the punishment of the people's sin and bearing their iniquities is salvific in that, through their solidarity with the servant, all the people undergo the punishment for sin together with him so as to be delivered from that punishment.²⁴ The church fathers generally applied Isaiah 53 to Christ on the basis of a physical doctrine of redemption: Christ "bore our sin" in that he took upon himself our sinful nature and then purified and healed it, restoring it to its sinless state.²⁵ All of these ideas can be and have been applied to 1 Cor 15:3 as well, as noted above, in addition to the penal substitution view.

While Isaiah 53 is quoted or alluded to in several places in the New Testament, only in 1 Pet 2:21–25 is the affirmation in v. 12 that the servant "bore our sins" applied to Christ's death. This passage, perhaps more than any other from the New Testament, has been cited in support of the claim that the early church looked to Isaiah 53 so as to understand Christ's death in substitutionary terms. In addition to telling his readers that Christ "suffered for you" (*hyper hēmōn*, v. 21), that he "bore our sins in his body on the tree," and that "by his wounds you have been healed" (v. 24*), the author affirms that Christ "committed no sin" (v. 22). Thus, it is claimed that this passage teaches that because "Jesus suffered innocently as the righteous One," his suffering unto death was "vicarious atonement," and that "Jesus bore our sins by suffering the judgment for them; he took the judgment *en tō sōmati*, i.e., in his bodily and human existence, upon himself."[26]

The idea that Christ "bore sins" obviously is not to be understood literally here, as if sins were some type of actual substance or entity that could have been removed from human beings of various times and places and transferred to Christ's body so as to be borne or carried by him. Therefore, most interpreters understand this passage in terms of Christ's bearing in the place of others the *judgment, penalty,* or *consequences* of human sins, namely, suffering and death in both a physical and a spiritual sense. Yet this involves reading into the passage all kinds of ideas that are the product of later theological reflection. In ancient Jewish and early Christian thought, it was not believed that each person dies because of that person's own individual sins, so that if one never sinned personally one would not suffer death. That possibility is never contemplated regarding anyone in Scripture, not even Jesus. The New Testament never implies that by nature Jesus was immortal or that, had he not died on the cross, he would have lived indefinitely because of some perfect or sinless nature he had assumed at the incarnation, or because he never committed a single sin. Nor does it provide any basis for the notion that "as righteous he did not need to die for his own sin," since, in biblical thought, eventually even the righteous inevitably die, and not even the righteous were thought to be perfectly sinless.[27] The claim that the judgment, penalty, or consequence of sins borne by Christ consisted of some kind of hellish experience of Godforsakenness in which he underwent untold spiritual agony and infinite torments in a way that no other person ever has is also absent from this passage and the rest of the New Testament.[28] Furthermore, when the author insists that Jesus "committed no sin," it is important to note that he is exhorting believers to follow Jesus' example rather than seeing this as unique to Jesus. They too will be approved by God by enduring pain while suffering unjustly for doing what is right and not committing sins (vv. 19–22; cf. 4:13–19). There is therefore no reason to read back into v. 22 the idea that Jesus' sinlessness qualified him to die for others, or that his death was due to the sins of others because he had no sins of his own. In fact, the passage is merely reminding the readers that Jesus had done nothing deserving the death sentence, as Pilate reportedly affirmed (Luke 23:13–17; John 19:6), not claiming that throughout his entire life Jesus never once committed a single sin.

If instead this passage is viewed against the background of the early Christian story of redemption, the idea would be that what Christ bore in his body on the cross was the consequence not of human sin per se but of his efforts to save God's people from their sins. While this still involves bearing in his body suffering and death, the reason for this is not that, according to some abstract theological truth, suffering and death are the inevitable consequence of human sin. Instead, Christ suffered and died because of his total commitment to bringing about the redemption of God's people from the plight to which they had become subject on account of their sins. His crucifixion here is thus attributed to the same reasons found in the Gospels, namely, the opposition that his activity generated and his refusal to put an end to that activity. In this case, "bearing sins" involves not only experiencing suffering and death but also assuming the responsibility or burden for doing what was needed in both relation to God and to others in order for God to forgive his people's sins. The idea would be similar to Heb 9:28 and various Old Testament passages that speak of offering up a sacrifice for sins, imploring God's forgiveness for others, but the focus here would be more on the bodily sufferings endured by Christ on the cross in order to attain forgiveness and redemption for others.

Several things in the context of 1 Pet 2:24 provide support for this interpretation of the passage. Above all, it is clear that the author has in mind specific parts of the story of Jesus' passion and death as we find it in the Gospels rather than some other "theological" story such as those considered in chapter 1. According to the Gospels, Jesus endured pain and suffered because he did what was right, as in v. 20 of this passage, and because he was committed to bringing others to put away sin and "live to righteousness," as v. 24 indicates. This was the objective, not so much of his *death*, but of the ministry that led to his death. In addition, it seems clear that the author is referring in these verses to Jesus' silence before the Jewish authorities and Pilate during his trial, as well as the mocking and beating he endured at the hands of the soldiers, together with the physical "wounds" or "stripes" that were inflicted on him (Isa 53:5). According to this interpretation, the idea of Christ's bearing sins in his body in v. 24 would fit in well with the idea running throughout the passage that Christ provides an example for believers: as he was willing to suffer bodily pain and be beaten and crucified in order to attain their redemption and healing, so should they be willing to endure beatings, pain, and suffering in their own bodies for doing God's will. When the author affirms that his readers have been healed by Christ's wounds, he must mean that Christ's willingness to suffer in order to attain their salvation has led to a situation in which those who form part of the community founded through his death have been "healed" in that they have now obtained the salvation Christ sought for them, which they experience to some degree even in the present. That this is the meaning of the phrase is made likely by the fact that in v. 25, the author has in mind the risen and glorified Jesus, their living shepherd and guardian to whom they have now returned; it is in this sense that they have been healed. And they can return to him now to be saved only because he was willing to suffer and die in order to attain their salvation, and for that reason was raised by God, who "judges justly" (v. 23).

Therefore, even if in 1 Cor 15:3 Paul has Isaiah 53 in mind, and interpreted it along the same lines as the author of 1 Peter, there is no basis for arguing that he understood Jesus' dying "for our sins" in terms of a substitutionary death. Rather, like the author of 1 Peter, Paul would have looked to the same basic narrative that we find in the Gospels to apply ideas from Isaiah 53 to Jesus' death. His efforts to save God's people from their sins had led to his being persecuted and put to death, being "counted among the lawless" (Luke 22:37) and "led to the slaughter" like a sheep, without opening his mouth (Acts 8:32–33). According to Matt 8:17, however, Isaiah 53 was applied not only to Jesus' passion and death but to his *entire ministry*; there, after mentioning Jesus' activity of healing and casting out evil spirits, the evangelist alludes to Isa 53:4: "This was to fulfill what had been spoken through the prophet Isaiah, 'He took our infirmities and bore our diseases.'"

This point is significant for interpreting 1 Cor 15:3. If Jesus' death was consistently interpreted in the context of his life and ministry in the early tradition, as has been argued previously, then the fact that Isaiah 53 is applied by Matthew to Jesus' ministry rather than to his death alone would provide further support for the argument that, in that tradition, it was not just Jesus' *death* that "dealt with sin," but *all* of the activity that led to his death. While it is no doubt possible that Paul was unacquainted with interpretations of Isaiah 53 such as that found in Matt 8:17, this is by no means certain. As David Wenham has shown, Paul does appear to be acquainted with much of the material found only in Matthew's Gospel.[29] In fact, in Rom 15:1–3, Paul himself seems to be alluding to Isa 53:4 when he speaks of bearing the weaknesses of others in the context of a reference to Christ's not pleasing himself, thereby employing the latter passage in the same sense that Matthew does.[30]

In any case, if in 1 Cor 15:3 Paul does have in mind the words from Isaiah 53 that speak of the servant's suffering for sin and becoming a sin offering, these ideas can be understood perfectly well according to the early Christian story outlined in chapter 3. In accordance with the divine plan foretold in the Scriptures, Jesus died so that people throughout the world might now have forgiveness of sins through him, as they live under the new covenant established through his death. Of course, this had been the objective not only of his *death* but also of his *ministry*: he *died* for what he had *lived* for, namely, that people might have access to God's blessings of salvation and forgiveness through him. Nevertheless, only by means of his death would these blessings become available for people such as the Corinthians and Paul ("*our* sins," referring to the sins of those such as the Corinthian believers and Paul who came to faith *after* Jesus' death and resurrection), since his death would lead to the proclamation of the gospel throughout the world and the incorporation of many more people into the church, where they would obtain forgiveness of sins. Had Jesus not been willing to die, this divine plan would not have been carried out, and what Jesus had lived for would not have become a reality, since there would be no proclamation of the gospel and no church in the present.

Therefore, by being faithful to his mission to the end and giving up his life to attain salvation and forgiveness of sins on behalf of those who would come to form part of the community under him, Christ has obtained what he sought for others in obedience to God's will. Strictly speaking, however, he attained this *when God raised him from the dead*, since his resurrection and exaltation ensured that the promises made by God of old would be fulfilled through him. For this reason, several verses later, Paul ties forgiveness of sins to Jesus' resurrection: "If Christ has not been raised, your faith is futile and you are still in your sins" (v. 17). As noted previously, the idea is that if God did not raise Jesus from the dead and he remains in the grave, he cannot bring the promised redemption and forgiveness, and in reality achieved nothing by giving up his life.

Viewed against this background, Jesus' death would be seen as sacrificial in that he offered himself up to God with the implicit petition that the divine promises of salvation and forgiveness of sins such as those found in Jer 31:34 and Isa 27:9 and 59:20–21 might be fulfilled through him. In this sense, he can be said to have "died for our sins." His death might therefore be seen as analogous to an expiatory sacrifice, in that he went before God seeking that God forgive and redeem those on whose behalf he was offering up his life. It might also be seen as a covenant sacrifice, in that he was seeking that through his death a new covenant be established in which many more might find the forgiveness of sins. However, this *Godward* activity on behalf of others must not be divorced from what can be termed the *humanward* activity he carried out, which consisted of calling people to repent of their sins and live in accordance with God's will as members of God's people under him. The formula "for our sins" could be employed to embrace *both* of these aspects of his activity.

In this case, the notion that Jesus died "according to the Scriptures" could be seen as fulfilling Isaiah 53, in that, like the servant, he was willing to suffer so that others might attain healing and salvation, and offered up his life to God, imploring God to accept his people and forgive their sins, like a sin offering. By his willingness to suffer and die in accordance with God's will, he obtained precisely what he sought for others, namely, their deliverance from their transgressions and iniquities. This is now found in him, so that it can be said that by his stripes they have been healed, and that Jesus "made intercession for the transgressors" (Isa 53:5, 12). In this sense as well, it could be said that "the LORD laid on him the iniquity of us all" (Isa 53:6), since he suffered for assuming the burden of saving others from their iniquities in obedience to God. Yet he suffered and died for this *precisely because he had dedicated his life to it*, bearing the people's infirmities throughout his ministry of service; just as the servant in Isa 53:11 sought to "make many to be accounted righteous" by his "knowledge," so Jesus dedicated himself to bringing about God's righteousness in others through his ministry of teaching and compassion. Nevertheless, it is probable that in 1 Cor 15:3 Paul has much more than Isaiah 53 in mind. The phrase "according to the Scriptures" would be taken as referring to *everything* that had been prophesied regarding the divine plan of which Jesus' death formed a part. For this reason, Paul adds that "he was raised on the third day in accordance with the scriptures" (v. 4). In this case, Paul would be saying here precisely what we find in Luke 24:44–47*: everything written about Jesus in the law and the prophets had to be fulfilled, in particular, "that the Messiah should suffer and rise from the dead on the third day, and that repentance and forgiveness of sins is to be proclaimed in his name to all nations." This was what Christ died for; and in that sense, he "died for our sins."

The same phrase *hyper tōn hamartiōn hēmōn* used in 1 Cor 15:3 is found in Gal 1:4*, where Paul writes that Christ "gave himself for our sins to deliver us from the present evil age, according to the will of our God and Father." Here we have the idea found in the early Christian story appearing in the Gospels that Jesus voluntarily gave up his life, in obedience to God the Father. In theory, the phrase "for our sins" could be understood in the sense that Christ gave himself up to make it possible for God to forgive "our" sins; yet this would require an argument to the effect that it was impossible for God to forgive sins without Christ's death, of which there is no hint either in Paul's letters or in the rest of the New Testament, not to mention ancient Jewish thought. Instead, if the phrase is understood according to the early Christian story, Jesus gave up his life so that others might now have forgiveness of sins through him, as they live under the new covenant established through his death. In obedience to his Father, he offered up his life to God seeking what he had sought throughout his ministry, namely, that through him God might save his people from their sins, both in the sense that they might be delivered from the plight that was the consequence of their sins and in the sense that they might no longer live in sin; and by doing so, Jesus attained that salvation and forgiveness for others. In the context of this epistle, Paul might have referred to this idea from the outset to remind both the "Judaizers" and the other believers in Galatia that they were no longer "in their sins," not because they had been obedient to the law but because Christ had died for them so as to enable them to attain through him the salvation they had not been able to attain through the Mosaic law.

The purpose of Christ's giving himself for the sins of others here is that they might be delivered from the "present evil age." It is important to note that Paul does not say that this deliverance has already come about or that the evil age is no longer a present reality for believers. Rather, this was Christ's objective in giving up his life: he sought that others might attain the life of the new age and be delivered from their sins. Of course, it can be said that they have already been delivered from the present evil age in the sense that they now have certainty regarding their future deliverance, and also have received many of the blessings associated with the new age, such as the gift of the Holy Spirit, who produces fruits in them (Gal 3:3; 5:22–23). Strictly speaking, however, their deliverance from the present age still awaits them.

In Rom 4:24–25* Paul writes that righteousness "will be reckoned to us who believe in him who raised Jesus our Lord from the dead, who was delivered up for our transgressions and raised for our justification." It is quite possible that Paul is also drawing on tradition here, and perhaps on Isaiah 53 as well.[31] This passage is different from the previous two in that it employs the phrase *dia ta paraptōmata hēmōn* instead of *hyper tōn hamartiōn hēmōn*: Christ died "on account of" or "because of" our transgressions.

According to the early Christian story, God allowed the Jewish and Roman authorities to arrest, mistreat, and crucify his Son without intervening on the Son's behalf, and in this sense "delivered him up." It seems doubtful that Paul is referring to Judas's betrayal of Jesus here, since in the phrases before and after this one, the allusion is to God as the one who raised Jesus from the dead. Behind Paul's words that Jesus was "delivered up for our transgressions" may be the idea that the reason Jesus was crucified was his commitment to saving God's people from the plight to which they were subject on account of their sins. In this case, the thought would be the same as in Isaiah 53, where the servant is sent by God to save his people from their sin and disobedience, and God wills that the servant endure the suffering, grief, and abuse that are the consequence of his carrying out this task in the midst of a sinful people. It is in this sense that God afflicts the servant (Isa 53:4–5, 10), since he does not save him from the consequences of his mission but has him be faithful to that mission unto death.

However, Paul seems also to have in mind the idea that God delivered up his Son so that those who were never able to attain salvation from their sins might now do so through Christ. In this sense, he was "delivered up for [their] transgressions," that is, so that through him they might now find the redemption from transgressions that the law had not been able to provide (cf. Acts 13:38–39). In fact, several ideas from the context support this interpretation. In Romans 4 Paul is discussing the promises made by God regarding not only believing Jews but also Gentiles who have faith like Abraham, "the ancestor of all who believe without being circumcised and who thus have righteousness reckoned to them" (4:11). Under the Mosaic covenant, Jews and Gentiles equally were unable to achieve forgiveness and righteousness before God; now, however, thanks to Christ's death and resurrection, they are able to do so as they live under him in faith. Paul's statement that Christ was "raised for our justification" (4:25) would communicate essentially the same idea: he was raised so that through him all who believe (both Jews and Gentiles) might now be justified by God. In the verses immediately following Rom 4:25, Paul speaks of having "peace with God through our Lord Jesus Christ," and having "obtained access to this grace in which we stand" (5:1–2). Because of their transgressions, neither Jew nor Gentile previously had peace with God nor access to God and his grace. This has changed, however, thanks to the fact that Christ gave up his life to attain these things for others and was consequently raised. Thus, the idea appears to be that God gave up his Son and consequently raised him so that many might come to find redemption from their transgressions and justification now through him by living as members of the new covenant community, composed of both Jews and Gentiles.

"For Sin"

A phrase somewhat similar to those just considered appears in Rom 8:1–4*, where Paul writes:

> There is therefore now no condemnation for those who are in Christ Jesus. For the law of the Spirit of life in Christ Jesus has set you free from the law of sin and of death. For God has done what the law, weakened by the flesh, could not do: by sending his own Son in the likeness of sinful flesh, and for sin [*peri hamartias*], he condemned sin in the flesh, so that the just requirement of the law might be fulfilled in us, who walk not according to the flesh but according to the Spirit.

Some have claimed that Paul here has the idea of a sin offering in mind, since *peri hamartias* is used in the Septuagint to refer to offerings for sin. If so, he would be saying that God sent his own Son "in the likeness of sinful flesh and as a sin offering."[32]

While this is certainly possible, once more the decision in favor or against such an interpretation will inevitably be based on a previously defined understanding of the nature and meaning of sin offerings, as well as a previously defined view of the redemptive significance of Christ's death. If sin offerings are understood according to a penal substitution scheme, for example, then the idea of penal substitution will be read back into Paul's words: God sent his Son to suffer in the stead of sinners the condemnation due them on account of their sin, just as the animal victims in the Old Testament were put to death in the stead of the sinners who presented them.[33] If the notion of substitution is combined with those of participation and representation so as to understand sin offerings as effecting not only a death *in the place* of the sinner but the death of the sinner in union with the animal victim that *represents* him or her, then Christ's death will be understood in the same terms: it is a sin offering in that believers undergo together with Christ the condemnation they deserved by dying together with Christ their representative.[34]

Although the problems raised by views such as these have already been discussed, several observations regarding this particular passage are in order. Above all, it should be stressed that Paul does not say here that sin was condemned in the flesh *in Christ's death*. In this regard, numerous ideas have been read back into this passage that are simply not there. Some who defend a penal substitution view have argued, for example, that sin was condemned in *Christ's flesh*.[35] Paul, however, says only that God sent his Son in the likeness of sinful flesh (literally, "flesh of sin"), and that God "condemned sin in the flesh." While the flesh in which sin is condemned is certainly "like" (*en homoiōmati*) that in which God sent his Son, Paul does not say that the condemnation of sin occurred in Christ's *particular* flesh. The idea is rather that sin is condemned in the flesh of human beings or believers in some general sense. Likewise, it has often been argued on the basis of this passage that God condemned *Christ* on the cross or that Christ underwent the condemnation due sinful human beings there.[36] Although such an idea is repeatedly mentioned by Pauline scholars, nowhere in the Pauline letters or in the New Testament as a whole is it ever said that Christ came under the divine judgment or the condemnation due human beings because of their sin. In fact, it is by no means certain that Paul is referring to Christ's death at all in this passage; in order to argue that he has the cross in mind, it must be shown that *peri hamartias* is a reference to a sin offering.

Whether or not Paul is in fact referring to Christ's death as a sin offering, a close look at the passage in its context reveals that *it is not by his death alone that sin is condemned in the flesh*. Rather, once again Paul's argument should be understood on the basis of the story of redemption outlined in the previous chapters. "Those who are in Christ Jesus," that is, who live in and under him as members of his body the church, are no longer under "condemnation" (8:1); God accepts them as righteous and forgives their sins by virtue of their relationship to Christ. Obviously, their situation is distinct from that of those who *are* under condemnation; and, according to Jewish thought and the Christian story handed down to Paul, those whom God condemns are those who live in sin, practicing unrighteousness and disobeying his commandments (Rom 1:18—3:20). In order to avoid condemnation, people must be delivered from this condition in which they are subject to "the law of sin and death" (8:2).[37] In other words, "the just requirement of the law" must be "fulfilled" in them, as in Jewish thought. However, as noted in chapter 4, Paul insists that the law was powerless to bring about in them this righteousness, because it was "weakened by the flesh" (v. 3). On account of their fallen condition (i.e., their subjection to the "law of sin and death"), those who aspired to live under the law could not fulfill the law's righteousness and thus be delivered from the plight in which they found themselves.

To remedy this situation, God sent his Son "in the likeness of sinful flesh and for sin"; Christ was born into the same existence shared by all human beings in this present age. The thought here is closely parallel to Gal 4:4–5, where God is said to have "sent his Son, born of a woman, born under the law, in order to redeem those who were under the law," and therefore under its "curse" as well, because of their inability to do what the law requires (Gal 3:10–13). Yet Paul does not explicitly say that God sent his Son *to die* either in Gal 4:4–5 or in Rom 8:3 (or anywhere else). Rather, according to Paul, God's purpose was to bring about the redemption of those who were under the law's curse and "deal with sin." This is accomplished *not merely by Christ's death* but *by all that God has done and continues to do in and through Christ*, as well as what God does *in and through the Spirit* (v. 4), who has been poured out on believers as a result of Christ's activity. Believers are saved as they live "in Christ," keeping the "law of Christ" in the sense of doing God's will in the way that Christ taught, and living under his present lordship in the power of the Holy Spirit.

In this way, the *dikaiōma* of the law is fulfilled in them. They are now under a different "law," the "law of the Spirit of life in Christ Jesus" (v. 2). The reason they are no longer under condemnation is that they are "in Christ Jesus" and walk "not according to the flesh, but according to the Spirit" (v. 4), thereby fulfilling the intention of the law. And the reason they can be in Christ

Jesus and walk according to the Spirit is that God sent his Son in the likeness of human flesh, directed him to carry out a ministry aimed at bringing about in others the righteousness he had commanded in his law, gave him over to death, and raised him from the dead as their Lord, so as then to pour out his Spirit through Christ. In this way God achieved his purpose: "sin in the flesh" is "condemned," not because it is "destroyed" through some mechanical process of transfer or exchange, or because its penalty has been inflicted on Christ as a substitute, but because those in Christ can now be certain that someday they will be liberated fully from its power, as they are now in part (for that reason, at present it is only "condemned" in their flesh, not actually "destroyed"). In Christ and the Spirit it is now possible to live under a new law in which one is no longer "hostile to God" (8:7), walking in sin, and thus to attain the life of the coming age. Believers are "alive because of righteousness" (8:10), that is, the righteousness they now have as they "put to death the deeds of the body" (8:13) in Christ and the Spirit; because of the presence of Christ and the Spirit in them, they can be certain that instead of being condemned on account of their sin, they will be delivered (8:9–17).

Such an interpretation does not necessarily rule out the possibility that Paul had in mind the idea of Christ's being a sin offering in v. 3, as long as Christ's death is seen in the context of his life and ministry. In this case, Paul would be saying that God sent his Son to offer up his life seeking the forgiveness of sins and redemption that he had sought for others throughout his ministry. However, a couple of factors weigh against this interpretation. First, in the general context Paul is speaking of Christ's work *in relation to believers* rather than his work *in relation to God on behalf of believers*. The objective is to deal with "sin in the flesh" rather than God's anger at sin. Second, behind the argument in favor of the "sin offering" translation of *peri hamartias* is usually the idea that Christ's death in itself fulfills some condition necessary for human salvation, and that God sent his Son for the express purpose of dying in order that this condition might be fulfilled. Thus, the "sin offering" translation probably would make sense only if some type of mechanical view of redemption is ascribed to Paul, and if the Jewish sin offerings are understood in mechanical terms. For this reason, it seems better to translate *peri hamartias* simply as "for sin," since it is not only Christ's *death* that deals with human sin, but *all* that God did through Christ after sending him into sinful flesh, as well as what God continues to do now and will do in the future through his Son (as well as the Spirit, through whom God might also be said to "deal with sin in the flesh").

Christ as *Hilastērion*

Sacrificial imagery is clearly behind Rom 3:24–26, where Paul uses the word *hilastērion* in relation to Christ. This passage presents a host of problems, not least of which is the translation. According to a literal translation, believers are "justified by [God's] grace as a gift through the redemption that is in Christ Jesus, whom God put forward [*proetheto*] as an expiation [*hilastērion*] in his blood through faith in order to show his righteousness on account of his passing over former sins in the forbearance of God, in order to show his righteousness in the present time, so that he might be righteous and justifying the one of the faith of Jesus." Among the difficulties related to this passage are the meanings of *proetheto* and *hilastērion* in this context, how "in his blood" (*en tō autou haimati*) should be understood and whether it modifies *hilastērion* or "faith," what "God's righteousness" refers to, and the translation of *kai* in the last phrase, which can mean either "and" or "also."[38]

With regard to the meaning of *hilastērion*, three alternatives have generally been proposed.[39] According to the first, *hilastērion* should be translated as "propitiation." In this case, the idea is that through his blood Christ appeases or exhausts the divine wrath. This interpretation is supported particularly by those who defend a penal substitution understanding of Christ's death.[40] Many of those opposed to such an idea have proposed a second alternative, arguing that *hilastērion* should instead be translated "expiation," or more precisely, "means of expiation" or "expiatory sacrifice."[41] Expiation has to do with *cleansing* or *purification*. According to this understanding, the purpose of Christ's death was not to put away God's wrath but to purify human beings from their sinful condition, either through some type of participatory union with him, through the renewal of the sinful humanity he assumed that is shared by all, or through the moving of human beings to repentance and greater love. The concept of expiation does not necessarily exclude that of propitiation, since when the sinner is purified from sin, God's wrath is put away. In this case, however, it is not Christ's sacrificial death itself that propitiates God but the change produced in the condition of sinners as a result of Christ's death.

A third possibility is that *hilastērion* refers to the "mercy seat" or "propitiatory" of the Tabernacle and first Temple; this is the meaning of the word throughout most of the Septuagint, where it is used to translate the Hebrew *kapporeth*.[42] This translation, like the one just considered ("expiation"), can be made to serve almost all of the doctrines of redemption outlined in chapter 1, since the rituals carried out at the mercy seat on the Day of Atonement had as their objective the propitiation of God's wrath and the purification of both the sanctuary and the people.

Intimately related to the question of how to translate *hilastērion* is that of how to translate *proetheto*.[43] The verb *protithēmi* can mean to "purpose" or "intend," or to "set forth" or "present," especially in a public way. Here the meaning is probably the second, although some commentators have argued for the first, either because they believe that Paul wished to emphasize the divine initiative in sending his Son to the cross, or because they accept the "mercy seat" translation of *hilastērion*.[44] In this case, the fact that the mercy seat was hidden from public view rather than exposed publicly might require the former translation, although it might also be argued that Paul was contrasting the "old" with the "new": Christ's sacrificial death on the cross was a very public act, in contrast to the old rites of atonement that were carried out behind the Temple veil.

The meaning of "in his blood" in this passage is also somewhat problematic. Most commentators agree that this phrase should be taken in conjunction with *hilastērion* rather than as the object of *dia pisteōs* (i.e., "through faith in his blood").[45] Either possibility can be reconciled with a penal substitution view, according to which Christ's blood refers to his death: if taken in conjunction with *hilastērion*, the idea is that God effected propitiation through Christ's death in that he sent Christ to die so as to put an end to his wrath at sin. If *en tō autou haimati* is taken as the object of *dia pisteōs*, then Paul means that God's wrath is put away when people believe in and accept Christ's substitutionary death on their behalf. Other views of Christ's work can also be reconciled with either of these interpretations, though the first seems to go better with them.

Paul's allusion to God's "passing over sins" in order to "show his righteousness" has often been understood in the sense that by sending his Son to suffer the penalty for sin or to overcome sin's power in the flesh, God has demonstrated that he does not take sin lightly.[46] Yet this interpretation leads to theological problems. If God put forward his Son as a propitiation *for the purpose* of showing his righteousness to human beings (i.e., showing that he punishes sin and takes sin seriously), then it would appear that his primary objective was not that his Son die for sins but that his Son's propitiatory death reveal some divine truth to human beings in order to bring about some change in them, namely, that they repent of their sins and believe in Christ. In that case, what ends up propitiating God's wrath is not Christ's death per se but the change occurring in believers by virtue of the new knowledge regarding the gravity of sin that they receive through Christ's death. If they do *not* change in the necessary way, God's wrath at their sins is still in force, and thus has not been taken away by Christ.

Rather than interpreting Rom 3:25–26 in the sense that in Christ's death God has shown that he takes sin seriously, many interpreters have argued that Christ's death manifests the "righteousness of God" in that it shows God's covenant faithfulness.[47] This view can be reconciled with any of the understandings of Christ's death outlined in chapter 1, since the idea is that God's righteousness or faithfulness is demonstrated by sending his Son to die in order to fulfill some condition for salvation that could have been fulfilled in no other way.

A close look at Paul's words here, however, reveals that for Paul it is not Christ's death or blood per se that is the *hilastērion*, but *Christ himself*, "*whom* God put forward as a *hilastērion*." This means that it is not an *event* that constitutes the *hilastērion*, but a *person*. If *en tō autou haimati* is taken in connection with *hilastērion* rather than as the object of *pistis*, as seems preferable, then the idea is that Christ became or was made by God a *hilastērion* through his blood. If a mechanical understanding of sacrifice is excluded, then it really makes no difference whether *hilastērion* is understood in terms of "propitiation" or "expiation." The reason for this is that according to Jewish thought, the offering of a sacrifice in itself neither put away God's wrath nor effected the purification of sinners. God was not *obliged* or *bound* to put away his wrath at their sins because a sacrifice had been offered to him; nor were sinners automatically *made* pure through expiatory rites so that God had no choice but to *accept* them as pure. As was argued in chapter 2, the basis for God's acceptance of sinners were the repentance and commitment to obedience that found expression in the sacrificial offerings presented to him by them or on their behalf. The same points must be stressed if this passage is taken to refer to the mercy seat (*kapporeth*), upon which blood was sprinkled on the Day of Atonement: it was not this rite in itself that put away God's wrath or effected the purification of the holy places and the people. Rather, God accepted and forgave his repentant people in response to the petition for acceptance and forgiveness that the priest made when he came before God's presence (symbolized by the mercy seat) with sacrificial blood. In the same way, by offering himself up to God seeking that God forgive and redeem those belonging to the (new) covenant community of which he was the head, Christ obtained that forgiveness and redemption for them.[48]

Any of the three proposed translations of *hilastērion* is acceptable, therefore, as long as Christ's death is viewed in the context of the early Christian story considered in the previous chapters. In fact, Paul's argument in the first three chapters of Romans follows the basic outline of that story closely. In Rom 1:18—3:20, Paul has argued that both Gentiles and Jews are under God's wrath and condemnation because of their sins. According to what we saw in chapter 2, this was precisely how the Jews understood their plight: the promised redemption had not yet arrived because of the people's sins and their lack of righteousness. For that redemption to arrive, God needed to put away his wrath at those sins and enable the people to practice the righteousness that he not only *commanded* from them but also promised to *give* to them. In Rom 3:21–26, Paul states that this promise (as witnessed to in the law and prophets) is now fulfilled through Christ: God's righteousness is manifested "through faith in Jesus Christ," or perhaps "through Jesus-Christ-faith" (*dia pisteōs Iēsou Christou*, v. 22), as was argued previously. Depending on the meaning given to *dikaiosynē theou*, Paul may mean either that God's faithfulness to his covenant promises is shown among believers, or that the righteousness God both demands and offers is given to them through their faith as a gift. If the latter interpretation is preferred, this should not be understood entirely forensically, but in the sense that believers are accepted by God as they live "by" or "out of" faith (*ek pisteōs*), accepting his gracious gift of a new life of righteousness. In this regard, there is "no difference" between Jews and Gentiles, since *all* have sinned: both Jews and Gentiles are accepted as righteous before God on the basis of the righteousness they receive through faith as a divine gift, and not through works of the law. As noted previously, in contrast to those who believed that stricter obedience to the commandments would bring about the promised redemption, Paul maintains that this redemption is to be found instead "in Christ Jesus" (v. 24), and thus that it is available to all who believe, both Jews and Gentiles.

Paul's allusion to Christ as *hilastērion* has rarely been seen in the context of his argument regarding the justification of both Jews and Gentiles through faith rather than works of the law.[49] According to the Mosaic law, only the Jewish people had a God-given *hilastērion* or means of expiation and propitiation, since the law prescribed that expiation be made in ceremonies and in a place in which full participation was open only to Jews.[50] It might be said, therefore, that the Jews had a *hilastērion dia ergōn nomou* that excluded uncircumcised Gentiles; this meant that Gentiles had no divinely prescribed way of obtaining forgiveness and acceptance from God. Now, however, in Christ, God had given to Gentiles as well as Jews a *hilastērion dia pisteōs*, since by believing in Christ and living under the new covenant established through his death, they could be certain of their forgiveness, acceptance, and justification before God. This was what Christ had obtained on their behalf through his sacrificial death (*en tō autou haimati*) when God raised him, thus responding favorably to the petition he in effect presented to God as he died, in which he sought that God forgive and redeem those living as members of his covenant people. The idea, then, would be that God has graciously put forward Christ as his instrument through whom *all* people, both Jews and Gentiles, may now draw near to him and be accepted by him through faith. Paul could expect that such an idea would be perfectly comprehensible to the Roman Christians if he assumed that they were well acquainted with the notion that everything found in the old covenant is now to be found in the new. Just as the old covenant had its temple (with a mercy seat), priests, and sacrificial means of atonement through blood, so now the same things were to be found in Christ, who was the fulfillment of these things and in some sense replaced them. Similar ideas are reflected in Eph 2:11–18*, which also speaks of Gentiles' being "brought near in the blood of Christ," and the "wall of hostility" and the "law with its commandments and ordinances" being done away with, so that those who formerly under the Mosaic law did not have access to God and the divine promises of salvation and forgiveness might now draw near to him through Christ and the Spirit. All of this is what Christ attained by giving up his life, since he was consequently raised and exalted.

The fact that Christ's blood is mentioned in Rom 3:25 has led most commentators to the conclusion that the verb *proetheto* refers to God's "putting forward" his Son to die on the cross. In that case, the idea would be that God sent his Son to offer up his life as a sacrifice, obtaining on behalf of others their forgiveness and acceptance before God in the context of the new covenant. If Paul's words are interpreted in this way, it is necessary to stress that this self-offering on Christ's part must be seen in the context of *all* of his activity, which was also God's activity through him. God put forward his Son to give up his life on behalf of others when the ministry Christ had carried out in obedience to God's will led to the cross, so that through him a new covenant might be established and people formerly outside of the covenant might obtain salvation and forgiveness. Thus, while God put Christ forward as a *hilastērion* in his death, it is not his death alone that propitiates God's wrath or expiates the sins of the people. Christ could be *hilastērion* through his death only because of everything else he had done before dying and would do after being raised.

Although this interpretation is possible and can be harmonized with the story of redemption being proposed here, it is perhaps more likely that behind the use of the verb *proetheto* is a reference not only to God's *sending* his Son and giving him up to die on a cross but also to his action of *raising* his Son from the dead as well. In this case, it is the *risen and exalted* Christ who has become the *hilastērion* by means of his blood, since by offering up his life on the cross, he attained from God the redemption that is now found in him (v. 24). This interpretation would place Paul's thought in line with that of the author of 1 John, who after describing Christ as the "advocate" whom believers now have, refers to him as the "*hilasmos* for our sins" (2:1–2).[51] There the idea is that Christ, now risen, puts away God's wrath at the people's sins by interceding on their behalf. Paul may have this same idea in mind when he speaks in Rom 8:34 of the risen Christ's intercession on behalf of believers. Although Paul does not specify that the content of Christ's intercession is that God forgives his people's sins, in the same context he does say that no one can "bring any charge against God's elect" or "condemn" them (vv. 33–34), so that the idea of being delivered from God's wrath at sin is not far from Paul's thought. Thus, in Rom 3:25 Paul may be saying that God put forward his Son, not only when he sent him to carry out a ministry on behalf of others and gave him up to death, but when he raised him as a result of his self-offering for others, so that he might now be the means given to both Jews and Gentiles to attain deliverance from God's wrath, forgiveness of sins, justification, and the promised redemption in the context of the new covenant established through Christ.

Behind Paul's words concerning the passing over of former sins in the forbearance of God may be the same idea found in Acts 17:30-31: "While God has overlooked the times of ignorance, now he commands all people everywhere to repent, because he has fixed a day on which he will have the world judged in righteousness by a man whom he has appointed." This may be why Paul uses *paresis* instead of *aphesis*, since the idea is not so much that God *forgave* previous sins but that he patiently *overlooked* and *tolerated* them until the time might come when he would send his Son and thus make known his righteousness, as he has now done (v. 26), as well as provide those whose sins he had overlooked for so long with a *hilastērion* through which they might now obtain his forgiveness for their sins.[52]

In spite of the numerous difficulties that Rom 3:21–26 presents, the basic idea is clear: redemption is to be found not through works of the Torah but through faith in Christ, whom God sent to be his instrument for bringing to pass the promised redemption. Through his death, Christ became the *hilastērion* or means of propitiation and expiation given by God to both Jews and Gentiles so that they might be forgiven and accepted by him as they live in faith. This idea can be understood perfectly well simply by looking to the early story concerning Christ. It is therefore not surprising that Paul could use such imagery when writing to Christians he had never met, many of whom were from a Gentile background. Even Gentile believers could readily understand the reference to Christ as a *hilastērion* given by God, since the general idea was common in both Jewish and Hellenistic thought.

Christ as Paschal Lamb

One other passage in which Paul uses sacrificial imagery to refer to Jesus' death is 1 Cor 5:7–8, where after exhorting the Corinthians to "cleanse out the old yeast" so as to be a "new batch," he writes, "For our paschal lamb, Christ, has been sacrificed. Therefore, celebrate the festival, not with the old yeast, the yeast of malice and evil, but with the unleavened bread of sincerity and truth."[53] While some have attempted to read ideas concerning propitiation and expiation back into this passage, this hardly seems plausible.[54] Strictly speaking, the paschal lamb was not a sin offering. By the first century virtually all sacrifices were viewed by the Jews as expiatory in some sense. This was not because animals were killed as substitutes, however, but because every petition offered up to God together with the sacrificial offerings implicitly included a petition that God overlook the sins of those offering it so as to grant what they were asking. When the paschal lambs were sacrificed in order to be consumed at the Passover celebration, one of the main petitions embodied in the sacrifice was that God bless and accept their celebration before him as they ate of what they had offered to him. This petition can therefore be understood as a request for divine acceptance and forgiveness, but no substitutionary mechanism is in effect.[55]

What may have inspired Paul (or his predecessors) to apply the image of the paschal lamb to Christ is the fact that according to the Synoptics, Christ had spoken of his death in sacrificial terms in the context of a Passover celebration. The Fourth Gospel gives evidence of another tradition, according to which Jesus died on the day the paschal lamb was sacrificed. In any case, Paul's concern in 1 Cor 5:6–8 is not to teach that sins are forgiven on account of Christ's death but to recall the need for the community to remain pure.[56] Just as those who participated in the Jewish Passover celebration needed to purify themselves and their homes by cleansing out the old yeast, so the new covenant people also needed to "cleanse out the old yeast" in a spiritual sense in order to "celebrate the festival." Whether Paul has in mind here the celebration of the Lord's Supper, the Christian fellowship in general that took place at the church's meetings, or the "eschatological banquet," the idea is that Christians celebrate their own version of the Passover feast as they live under the new covenant centered on a sacrificial lamb (Christ), and need to purify themselves in order to do so. If Paul's allusion here is not merely to the later Passover celebrations but to the original Passover celebrated by the Israelites in Egypt, then the comparison would be that just as the paschal lamb was offered and its blood shed so that those who partook of that first Passover feast might be redeemed from their bondage in Egypt, so Christ offered up himself and shed his blood seeking that the new covenant people might be redeemed from their bondage to sin and death.[57] In either case, the allusion can be understood perfectly well on the basis of the story of redemption that has repeatedly been outlined.

Christ's Death, Righteousness, and Justification

As noted in chapter 4, in Jewish thought justification had to do with the distinction between the "righteous" (Heb. *tsaddiqim,* Gk. *dikaioi*) and the "unrighteous," "wicked," or "sinners" (Heb. *reshaim,* Gk. *asebeis, hamartōloi*), rather than between the "innocent" and the "guilty."[58] To be "justified" was to be counted as belonging to the community of the righteous, both in the present and at the final judgment.[59] What distinguished the righteous from the unrighteous was not that the former were perfect or sinless but that they were committed to living in obedience to God's will. The fact that the righteous were not entirely without sin meant that in order to be justified, they also needed to be forgiven. Yet while there was certainly a forensic aspect to justification, it must not be reduced to this, as if those justified were merely forgiven independently of any life of righteousness on their part. One needed to *live* righteously in order to be *accepted* by God as righteous, even though this righteousness would inevitably be imperfect.

When Paul insists that justification is by grace, therefore, he has *both forgiveness and the new life of righteousness* in mind: God's "free gift" consists not merely in the forgiveness of sins and the acceptance of the "ungodly" but in the righteous way of life and the obedience graciously brought about by God through Christ and the Holy Spirit. In Paul's thought, even though one must live righteously in order to be forgiven and justified, as all faithful Jews recognized, one does not earn or merit one's own justification through one's works or deeds, since the ability to live righteously is a gracious gift of God rather than a human achievement. Because justification involves both a change of life in sinners and a gracious disposition on God's part to accept and forgive those sinners who receive that change of life through faith, when Paul speaks of God's work in Christ leading to justification, he must have both of these aspects in mind: Jesus sought to bring about the new life of righteousness in others, yet he also sought that God would accept and forgive them.

Paul relates the justification of believers to Jesus' death in Rom 5:9–10*, where he writes, "Much more surely, then, now that we have been justified by means of his blood [*en tō haimati autou*], will we be saved through him from the wrath of God. For if while we were enemies we were reconciled to God through the death of his Son, much more surely, having been reconciled, will we be saved by his life." These words appear almost immediately after Paul has affirmed that "while we were still weak, at the right time Christ died for the ungodly," and that "God proves his love for us in that while we still were sinners Christ died for us" (vv. 6, 8).

The allusion to Christ's "blood" here should be understood in the context of the passage as a whole. Paul clearly has in mind not merely the fact that Jesus *died* but the fact that he *gave up his life in love sacrificially*, seeking something on behalf of others.[60] As we have seen, according to the early Christian story, one of the things that Jesus had been seeking in his ministry was to form around himself a community of righteous people who would live according to God's will. In Pauline language, it might be said that *Jesus dedicated his life to seeking the justification of others.* Yet it was not the shedding of his blood or his death in itself that was to bring about this justification, as if it fulfilled some condition necessary for God to declare the ungodly righteous. Rather, Jesus' death must be seen against the background of the rest of the early Christian story with which Paul no doubt expected his Roman readers were well acquainted. If so, then they would have known that Jesus' efforts to bring about God's righteousness in others had led to his death. Yet by being faithful unto death in seeking this, together with God's gracious acceptance of his followers, Jesus attained these things when God raised him from the dead, since by exalting Jesus, God was ensuring that the members of his community would be among those to be declared righteous and thus redeemed in the end. In this sense, believers are now "justified by means of his blood." Paul may also have had in mind the idea that just as in the old covenant sacrificial blood was shed on behalf of others to attain forgiveness of sins, so also according to the new covenant Christ had shed his own blood seeking that others be forgiven. Thus, through Christ and his death on their behalf, those living under the new covenant could now find forgiveness and justification.

Undoubtedly, there is a forensic aspect to this justification, since Jesus offered up his life seeking the justification of the "ungodly" (v. 6), the "sinners" (v. 8), and those who were God's "enemies" (v. 10). Paul no doubt is thinking of both Jews and Gentiles here, although his language is probably directed particularly at Jewish believers so as to remind them that they too were ungodly and sinners, living as God's enemies. Like the Gentiles, the Jewish believers have come to be justified, not because they have been faithful in observing the law or have merited their justification, but only because Christ gave up his life in love for them. However, that this justification is not exclusively forensic is evident from the fact that Paul uses the past tense in referring to believers as "sinners" and God's "enemies"; though they *were* sinners and enemies, and *were* "weak" (v. 6), in some sense they are no longer so.

Particularly significant in this passage is Paul's use of the word "now," which appears in the context of references to what Christ did *in the past*, namely, dying "for us" and offering up his life by shedding his blood. Paul does not say that believers *were* justified when Christ died, as if justification followed directly from his death; rather, he says that they are justified "now" as a result of Jesus' sacrificial self-giving unto death ("blood"). In other words, those who have come to form part of the new covenant community for which Christ gave up his life are accepted by God as righteous or justified *now,* thanks to the fact that Christ laid down his life to obtain their forgiveness, salvation, and justification.

Several verses later, Paul writes that Jesus' "act of righteousness [*dikaiōma*] leads to justification and life for all" and that "by the one man's obedience the many will be made righteous" (Rom 5:18–19). Here Paul evidently has Jesus' death in mind: this is his act of righteousness and obedience. This passage, like the one just considered, can be understood on the basis of virtually any of the views of redemption examined in chapter 1. In fact, all it affirms is that there is some relation between Christ's act of righteousness and obedience in giving up his life, on the one hand, and the justification of others, on the other. According to those views, Christ's act of righteousness and obedience is salvific because through it he makes satisfaction to God for human sin, because it qualifies him to be a sinless substitute so as to die in the place of others, because it was offered up to God in the stead of believers, because believers participate in it, because it provides them with a model or example to imitate, or because his righteousness is imputed or imparted to believers.[61]

Instead of looking to one of these stories to interpret Paul's thought here, however, we can fill in Paul's argument by looking to the story of redemption told by the first Christians. Christ's act of righteousness consisted of obediently giving up his life, seeking to bring about God's righteousness in others and obtain from God their justification. His death would also lead to a new covenant in which many more would receive this righteousness and be justified, as the gospel would be proclaimed throughout the world. As a result of that act, God raised him from the dead so that what he had sought in life and death might become a reality. Thus, because of what Christ did, many people throughout the world have obtained "justification of life" and will be "constituted righteous," since through their relationship to Christ they have obtained certainty of both a new life of righteousness and their acceptance before God.[62]

In this passage Paul contrasts Christ with Adam, whose sinful act led to the opposite result: sin came into the world and, with it, God's condemnation. Yet for Paul this should not be understood automatically or mechanically, as if there were some "cause-and-effect link between the one act and the many's destiny."[63] Nor should Paul's words be understood in the sense that all human beings or believers have somehow participated in a past event, be this Adam's fall or Christ's act of righteousness and obedience.[64] Rather, Paul's argument should be understood *historically*: according to the Old Testament story, as a result of Adam's trespass, sin came into the world, and along with it death and condemnation. As a result of Christ's righteous act and obedience unto death, however, many throughout the world are now accepted by God as righteous, since his obedience and faithfulness unto death to the task of forming around himself a righteous people resulted in both his resurrection by God and the existence of such a people throughout the world, who now are righteous as they live in and under him under the covenant established through his death. For Paul, Adam's trespass does not lead to sin and death in the same way that Christ's act of righteousness and obedience leads to justification and life. The point of comparison is merely that the act of each one has had consequences for others.

The same ideas are probably behind Paul's words in 2 Cor 5:21, where he writes that "for our sake [God] made him to be sin who knew no sin, so that in him we might become the righteousness of God." This passage has often been interpreted according to some type of mechanical understanding of redemption, as if in itself the sinless Christ's being "made sin" led to believers' becoming "the righteousness of God." Ralph Martin, for example, speaks of Paul's "carefully worked-out explanation of the 'mechanics' of God's action in verse 21" and says that the idioms of 2 Cor 5:21 "state simply a substitution-ary change."[65] While this can be understood in a forensic sense, some have argued instead for some type of real exchange or "interchange": human sin collectively (or the penalty due humans because of that sin) was transferred to Christ, and Christ's righteousness or purity in turn was transferred to believ-ers.[66] Such views are mechanical in that they make the process automatic: sin or its punishment is "dealt with" merely by being passed from believers onto Christ in some mysterious fashion, while righteousness tends to be regarded either as some type of actual substance or power imparted to believers or as a status that is imputed to them. Not only are ideas such as these absent from the story we find in the early kerygma; they also involve replacing that story with a very different one. In that case, Paul is departing radically from the early story of redemption and making up his own.

Rather than looking to ideas such as these and ascribing them to Paul, all we need in order to understand his thought in 2 Cor 5:21 is the story found in the early tradition. According to that story, God sent his Son in "sinful flesh" to carry out a ministry aimed at bringing others to fulfill the *dikaiōma* of the law (Rom 8:3–4) and had him persevere in that ministry all the way to the cross, thus "giving him up" rather than "sparing" him (Rom 8:32). Either of these ideas may be behind Paul's affirmation that God "made him to be sin who knew no sin." If Paul is thinking of Christ's coming in human flesh, the idea is that God sent his Son, who previously "knew no sin," into an existence in which all are under sin. If Paul instead has in mind Christ's passion and death, however, then the idea is that God treated his Son, who had committed no sin, as if he were a sinner when he had him suffer the consequences of his activity on behalf of others by dying on the cross. This does not mean that God *judged* or *condemned* Christ on the cross, or made him the object of his wrath, but rather that God gave him over to death at the hands of evildoers. As the Old Testament repeatedly insists, God hears the prayers of the righteous but refuses to listen to the prayers or come to the aid of those who practice sin and evil. According to the Gospel passion accounts, this seemed to be precisely what had occurred on the cross: God had apparently abandoned his Son, turning a deaf ear to his cries and failing to rescue him from death, contrary to the hopes of many of the onlookers. Initially, then, God treated Christ as an evildoer, as "sin," even though three days later God raised him from the dead.

Whether Paul has in mind Christ's coming or his death on the cross in 2 Cor 5:21, what is important is the objective stated by Paul: "that in him we might become the righteousness of God." This phrase has generally been understood as a synonym of justification: in Christ, believers are accounted righteous before God.[67] It is also possible that Paul is thinking more in collective terms: the righteousness of God to which the law and prophets bore witness (Rom 3:21) is now practiced by God's new covenant people. Once again, it should be stressed that in either case what is involved is not merely some change in status before God or a forensic declaration. Paul nowhere says or implies that God sent his Son and gave him up to death simply to make it possible for him to forgive or acquit sinners, as if previous to Christ's death his holy and righteous nature prevented him from doing so. Rather, God's objective was to bring about in them a new life of righteousness, on the basis of which they might become acceptable to him. Furthermore, it is not Christ's incarnation or death in itself that accomplishes this, as if some change had been effected in human nature or in the way God looks upon sinners merely because Christ became human and died on a cross. Instead, according to the early story of redemption, God's objective of bringing about a new, righteous people has been achieved thanks to his sending the Son to bring about in others the righteousness he desired, giving him over to death when he was faithful to this task, and pouring out his Spirit on them after exalting Christ to his side in heaven.

One final passage from Paul's letters that relates Christ's death to the justification of believers is Gal 2:21, where Paul writes, "I do not nullify the grace of God; for if justification comes through the law, then Christ died for nothing." Here again, rather than claiming that Paul considered Christ's death as fulfilling a necessary condition for justification, as if justification followed from it automatically,[68] we need only look to the early Christian story to understand Paul's thought. In spite of all their efforts to attain the promised redemption by strict submission to the law, the Jewish people had never been able to attain the righteousness necessary for God to redeem them (cf. Acts 13:39; 15:10–11). Through Christ, however, that righteousness is now freely given by God as a gift, along with the justification and certainty of redemption that go along with it. Christ attained all of this at the cost of his life, since his efforts to bring it about led to conflict and the cross, to which he willingly submitted out of love for those whose salvation he sought. And by making that supreme sacrifice, he now obtained a way for others to be justified apart from the law, by living under him in a new covenant. However, if the righteousness necessary for justification must still be attained by human beings on their own through literal obedience to the Torah's commandments (such as circumcision), independently of the activity of Christ and the Holy Spirit now given to believers, then in reality Christ accomplished nothing by giving up his life, and all his efforts were in vain; everything remains precisely as it was before Christ came. This would be to nullify God's gracious gift given through Christ.

Christ's Death and Reconciliation

In the undisputed Pauline letters, the language of reconciliation occurs in the context of allusions to Christ's death in only two passages, a portion of each of which was just examined: Rom 5:10–11, part of which was quoted at the outset of the previous section, and 2 Cor 5:17–21. In Rom 5:10–11, after affirming that believers have now been justified through Christ's blood and will be "saved through him from the wrath of God," Paul adds, "For if while we were enemies, we were reconciled to God through the death [*dia tou thanatou*] of his Son, much more surely, having been reconciled, will we be saved by his life. But more than that, we even boast in God through our Lord Jesus Christ, through whom we have now received reconciliation." In 2 Cor 5:17–20*, the language is somewhat similar:

> So if anyone is in Christ, that person is a new creation: the old things have passed away; see, they have become new. All this is from God, who reconciled us to himself through Christ, and has given us the ministry of reconciliation; that is, in Christ God was reconciling the world to himself, not counting their trespasses against them, and entrusting the message of reconciliation to us. So we are ambassadors for Christ, since God is making his appeal through us; we entreat you on behalf of Christ, be reconciled to God.

Although in these particular verses from 2 Corinthians Christ's death is not mentioned, allusions to the cross appear in the preceding verses (vv. 14–15), and perhaps in v. 21 as well, if "[God] made him to be sin" is understood as an allusion to Jesus' passion and crucifixion.

Both of these passages have traditionally been interpreted on the basis of stories of redemption like those considered in chapter 1. Some have argued that Christ's death reconciles believers to God in that he took humanity's judgment upon himself, thereby exhausting God's wrath at sin and sinners and satisfying the need for human sin to be condemned. Others have instead claimed that Christ's death produces some change in human beings themselves or their condition by acting upon their hearts, bringing Satan's rule to an end or destroying sin in the humanity Christ shares with all so as then to exalt that humanity to God's presence. Those who maintain the latter have often stressed that Paul speaks of human beings being reconciled to God, not God to human beings.[69] These interpretations of Paul's thought are based on the supposition that Christ's death in itself has some salvific consequence or effect, fulfilling some condition that makes reconciliation with God possible. Once again, the brevity and compactness of Paul's allusions to reconciliation through Christ's death make it possible to understand them on the basis of virtually any narrative framework such as these.

The idea of God and his people being reconciled is not a particularly prominent one in ancient Jewish thought. It is all but absent in the Hebrew Bible, but it does appear several times in 2 Maccabees, which tells of the oppression of the Jews at the hands of Antiochus Epiphanes. There reconciliation clearly has to do with God putting away his wrath at his people. One of the Jewish martyrs, for example, states, "And if our living Lord is angry for a little while, to rebuke and discipline us, he will again be reconciled with his own servants" (2 Macc 7:33). Further on, it is said that the people "made common supplication and implored the merciful Lord to be wholly reconciled with his servants," that is, to deliver them from the oppression they were suffering (8:29; cf. 1:5; 5:20). To understand the ideas behind these passages, we need merely look to the Jewish story of redemption considered in chapter 2: when the people of Israel suffered and were oppressed, they believed themselves to be under God's wrath at their sins; God was chastising them. However, they trusted that God's wrath would come to an end as they repented, became more obedient, and offered up prayers and supplications to him, asking him to put away his anger. In the case of the persecution under Antiochus Epiphanes, this occurred when God slew Antiochus and delivered them from their suffering under his rule. Thus, the "reconciliation" that the people were awaiting was simply their redemption and deliverance; when God put away his wrath at their sins, they would be redeemed.[70]

While ideas such as these may be behind Paul's language in Rom 5:10–11, it is important to note that there Paul says that believers have been reconciled to God, rather than God to believers. If we look to the early Christian story rather than to some version of one of the various stories of redemption presented in chapter 1, the idea in this passage would be that both the Jews and the Gentiles to whom Paul was writing were still "enemies" of God when God sent his Son, since they had not yet been living according to God's will. Nevertheless, they were "reconciled to God by the death of his Son" in the sense that, in obedience to his Father, Christ gave up his life seeking the reconciliation of others to God, particularly those who would come to form part of the community under him. This was something God had sought through his Son, not just in his death but also in the ministry that led to his death, since Jesus called people to repentance and a new life of righteousness as well as laying the foundation for what would come later. By giving his Son up to death according to the divine plan (*kata kairon*, 5:6), God made it possible for a new covenant to come into being, in which those who were "enemies" might now live as God's people in the context of the church, as was the case in Rome; believers now no longer live as enemies of God. Thanks, then, to the new reality in which they live as a result of Christ's death on their behalf, they have "peace with God" and have "obtained access" to the grace in which they stand (Rom 5:1–2); and as they live in this new reality, reconciled with God, they can be certain that in the end they will be saved by Jesus and delivered from God's wrath (5:9–10), since Jesus is alive. Several of these ideas are found also in Eph 2:11–22 and in Col 1:19–23, both of which speak of reconciliation taking place through (*dia*) Christ's death, blood, or cross, and of the new community of holy and righteous people embracing both Jews and Gentiles who now live in peace with God and one another as a result of what Christ has done.

In 2 Cor 5:17–20, Paul relates reconciliation not only with God's activity through Christ but also with the activity of those who serve as his "ambassadors," to whom he has "given the message of reconciliation" and who thus carry out "the ministry of reconciliation." Here it is not merely Christ's death that leads to believers' being a "new creation," but the fact that they are now "in Christ" (v. 17). Likewise, when Paul writes that God "reconciled us to himself through Christ and has given us the ministry of reconciliation" (v. 18), he seems to be alluding not only to Christ's life and death but also to God's commissioning of apostles through Christ. This too formed part of the divine plan, as we have seen, and has led to the reconciliation of the Corinthian believers with God. Paul's use of the periphrastic imperfect in Greek, *ēn katalassōn*, in v. 19 may indicate that he had in mind not simply one past moment or event but all of the activity God carried out through Christ, including not only his death but his ministry and perhaps even his resurrection, together with his sending out of apostles.

The fact that Paul here speaks of reconciliation as something already accomplished (the "indicative") yet still calls on his readers to be reconciled to God (the "imperative") has often been seen as supporting the objective/subjective distinction considered previously.[71] It is thus said that "the Christ-event (vv. 14, 21) in principle effected the reconciliation in an objective fashion, prior to any consequent human response," but that this reconciliation "is not complete without the individual human response."[72] Lying behind these distinctions has usually been a mechanical understanding of Christ's work, according to which Christ's death fulfills a first condition for reconciliation with God, and the response of believers fulfills a second condition. The question then becomes whether, in fulfilling the first condition, Christ fulfilled this for *all* people (the "world") or only for some. This question has led to the theological debates over whether the atonement wrought by Christ is *unlimited* or *limited*.[73]

According to the early Christian story of redemption, however, what Jesus was seeking from God as he offered up his life was reconciliation and redemption *for his community of followers*, the (new) covenant people. At the same time, however, his objective was that people from around the world, including especially Gentiles, come to form part of that community. His death and resurrection would lead to a new covenant and the incorporation of people from among the nations through the proclamation of the gospel. That this is what Paul means by speaking of the "world" being reconciled to God is evident from Rom 11:15, where he says that the rejection of the gospel on the part of the Jews means "the reconciliation of the world," that is, the rest of the world, embracing the Gentile peoples.[74] As has been shown previously, according to the early Christian understanding of the divine plan, both Jesus' death as well as the rejection of the gospel on the part of many Jews led to the mission to the Gentiles, who are now also brought into reconciliation with God as they live in faith and obedience under a new covenant. This reconciliation does not result automatically from Jesus' death but is the result of the proclamation of the gospel following the establishment of the new covenant through his death.

Thus, while it can certainly be said that for Paul God reconciled believers to himself in Christ "prior to any consequent human response," this response was *presupposed* in God's acceptance of Christ's self-offering on behalf of believers. That is, those reconciled to God are those who would come to live obediently in faith under Christ. While *temporally* the objective reconciliation precedes the subjective reconciliation and the indicative precedes the imperative, *logically* it is the reverse: those who were reconciled to God through Christ's death are those who through God's grace would respond affirmatively to the call to live in faith and obedience in Christ. The imperative thus does not simply follow upon the indicative but is the condition upon which the indicative can be used regarding them.

To say that only those who would come to form part of the community of believers were reconciled to God through Christ's death is not necessarily to claim that Paul thought that only believers will be saved in the end. While it is doubtful that Paul was a universalist in the sense of maintaining that ultimately all people without exception will be saved, he may have held the Jewish belief in an "eschatological ingathering" of peoples from all around the world. In that case, he would have thought that those who practiced righteousness in various times and places without knowing Christ might also be reconciled to God through Christ, since someday when he comes in glory they *will* live in and under him as Lord.[75] He may also have believed that many of the Jews who do not accept Jesus as the Messiah will be saved.[76] Thus, in addition to referring to Paul's belief that both Jews and Gentiles from around the world share in this reconciliation with God, his mention of the "world" in 2 Cor 5:19 and "all" in 5:14–15 may imply that he believed that in the end people from all over the world will attain salvation in Christ, when "every knee shall bend" and "every tongue confess that Jesus Christ is Lord" (Phil 2:10–11*). Because this is now a certainty by virtue of Christ's resurrection, Paul can use the past tense: the "world" and "all" were reconciled to God when Christ offered up his life on their behalf and God responded by raising him from the dead; in this way, God ensured that what Christ had died seeking for all people in obedience to God would come to pass. This idea may also be behind Paul's affirmation that God was "not counting their trespasses against them" (2 Cor 5:19). Although this may refer to the forgiveness that is now found in Christ, it is possible that Paul instead had in mind the idea that in spite of the sin of both Jews and Gentiles, God graciously reached out to them in Christ to reconcile them to himself: God had patiently overlooked and tolerated their sin until the time when he would carry out his plan of reconciliation throughout the world (cf. Acts 17:30).

Redemption through Christ's Death

Throughout this study, the word "redemption" has been employed in the sense in which it was commonly understood in Judaism, where it generally referred to the salvation and deliverance that Israel was expecting (see Luke 2:38; 21:28; 24:21). Undoubtedly, the language of redemption was used in other contexts, particularly to refer to the liberation of slaves through some type of payment.[77]

On this basis it has been argued that whenever Paul speaks of redemption, he has in mind the payment of some price, generally in substitution or exchange for something or someone.[78] This argument is particularly common among those adhering to a penal substitution view, many of whom claim that the same idea is found in the *lytron* saying attributed to Jesus (Mark 10:45; Matt 20:28) and in the affirmation that Christ "gave himself as a ransom for all" (*antilytron hyper pantōn*) in 1 Tim 2:6.[79]

There is no reason, however, to ascribe all of these ideas to Paul. At times, redemption may simply involve deliverance or liberation, as when God "redeems" his people from bondage such as that which they suffered in Egypt. In this case, no cost was involved for God; to say that God had to exert some effort to redeem the people, and that this represented some type of cost or sacrifice to God,[80] seems to be totally alien to Old Testament thought, where God is regarded as sovereign and omnipotent. In the case of the redemption of slaves, of course, some price was generally paid to the person who had legal rights over the slaves. But this idea can hardly be applied to the people of Israel or humanity as a whole, unless it is said that Satan had legal rights over them.

It is evident from 1 Corinthians that Paul was well acquainted with the idea of ransoming or acquiring slaves through the payment of a price. In 1 Cor 6:19–20, he tells the Corinthian Christians, "You are not your own . . . you were bought with a price." A chapter later he reminds them once more that each of them is "a slave of Christ" rather than of human beings, because they were "bought with a price" (7:22–23). A similar idea is attributed to Paul by Luke in Acts 20:28, where Paul exhorts the leaders gathered at Ephesus to "shepherd the church of God that he obtained with the blood of his own Son."[81] While only in this last passage is Christ's death or blood explicitly mentioned, there can be little doubt that the "price" Paul has in mind in 1 Corinthians is also the suffering and death of God's Son.

To speak of Christ's death as a "price" might be taken as implying that his death itself obtained or purchased the salvation of others. This could be understood as supporting one of the stories considered in chapter 1, where Christ's death is a price paid to obtain divine forgiveness or deliverance from the penalty or consequences of sin for others, or to ransom human beings from the forces of evil that held them in bondage. Such views, however, end up regarding Christ's death as some type of personal transaction between

God and the devil or between God and himself through his Son, or else as an impersonal transaction in which Christ's death meets some requirement that had to be fulfilled in order for humanity to be redeemed.

Once more, however, ideas such as those found in 1 Cor 6:19–20 and 7:22–23 can be understood perfectly well on the basis of the early Christian story of redemption. According to that story, what God sought was a people of his own who would do his will as his servants. This idea is found throughout the Hebrew Scriptures, where Israel is repeatedly spoken of as God's own possession and servant. In Old Testament thought, however, the people became God's possession and servants when God redeemed them from bondage in Egypt.[82] When the first Christians took over the Jewish story of redemption, they applied some of these same ideas to the Christian community, now understood as the new covenant people. As such, they must also have been obtained by God at some point, redeemed from their own former existence of bondage to sin and death in order to become God's people and servants. For them, this had occurred when God sent his Son to dedicate himself to the task of establishing this community committed to serving God in righteousness. As in the parable of the wicked tenants (Matt 21:33–41), however, the result of sending his Son to carry out this task in the midst of evildoers was the Son's death. Because Christ was faithful unto death in seeking to form such a people around himself, and because he gave himself up according to the divine plan so that a new covenant might come into place for the benefit of many throughout the world, when he was raised by God, this new community of obedient servants became a reality. These same ideas are reflected in Titus 2:14, where it is said that Jesus Christ "gave himself for us that he might redeem us from all iniquity and purify for himself a people of his own who are zealous for good deeds"; this was what Christ had lived and died for. Thus, by paying the price that he did, namely, sending his Son to carry out a ministry that would result in his Son's violent death (i.e., his "blood"), God obtained the people he desired (Acts 20:28). Their redemption thus "cost" him his Son's life.

Because of this, Paul can tell believers that they were "bought" or "purchased" with a price. They are now God's own possession and belong to him; they are God's *douloi*, since they obey his will as slaves of old obeyed their owners. Although this is true of each of them individually, strictly speaking, what God "purchased" or "acquired" was the church (as in Acts 20:28), that is, the community of people who live in obedience to him. As individuals become part of that community through faith, they too are counted among those whom God made his own at the cost of his Son's blood or death, and for whom Christ died (1 Cor 8:11; Gal 2:20). While the redemption of God's people thus "cost" God something, since the "price" both God and his Son "paid" was the Son's death, this does not mean that this price was paid *to* someone, such as the devil or God himself. Instead, the idea is similar to that of an athlete who pays a high price to win a competition by making many sacrifices in order to prepare for that competition, or of the soldier or police officer who pays the ultimate price of his or her life to defend or protect someone else.[83] This is what Christ did to obtain the salvation of God's people: he gave himself up as a "ransom for all" (1 Tim 2:6) in the sense that, in exchange for the giving up of his life, he obtained the redemption he had sought for others in life and death when God raised him from the dead. What is involved is doing something not in the place of others but on their behalf.

Paul uses a variation of the verb *agorazein*, found in 1 Cor 6:19–20 and 7:22–23, in two passages in Galatians to speak of redemption through Christ. In the first, Christ's death is mentioned explicitly: "Christ redeemed us from the curse of the law, having become a curse for us—for it is written, 'Cursed is everyone who hangs on a tree'—in order that in Christ Jesus the blessing of Abraham might come to the Gentiles, so that we might receive the promise of the Spirit through faith" (Gal 3:13*). Several verses later, Paul writes, "But when the fullness of time had come, God sent his Son, born of woman, born under the law, to redeem those who were under the law, so that we might receive adoption as children" (Gal 4:4–5).

Most interpreters from the time of the church fathers to the present have continued to look to various versions of the stories of redemption considered in chapter 1 to interpret Paul's words in these passages.[84] What Paul writes here, however, can be understood perfectly well by looking instead to the story told by the first Christians and Paul that was outlined in chapters 3 and 4. The people of Israel had been seeking to obtain the promises of redemption made to the patriarchs by obedience to the law, but they had not achieved what they sought. According to Paul, this was because they had not kept the law, and because the law itself was powerless to bring about in the people the obedience and righteousness God desired and commanded. For this reason, they remained under the curse that the law pronounces on all who disobey (Gal 3:10). God, however, sent his Son "to redeem those under the law" (4:4), so that they might attain what God had promised. Jesus dedicated himself to that task throughout his ministry, and as a result faced the possibility of being executed on a cross, a kind of death over which the law pronounced a curse (Deut 21:23). Rather than attempting to escape or avoid such a death, however, he willingly submitted to it, thereby becoming a curse on behalf of others (3:13). By doing so, he obtained the fulfillment of the promises he had sought for others when he was raised by God, including the gift of the Holy Spirit and the blessing of the Gentiles promised to Abraham (3:14). By submitting to such an accursed death, Jesus has redeemed from the law's curse those who could not attain the promised blessings of salvation through that law by making it possible for people to live as part of God's people under the new covenant founded through him. Thus, they now can receive through faith what they were not able to receive through the law. In particular, they receive the righteousness that they could not previously attain; this is theirs as they live "out of faith" (*ek pisteōs*, 3:11), as Abraham did (3:6). They become Abraham's children, members of God's chosen people (3:7, 29), and as his heirs, they inherit the promises made to him (4:7).

It is important to stress that Paul does not say in this passage that the "curse borne by Christ (3:13) is the same curse previously borne by Christians";[85] rather, he speaks of *two different curses*. The curse Christ underwent was not the curse pronounced in Deut 27:26 on "anyone who does not uphold the words of this law by observing them," but the curse pronounced in Deut 21:23 on those who were hanged on a tree. In other words, Christ came under the curse pronounced on those hanging on a tree in order to save those who were under the curse pronounced on those who did not obey the law. Undoubtedly, it was the *same law* that pronounced both of these curses, but the two were not the *same curse*. It might also be said that Jesus was condemned and crucified for breaking the law and perhaps teaching others to do the same as a "servant of sin" (Gal 2:17; see Mark 14:64; Luke 22:37; 23:5, 14; cf. John 18:30; 19:7); yet because the curse of Deut 21:22–23 is also pronounced on one who commits "a crime punishable by death," his death would still be seen as a fulfillment of this curse rather than the one mentioned in Deut 27:26. On the basis of this distinction between the two curses, many of the traditional readings of Gal 3:13 must be ruled out, since they depend on the idea that Christ suffered in the place of others the same curse they had merited by their sins, or that believers are redeemed by undergoing together with Christ the same curse through some type of participation in his death. This distinction also rules out the translation of *hyper hēmōn* as "in our place"; this phrase should simply be translated "on our behalf" or "for our benefit."

The use of the aorist participle *genomenos* also supports the reading proposed here: Christ delivered others from the curse pronounced by the law on those who do not obey it, *when he had become* a curse for them by hanging on a tree. It has often been argued that temporal force should not be ascribed to the aorist participle, but that instead it should be "taken in a modal sense" or in some other way.[86] This is precisely because to understand the aorist participle in a temporal sense raises difficulties for the substitutionary and participatory readings of this verse, according to which *it is when Christ dies* that those under the curse are redeemed, since Christ's death in itself satisfies the condition necessary for their redemption. According to what has been argued here, however, Christ attained the redemption of others *when he was raised by God in response to his obedience unto death in seeking that redemption*. Although Paul does not mention Jesus' being raised here, his allusion to the outpouring of the Holy Spirit on believers in the verses immediately following both Gal 3:13 and 4:4–5 indicates that he certainly had it in mind, since the Spirit was given *after* Christ had been raised.

Outside of these passages in the undisputed Pauline letters, the language of redemption occurs in only three places. In each of these Paul uses the noun *apolytrōsis*. This word is used in Rom 8:23 to speak of the "redemption of our bodies" and in 1 Cor 1:30, where Christ is said to have been made from God "our wisdom . . . and righteousness and sanctification and redemption." Neither of these two passages mentions Christ's death explicitly, in contrast to Rom 3:24–25, where Paul speaks of "the redemption that is in Christ Jesus" immediately before referring to Christ as a propitiation in his blood. All three of these passages are perfectly comprehensible when viewed against the framework of the early Christian story. By virtue of his death and resurrection, Christ has become the source of redemption (as he has also become the source of wisdom, righteousness, and sanctification, 1 Cor 1:30), so that believers can now be certain that someday their bodies will be redeemed together with the rest of the created order (Rom 7:24; 8:19–23). Redemption is thus to be found now "in Christ Jesus" as a result of God's gracious activity in sending his Son; but it is also to be attributed to Christ's death or "blood," since his commitment to the end in attaining that redemption for others has led to a situation in which it is now theirs through him (cf. Eph 1:7; Col 1:14).

CHAPTER 6

Dying with Christ

If the early Christian story of redemption as outlined in the previous chapters is behind Paul's "cultic-juristic" or "forensic" language regarding Christ's death, is it also behind his so-called participatory language? Initially, this seems unlikely, since the idea that believers actually participate or share in Christ's death is absent from that story as best as we can reconstruct it. Nowhere in the Synoptics or Acts is it explicitly said that believers collectively die with Christ; nor do we find there anything similar to Paul's "in Christ" language. If Paul did not get these ideas from the early tradition, then either he or others in the Christian communities of which he formed part must have developed them independently from that tradition by looking outside of it.

No matter how the question of the origin of Paul's so-called participatory language is resolved, the problem of the narrative framework underlying that language remains; obviously, there must be *some* story of redemption underlying it. In order to argue that the story behind such language is the same as that found in the early Christian tradition, it is necessary to show not only that this story provides all the elements necessary to understand the participatory language in Paul's letters but also that such language developed directly and naturally out of the early story, rather than originating in some other source. However, if it is instead claimed that lying behind Paul's participatory language is a story distinct from the early Christian story of redemption, then besides demonstrating that this other story can make sense of Paul's words in the relevant texts, it is necessary to answer convincingly the question of where the ideas that provide the basis for this other story came from. In this chapter, after a brief review of the history of the interpretation of Paul's participatory language, we will consider the possibility that behind this language is a story of redemption distinct from the early Christian story—one based on ideas taken from ancient Jewish or Hellenistic religious thought, but not directly from the early Christian tradition itself. Following this, we will consider the other possibility, namely, that Paul's so-called participatory language has its roots in ideas taken from the same story of redemption repeatedly outlined, and that all the elements necessary to understand that language are found in that story.

The Notion of Participation in Pauline Scholarship

As noted toward the end of chapter 1, throughout most of the twentieth century Paul's so-called mystical or participatory language was the subject of a great deal of attention on the part of Pauline scholars. One of the first to focus on this language was Adolf Deissmann, who pointed out the importance of the "in Christ" formula for Paul.[1] Deissmann argued that Paul understood this formula "vividly and mystically," and that in Paul's thought Christ is "not a 'historical' personage, but a reality and power of the present, an 'energy.'"[2] He also claimed that all the passages from Paul's letters that speak of suffering, dying, and being crucified and buried with Christ should be understood against the background of Paul's "passion mysticism": as a member of the body of Christ, Paul "mystically experiences all that that Body experienced and experiences."[3]

These ideas were developed further by Albert Schweitzer in his influential work *The Mysticism of Paul the Apostle*. According to Schweitzer, Paul taught that through baptism into Christ believers were "united in one corporeity" with Christ and underwent with him his dying and rising again.[4] Because of the union between Christ and believers, the latter share in the same process and experiences that Christ underwent, and actually form part of the same body, so that they "no longer carry on an independent existence, but are now only the Body of Christ."[5] Schweitzer also claimed that Paul understood the relationship between Christ and believers in ontological and realistic terms, even going so far as to claim that Paul conceived of the union of believers with Christ as "a physical bodily union."[6] Ideas such as these were taken up by a number of other scholars. John A. T. Robinson, for example, wrote that "it is almost impossible to exaggerate the materialism and crudity of Paul's doctrine of the Church as literally now the resurrection *body* of Christ."[7]

As was noted in chapter 1, both Karl Barth and Rudolf Bultmann developed these same ideas, but in very different ways. Barth claimed that in New Testament thought, Christ had taken our same humanity (i.e., "man") at the incarnation, and then by dying and rising in that humanity, effected the destruction of the "old man" and brought into existence a "new man." According to Barth, because all human beings share the same humanity with Christ, "the totality of all sinful men" died with Christ on the cross; the participation of human beings in Christ's death is thus an *ontological* one, involving "the *humanum*, the being and essence, the nature and kind, which is that of all men."[8]

In contrast, according to Bultmann's interpretation of Paul, participation in Christ and his death involves neither an ontological union between believers and the past event nor some type of mystical union with Christ. Instead, the union between Christ and believers occurs when the proclaimed word "accosts the hearer and compels him to decide for or against it."[9] What becomes "present" for the believer is not so much Christ himself but the "cosmic event" of the cross, which "may no longer be considered as just the historical event of Jesus' crucifixion on Golgotha. For God made this event the eschatological occurrence, so that, lifted out of all temporal limitation, it continues to take place in any present moment, both in the proclaiming word and the sacraments."[10] According to Bultmann, "'In Christ,' far from being a formula for mystic union, is primarily an *ecclesiological* formula." Similarly, while "baptism grants participation in the death and resurrection of Jesus," it does so in no other way "than the word proclaimed and heard in faith."[11] There is no mystical relationship between Christ and the baptized; nor does baptism have a magical effect.

Following other scholars of his day, Bultmann claimed that while Paul's cultic language was passed down to him from the early church, his participatory language had its roots in ideas taken from the mystery religions and Gnosticism.[12] On this basis, Bultmann argued that for Paul baptism "unites the baptized with Christ into one *soma*" so that Christ is "not really an individual person," and what happened to Christ "happens to his whole *soma*." This means that what is true of Christ is true of the members of his body, who are "bound up with him into one body": as he suffered and has been raised from the dead so as to return to the heavenly home and be released from the sinful powers ruling the world, so have they.[13]

These basic ideas have continued to be popular among Pauline scholars, as noted in chapter 1. In the English-speaking world, among the most influential works that have stressed the importance of the notion of participation for Paul's soteriology have been those by D. E. H. Whiteley, Robert Tannehill, E. P. Sanders, Morna Hooker, James Dunn, N. T. Wright, and Richard Hays.[14] Undoubtedly, there are important differences among these scholars. Nevertheless, throughout their writings we continually encounter many of the same ideas concerning Paul's soteriology that are present in the thought of Deissmann, Schweitzer, Barth, and Bultmann. The most important of these is that Christ represents or incorporates others in some way so that what is true of him is also true of them; this latter idea is repeated frequently.[15] Many of these writers posit some type of corporate reality through which Christ is united to believers so as to be one with them, so that his death and resurrection are not his alone but theirs as well; with Christ they are "transferred" from this age to the next, undergo the penalty or curse of sin, and are redeemed from their fallen condition. This union may be seen as being effected either through some type of mystical relationship; through some entity called "humanity" in which both Christ and believers (or all people) share by virtue of Christ's incarnation; through the Holy Spirit, who unites Christ to believers; or through the sacraments. Likewise, following Bultmann, Christ's death and resurrection are commonly spoken of in terms of an "event" (the "Christ-event"), which is said to be salvific by virtue of the "effect" it has (or had) on those participating in it by means of their union to Christ or his death. Reflecting ideas found in the writings of Deissmann and Schweitzer, a number of Pauline scholars still make reference to Paul's "mysticism" and affirm that Paul taught that believers share the same "experiences" as Christ.

In spite of the popularity of this interpretation of Paul, a number of serious problems associated with it have continued to plague its adherents. These problems are of both a theological and a historical nature.

Theological Difficulties

The term "participation" is commonly used by Pauline scholars to describe a relation to both a *person* (Christ) and an *event* (the "Christ-event"). Yet what does it mean to participate in Christ or in his death and resurrection? The first of these phrases is problematic in that in normal English, people are not said to "participate" in other people: we do not speak of "participating" in Mary or "sharing" in John. We may participate in *groups* or *communities* of people (e.g., the church), but not in other persons themselves. Paul, in fact, never uses such a phrase. Although in 1 Cor 1:9 he does speak of the *koinōnia* of God's Son, Christ Jesus, the idea seems to be that of a fellowship or communion relationship with Christ, not a "participation" in him. Thus, what it might mean to participate or share in Christ is not at all clear.

One way of attempting to make sense of the notion of participation in Christ has been to look, consciously or unconsciously, to the Platonic doctrine of participation, according to which particulars participate or share in the universal forms or ideas (e.g., "men" participate in the idea of "man").[16] Participation in Christ would then involve a relation to Christ through some type of universal, such as "man," "humanity," "body," or "flesh," that is common to all human beings, including Christ. In fact, it is possible to regard Christ himself as some type of universal figure or archetypal "man" in whom others participate. Such views raise the same problems as Plato's doctrine of ideas. Precisely how particulars can participate in universals is a question that neither Plato nor his later interpreters were able to resolve satisfactorily. Furthermore, there is no clear evidence in Paul's letters that he drew on Plato's teaching or was heavily influenced by it, so as to speak of "man" as some type of universal in which all share.

Other attempts to define the relationship between Christ and those who participate in him have proven equally problematic. Deissmann's idea that for Paul believers participate in Christ as if he were the "air" that they live in and breathe tends to reduce Christ to some type of mysterious material substance, ether, or energy, so that Christ ceases to be "a 'historical' personage." The mystical interpretation proposed by Schweitzer raises the same difficulties: What does it mean for believers to share "the same corporeity" with Christ? Here Christ's body ceases to be an "isolated entity" and becomes some type of inclusive amalgamation.[17] According to conceptions like these, Christ and believers are dissolved into each other, so that they lose their individuality. This denial of either the personhood of Christ or that of believers is found explicitly in the writings of Pauline scholars adhering to the notion of participation in Christ. Bultmann, for example, while rejecting a magical or mystical understanding of the union between Christ and believers, nevertheless claimed that in the Gnostic thought that influenced Paul, the Redeemer "is a cosmic figure and not really an individual person."[18] Other Pauline scholars who speak of "participation in Christ" maintain that in some way for Paul believers become "one person" with Christ;[19] but what does this mean? Christ ends up being some*thing* rather than some*one*, and believers also cease to be seen as unique persons.

Perhaps even more problematic is the affirmation that believers participate in Christ's death. How can those existing in other times and places participate in a particular, unrepeatable historical event that took place at a time and in a place in which they were nowhere to be found? To speak in such terms requires that the past event be "universalized" or made omnipresent by being "lifted out of all temporal limitation" in some way, as Bultmann argued, or else that people of other times and places be mysteriously included in the unique event of Golgotha, so that they literally die with Christ there, as Barth claimed. If this participation is regarded as real or ontological, then some new conception of time and space is necessary. In either case, just as the phrase "participation in Christ" implies a loss of particularity on the part of Christ and/or believers, so the notion of participation in the Christ-event tends to make of Christ's death and resurrection an abstraction rather than a concrete historical occurrence. The idea that believers participate in Christ's "experiences" is equally unclear. How can people of various times and places participate in the unique experiences of a historical individual of a time and place distinct and distant from their own? We end up making abstract generalities of those experiences.

Pauline scholars have repeatedly attributed ideas such as these to Paul without making any attempt to clarify what Paul supposedly meant. The few who have attempted to tackle this question have generally ended up concluding that Paul's thought in this regard is impossible to understand, particularly for people of our day and age, thus attributing our inability to grasp such ideas to the cultural distance separating us from Paul, as if people of Paul's time would have had no difficulty thinking in such terms. At one end of the spectrum we find those such as Deissmann, Schweitzer, and Robinson, who argue that we must look to some type of ontological or mystical realism to interpret Paul's thought, so as to speak of an "ontological participation" in Christ, as J. Christiaan Beker does.[20] At the other end of the spectrum are those such as Bultmann, who rejects the ontological idea according to which there is some substantial union between Christ and believers in order to define the relationship more in terms of some type of moral influence of Christ or the Christ-event on believers.[21]

Many contemporary scholars have sought to take a stand somewhere in the middle of these two positions. E. P. Sanders, for example, agreed with Bultmann in rejecting the idea that participation in Christ or the Christ-event involves some type of "magical transfer," but he claimed that Bultmann's existentialist interpretation, in which being "in Christ" involves "constantly accepting a revised self-understanding," also failed to do justice to Paul's thought. Instead, he argued that it is "best to understand Paul as saying what he meant and meaning what he said: Christians really are one body and Spirit with Christ," and the transformation of the world and of individual believers should be understood in real terms.[22] Yet what are these real terms? Ultimately, Sanders was unable to provide an answer and merely responded that "we seem to lack a category of 'reality'—real participation in Christ, real possession of the Spirit—which lies between naive cosmological speculation and belief in magical transference on the one hand and a revised self-understanding on the other. I must confess that I do not have a new category of perception to propose here." Thus, Sanders concludes that "what Paul concretely thought cannot be directly appropriated by Christians today."[23]

Richard Hays has proposed an alternative understanding of participation, according to which it involves an identification with the story of Christ on the part of believers. Hays argues that this "story participation" involves a transformation that is "real" yet "neither automatic nor magical." He insists that this participation cannot be reduced to some type of ethical *imitatio Christi*, since "the gospel story works a subtle transformation" in those who hear it, and the Holy Spirit "effects a mysterious personal union with Christ."[24] Yet his insistence on the "reality" of this participation ultimately leads him back to what appears to be a mystical or magical understanding of Christ's work, in spite of his stated rejection of such a view. Thus, as noted previously, he writes that "Jesus' death/resurrection has put an end to the world as it was and has adumbrated the 'new creation,'" and that "Jesus' death terminates the old age and ushers in a new one, in such a way that the very structure of reality is transformed"; this enables believers to "participate in the blessings and power of the new age . . . not only because a cosmic revolution is under way but also because they are personally united with Jesus and thus mysteriously transformed."[25] This implies that some type of ontological change occurs in believers and the world as a whole through their relationship to Christ and his death and resurrection.

Like Hays, Morna Hooker claims that Paul had more in mind than an *imitatio Christi*, arguing instead for some type of "conformity" to Christ's life on the part of Christians, in which they "share in Christ's experience." She does not explain precisely how the latter phrase should be understood, although it appears she has some type of ethical participation in mind.[26] James Dunn repeats the affirmations of both Hooker and Hays in speaking of believers' sharing in Christ's experience and participating in his passage from the old age to the new. But Dunn also claims that for Paul the event of Christ's passion and resurrection is reenacted in believers, in whom there is a real "indwelling" of Christ.[27] Once again, however, he offers no clear explanation of what all of this means, and he must admit that in these matters "conceptual clarity remains elusive."[28] N. T. Wright ascribes to Paul the idea that Jesus "sums up his people in himself" as an "incorporative Messiah" but makes no effort to define how this should be understood.[29]

It therefore seems that if we wish to make sense of Paul's language, we must choose between two alternatives: either an ethical understanding of participation in Christ and his death that merely involves a decision to identify with him as a person or with the past event of the cross, or else a real, ontological participation. The latter clearly implies some type of mystical or even magical transformation of believers, since Christ's death (or death/resurrection) is salvific in that it produces some mysterious "effect" on those who participate or share in it, altering their being or situation in some way. If one claims, as Karl Barth did, that Paul taught that *all* people actually participated in Christ's death and resurrection in some way, the problem becomes even greater: in that case, it is not clear what role faith and baptism play in salvation, other than that of enabling people to know or recall that they have already died and risen with Christ, and are thus already saved.[30] Even when faith is regarded as necessary for the Christ-event to produce some salvific effect on a person, the idea can still be magical or mechanical: faith becomes part of the "formula" necessary for Christ's death and resurrection to "work" or bring about some mysterious change in believers. Thus, for example, even though Bultmann rejects a magical or mystical understanding of participation in the Christ-event, ultimately he comes close to slipping back into the same kind of view. He maintains that the proclamation of the Christ-event has some mysterious "effect" on the hearer, producing a change in her or him; it "accosts" and even "compels" the hearer to alter her or his life. Thus, for Bultmann it seems that merely hearing about Christ's death and resurrection effects some mysterious change in people.

In addition to the ethical and the ontological understandings of participation, however, there is a third alternative. Believers can be said to have "died with Christ in God's decision" or "in God's sight."[31] This involves God's merely looking upon believers as having died when Christ did, in the sense that God regards them as having undergone the penalty or consequences of sin together with Christ their substitute. In this case, there is neither an actual ontological participation in Christ's death nor an ethical decision on the part of believers to die with Christ, but a forensic dying with Christ. Yet few of those who claim that Paul's soteriology is primarily participatory would agree that Paul understood participation solely in a forensic sense.

The notions of substitution and participation can be combined not only in a forensic view but in an ontological view, such as that of Karl Barth, for whom Christ was both "our Representative and Substitute."[32] As our substitute, Christ died in our place, but because he also represented us, we died with him, so that it is possible to speak of "our participation in that event."[33] The fact that Christ undergoes the divine judgment on human beings "does not mean that it is not executed on us but that it is executed on us in full earnest and in all its reality. . . . That Jesus Christ died for us does not mean, therefore, that we do not have to die, but that we have died in and with him."[34] James Dunn follows Barth in combining these two ideas, even recognizing his dependence on Barth.[35] Similarly, N. T. Wright attempts to combine the two notions: "'Participation' does not of itself exclude 'substitution,' however frequently that spurious 'either-or' is asserted."[36] The problem, however, in combining the ideas of substitution and participation is that according to the first, believers *do not* die because Christ dies in their stead, but according to the second, believers *do* die together with Christ by sharing in his death. It is hard to see how these two ideas are not mutually exclusive, unless "dying" is understood in two different senses.

One final theological difficulty has to do with the idea that Christ's death was necessary because only in that way could others die and rise with Christ so as to be transferred from the present age into the new one. According to this idea, Christ died for the *purpose* of making such a dying and rising possible.[37]

In Jewish thought, however, for people to die and to rise from the dead, it was not necessary that some representative figure first undergo such a dying and rising on their behalf. All people already die, independently of Christ; and all that was necessary for the dead to be raised at the last day so as to enter into the life of the new age was that God bring about such a resurrection, which in Judaism was always believed to be entirely within God's power. Although the New Testament affirms that God has now given the Son power and authority to usher in the new age and raise the dead, this affirmation is not based on any argument for necessity, as if it were impossible for God to accomplish these things without Christ's death and resurrection. Furthermore, there is no evidence in the New Testament that Jesus or his followers understood his death and resurrection as having the purpose of making it possible for others to die and rise in union with him by participating in those events. All of these ideas have their origin in later atonement theology, but not in the New Testament itself.

Historical Difficulties

While these understandings of the notion of participation are problematic in themselves, they become even more so when ascribed to Paul. For then the question arises, where did Paul get his ideas concerning participation in Christ and his death and resurrection? He apparently did not get them from the early Jesus-tradition, and it is hardly plausible that either he or the Christian communities of which he formed a part came up with such ideas totally "out of the blue." Therefore, some type of pre-Christian Hellenistic or Jewish background for the notion of participation must be posited.

For a long time, the general consensus among those ascribing to Paul a participatory soteriology was that either Paul or the community of which he formed a part had looked to some Hellenistic pagan source for the ideas behind his language, particularly Gnosticism or the mystery religions. It seems quite unlikely, however, that Paul took his ideas directly from a pagan source on his own, since this would have set him off entirely from the rest of the early Christian community. He could hardly have expected widespread acceptance of his gospel among Jews and Jewish Christians (like those in Rome, whom he had never met and whose support he sought for his work) if he were overtly drawing on pagan ideas. To avoid this difficulty, Bultmann argued that "gnostic motifs" as well as ideas taken from the mysteries were already present in the kerygma of the Hellenistic church prior to Paul; thus, Paul was merely developing what he had already received from the early Christian tradition when he spoke of participation in the salvation occurrence, Christ's death and resurrection.[38]

Several recent studies, however, have raised serious doubts regarding the possibility of a Hellenistic source for the participatory soteriology supposedly found in Paul. The claim that this soteriology was based on Gnostic ideas has been shown to be particularly problematic. There is no clear evidence for the existence of Gnostic myths concerning redemption and a "primal man" in Paul's day; on the contrary, "it is extremely doubtful whether the Redeemer myth existed until a couple of centuries after Paul."[39] Dunn goes so far as to speak of "the wild-goose chase for a pre-Christian Gnostic redeemer myth," observing as well that "the quest for a pre-Christian Gnostic primal man has now almost entirely been abandoned."[40]

The view that Paul's soteriology (or that of the early church) was heavily influenced by ideas from the mystery religions has also come under attack, although it still finds a number of adherents. A. J. M. Wedderburn in particular has presented a strong case against the view that Paul's language regarding dying and rising with Christ is derived from the soteriology of the mysteries. Without denying the fact that there are certain parallels between the two soteriologies, he concludes that "the mysteries were not saying the same thing as Paul, nor was Paul borrowing his ideas from the mysteries."[41] Besides the fact that there appears to be no basis in the mysteries for speaking of dying and rising with Christ in the way Paul does, or for his "with Christ" language and his teaching concerning baptism, it is not at all clear that the so-called mystery religions actually constituted a unified phenomenon.[42] Furthermore, in other Jewish and Christian texts of the same period, there is no clear evidence that the mystery religions had any significant influence on Jewish or Christian thought. For these and other reasons, it now appears unlikely that either Gnosticism or the mystery religions are behind Paul's thought.

Because of the general lack of evidence that Paul's soteriology drew on ideas found in the beliefs and practices of Hellenistic religions, many Pauline scholars now turn to ancient Judaism in order to argue that the basis for Paul's thought is to be found in Jewish beliefs concerning corporate figures, particularly Adam. Both John Ziesler and James Dunn, for example, look to the Genesis story and later Jewish literature to argue that Adam was regarded in Jewish thought as a representative man who incorporated others into himself.

Ziesler has claimed that in some ancient Jewish circles, Adam was regarded as the equivalent of humanity in general, so that "his individuality is almost totally eclipsed" and "he stands for all humanity" or "Everyman."[43] Similarly, Dunn argues that for Paul, as for other Jews of his time, Adam denoted humankind as a whole.[44] N. T. Wright rejects the idea that Jewish thought concerning Adam was about humankind in general, instead arguing that Adam is embodied only in Israel. Nevertheless, he agrees that Jewish "Adam theology" is the source of Paul's participatory language, claiming that just as in Jewish thought Adam embodied or incorporated others, for Paul Christ "sums up his people in himself, so that what is true of him is true of them."[45] Ziesler draws on these same sources to claim that for Paul "Christ is not just an individual, but in some sense an incorporating figure, so that what is true of him is true also of those who belong to him, who are in him."[46] Here again we find the attempt to equate Christ with believers, so that what is posited of Christ can automatically be posited of them as well.

Yet a close look at the passages from ancient Jewish literature that these scholars quote in support of their positions reveals little if any evidence for the existence of a Jewish doctrine of participation that might have provided the basis for Paul's participatory language. While in Jewish thought Adam's sin had universal consequences for all of his descendants, this did not mean that Jews believed that they had all mysteriously "participated" in his act, or that they somehow constituted a single corporate person with him. To say that Adam is the father of all people, that all human beings are born from his seed, or that his actions affected his descendants permanently in some way, is not the same as saying that Adam *is* all people rather than a particular individual, or that he incorporates them in himself. If Adam can be called "Everyman," it is only in the sense that he is the "type" of those who have followed, who have sinned as he did. Ziesler himself makes this clear:

> "Corporate personality" as a Hebrew notion is now under grave question. . . . While the Old Testament and later Judaism easily conceived of representative figures, it is not clear that they ever envisaged corporate figures, whether kings, patriarchs, Adam, or anyone else. We saw that Adam could be Everyman, but found no good reason to suppose that as an individual he could include other individuals. It is now very doubtful whether there ever was a Hebrew idea of corporate personality which could explain Paul's language.[47]

Ziesler therefore rightly concludes, "It thus does not seem that there was a key either in Gnosticism or in Hebrew corporate thinking which can unlock Paul's ideas for us."[48]

In fact, the evidence in support of a Hellenistic or Jewish origin for Paul's participatory language is very weak, and appears to be based on a faulty methodology. Everett Ferguson rightly observes that Pauline scholars have worked backwards, constructing a "general 'mystery theology' or common 'mystery religion'" that never actually existed as such, and "(unconsciously) starting with Christian ideas, using these to interpret data about the mysteries, and then finding the mysteries as the source of the Christian ideas."[49] The same appears to be true of the attempts to find a Jewish origin for Paul's participatory language: it is assumed from the start that Paul was working with some concept of "corporate personhood," and then efforts are made to find a basis for such a notion in ancient Jewish thought, in effect searching there for the "primal man" that neither Gnosticism nor the mysteries could provide. This involves reading ideas back into passages that are sufficiently ambiguous to lend themselves to such interpretations, although those ideas are never mentioned explicitly there. Furthermore, the Jewish texts purported to contain such ideas were generally not particularly influential or prominent in first-century Judaism; in some cases, they are actually from a later period. Thus, it can hardly be claimed that the idea of corporate personality was so widespread in Jewish thought in Paul's day that he could readily have expected his readers (particularly in Rome) to look to such an idea to interpret his teaching regarding Christ.

In addition to the lack of evidence, other serious problems exist for those who wish to claim that Paul looked to Hellenistic or Jewish religious beliefs and practices for the ideas behind his participatory language. As noted above, many of the proposed interpretations of "participation in Christ" reduce both Christ and his death and resurrection to abstractions. Besides the theological and conceptual difficulties such interpretations raise, there is also the historical difficulty of how Paul and others could have come to understand the events surrounding Jesus' death in that way only a few years after they had taken place. Supposedly, shortly after those events, either Paul or the first believers had converted a concrete, historical person into some nebulous, mythical corporate figure in whom others might participate or be included, and his death and resurrection into some cosmic, ubiquitous event transcending human history. In contrast, the Gospel narratives speak of a particular individual, Jesus of Nazareth, a Galilean Jew and carpenter's son, being crucified on a hill called Golgotha outside Jerusalem under orders from Pontius Pilate, who sentenced Jesus to death after Jesus had been sent to him by the Jewish authorities around the year 30 C.E. Likewise, those accounts affirm that Jesus was raised by God three days later from the sepulcher where he had been laid, which originally belonged to Joseph of Arimathea. When these events are viewed in their historical particularity, it is obvious that these things can be said only of Jesus himself, and not of believers; thus, what is true of Christ is *not* true of others. Therefore, to say that Paul believed that people of other times and places participate (or participated) in Christ, or in his death and resurrection, is to affirm that either for Paul or those before him, Jesus Christ had been dissolved into some kind of impersonal power or corporate entity into which others could enter, and that his death and resurrection had become some timeless mythical occurrence that could be reproduced or made present in other times and places, or that could be entered into by people who were nowhere to be found in the time and place in which those events actually occurred.

Views such as these present us with a Paul who is no longer a first-century Jew but a teacher of abstract metaphysics who worked with an extremely elaborate ontology of his own unlike anything known to us in the early church. In other words, *they present us with a Paul who is in radical discontinuity with the early tradition as we know it, and with his contemporary fellow believers.* The Gospels, for example, written years *after* Paul's letters, do not conceive of Jesus in such impersonal or abstract terms; on the contrary, he is consistently presented as a unique, historical individual, even in the Fourth Gospel. Nor do they view Jesus' passion, crucifixion, and resurrection as some type of supra-historical or mythical occurrence but as a concrete and unique historical event.

This means that if we are to ascribe to Paul the idea that believers actually participate in Christ and his death and resurrection, then we must believe that Paul stood virtually alone in the early church in his doctrine, either because he combined Greek religious ideas with what he believed about Jesus Christ in syncretistic fashion or because he interpreted the Jewish faith in a way unique to himself so as to speak of Christ as an "inclusive person" who actually incorporated others into himself. In either case, Paul worked with a system of thought that was virtually unknown elsewhere in the early church, and for which *there is no clear evidence outside of the writings traditionally attributed to him.* He took a few details from the early story regarding Jesus' life and death and combined them with soteriological ideas that were unlike anything else found in that early story, so as to come up with a story of his own. Then he expected believers whom he had never met, such as the Roman Christians, to understand those ideas perfectly well when he wrote to them. Nevertheless, while the letters attributed to Paul were preserved in many of the Christian communities in the years following his death, his understanding of salvation as participation in Christ and his death was almost immediately forgotten or abandoned. For this reason, outside of the deuteropauline epistles, there is virtually no trace of such ideas in the other New Testament writings that were composed later on. Frankly, this is all difficult to believe.

In order to support the participatory reading of Paul proposed by many Pauline scholars, it has been necessary to disassociate him from the "mainstream" apostolic tradition, in which Jesus was conceived of in concrete, historical terms. This has been done in several ways. As observed in chapter 4, scholars have argued from Paul's virtual silence regarding the life and teachings of Jesus to conclude that he was uninterested in the historical Jesus. In that case, he came up with his own story of the cross and invented a Christ-figure who in general had little to do with the Jesus of Nazareth we find in the Gospel accounts. It has also been common to stress Paul's conflicts with other apostolic figures in the early church, as well as those believers who came from Jerusalem, in order to argue that Paul not only was at odds with the other apostles but also proclaimed a gospel that was fundamentally different from theirs. Likewise, it becomes necessary to deny the essential historicity of what we read in Acts concerning Paul, since there we find a Paul who is generally in close continuity with Peter and the other apostles.

Yet these arguments no longer seem to hold water. As noted in chapter 4, a number of scholars are beginning to claim that the historical Jesus did in fact play an important role in Paul's theology. It also appears quite unlikely that Paul preached a gospel entirely distinct from that which the apostles and those from Jerusalem proclaimed. There is considerable evidence in Paul's letters that he knew the apostles and spent time with them, and that he also knew and worked with the "pillars" of the early church, who were well acquainted with the historical Jesus. The book of Acts, as well as Paul's letter to Philemon and the deuteropauline epistles, relate Paul to both Mark and Luke (Philem 24; Col 4:10, 14; 2 Tim 4:11). If in fact either Mark or Luke (or both) were involved in the composition of the Gospels traditionally ascribed to them, and the traditions linking one or both of them to Paul were correct, this would make it likely that Paul viewed Jesus in roughly the same terms as those writings do—as a concrete, historical person rather than an abstract or mythical messianic figure. Similarly, like the Synoptics, Paul would view Jesus' passion and death as a particular, unrepeatable historical happening, rather than some distant, abstract "cosmic event" in which others participate.

In conclusion, the theological and historical problems associated with the participatory soteriology that many Pauline scholars have ascribed to Paul are considerable. If we wish to understand properly Paul's doctrine of salvation, we must not begin with the assumption that he thought in terms of participation in Christ and his death and resurrection so as then to look for the origins of such an idea in ancient Hellenism or Judaism. Instead, we must take as our starting point the most basic and general points of the tradition that we know Paul received, in order then to explore whether these are sufficient to understand his so-called participatory language.

Christ Crucified

Perhaps the best place to begin in order to attempt to understand the Pauline passages generally classified as "participatory" is Paul's language concerning Christ crucified. On three occasions, Paul refers to Christ as "the crucified one" by making use of the perfect participle *estaurōmenos*. Two of these occur in the same context, 1 Cor 1:23 and 2:2, where Paul claims to know and proclaim only Christ crucified. In Gal 3:1 he tells the Galatians that Christ crucified was presented before their eyes; this is probably a reference to Paul's preaching as well.[50] As scholars generally recognize, Paul's use of the perfect tense of the participle indicates that he has in mind *the risen and exalted Christ*: it is the living Christ who has been and *remains forever* crucified. It is important to stress that in these passages Paul does not say that he proclaims *an event* but *a person*: he does not merely announce the crucifixion of Christ or that Christ was crucified but proclaims Jesus of Nazareth as Christ or Messiah, the same man who was crucified and who is thus, even now as risen, the "crucified one."

In speaking of Christ in this way, Paul is not alone in the New Testament. In the resurrection accounts of both Matthew and Mark, the same perfect participle is used to refer to the risen Christ, who is proclaimed by the angel or the young man at the tomb as Jesus "the crucified one" (*ton estaurōmenon*;

Matt 28:5–6; Mark 16:6). While neither Luke nor John refers to Jesus in this way, both of these Gospels allude to the marks in the hands and feet of the risen Jesus (Luke 24:39; John 20:25, 27), indicating that for them the risen Jesus remains forever crucified. Paul also seems to be aware of the tradition of the marks in the risen Jesus' body, since he speaks of bearing "the marks of Jesus branded on [his] body" in the context of alluding to his having suffered persecution "for the cross of Christ" and being crucified to the world (Gal 6:12, 14, 17).[51] Finally, in Revelation the perfect participle is also used in three passages to speak of Christ as the Lamb who was (and remains) slain (*esphagmenon*; 5:6, 12; 13:8).

All of this would indicate that Paul is in close continuity with the tradition that proclaims as salvific, not so much the *event* of the cross, but the *person* of Christ, crucified and risen. As in Acts, what is stressed is that the one who is now Lord and Christ is the same man who was crucified, "this same Jesus" (Acts 2:23, 32, 36). If this is Paul's thought, then we can conclude that when he uses the perfect tense of the participle to speak of the crucified Christ, he has in mind an *ongoing status* or *condition*: in his risen state Christ *remains* crucified. Obviously, this status or condition is dependent on a past event, Jesus' actual crucifixion on Golgotha.

Baptism, Salvation, and the Church in the Early Christian Tradition

As has been argued throughout this study, the early Christian proclamation was relatively simple. It maintained that Christ, who had died seeking the salvation of God's people, had been exalted to God's right hand following his death and would come in glory as God's instrument to establish God's reign definitively. Thus, in order to be saved, what was necessary was to be incorporated into the community of those living under Christ's lordship, that is, the church. Baptism was the sign and seal of this incorporation. A closer look at these ideas will provide more of the background needed to understand Paul's so-called participatory language.

If we wish to understand Paul's teaching concerning baptism into Christ, the first place to turn is not to the brief, formulaic allusions to baptism that appear in his letters, since these are easily adapted to all sorts of interpretations. Instead, we must begin with the meaning of baptism in the early Christian communities, a subject already briefly touched on in chapter 3. The fact that Jesus was apparently originally a disciple of John the Baptist and that according to the Gospels and Acts there were close ties not only between John and Jesus but also among their respective followers (Luke 5:33; 7:18–30; 11:1; John 10:40–42; Acts 18:24—19:7) indicates that Jesus' followers most probably understood baptism in terms similar to those ascribed to John in the Gospels. Indeed, many of the ideas associated with John's baptism are also associated with baptism into Christ: repentance and a consequent new life of righteousness, forgiveness of sins, and, above all, eschatological redemption (or deliverance from God's coming wrath).[52] Of course, as noted previously, forgiveness of sins was essentially another way of speaking of the coming redemption. In the case of John's baptism of *metanoia*, then, those who were baptized gave public expression to their break with their past life, characterized by sinfulness and disobedience to God's will. At the same time, they pledged to begin a new life so as to be counted among the community of the righteous or elect that would be saved and forgiven when God came to judge the world and establish his kingdom.

Among the followers of Christ, the meaning of the baptismal rite was essentially the same, with a couple of significant differences. First, they believed that the community of the righteous was now to be defined on the basis of faith in Jesus as the promised Messiah designated by God to establish his reign; thus, baptism was in Jesus' name. Second, they believed that those who formed part of this community received the Holy Spirit, who empowered them to live a new life pleasing to God in obedience to Jesus' teaching. Thus, while baptism in the name of Jesus was still a baptism of repentance or renewal, as well as a baptism of forgiveness, it was also a baptism of the Holy Spirit and "fire" (Matt 3:11; Luke 3:16).

Yet it is important to recall the eschatological tension in early Christian soteriology based on the belief that in Jesus the promised Messiah had already come but nevertheless needed to come again. On the one hand, in spite of the coming of the Messiah, the change of aeons had not yet occurred; essentially, the world remained the same as it had been previously. On the other hand, believers now had a certainty of salvation they previously did not have: because Christ had been enthroned in power at God's right hand as a result of his faithfulness unto death in seeking their redemption, that redemption was now certain to come through him. This meant that they could say that they had *already* been saved when Christ died and rose, and that they had *already* been forgiven, delivered, and justified by God when he raised his Son on their behalf, since that act guaranteed their coming salvation, forgiveness, deliverance, and justification.

Furthermore, the fact that the life of the new age was certain to come now through Christ meant that, by living under his lordship, in some sense they disassociated themselves from the life of the present age of sin, death, and evil, and conversely identified with the coming age. By receiving the Holy Spirit, practicing righteousness and obedience in a God-pleasing way, living in communion with God and others, and experiencing in their communities the love, joy, wholeness, and peace that were believed to characterize the life of the coming age, they not only anticipated the life to come but even had a taste of it in the present. Thus, as Paul writes in Phil 3:20–21, they considered themselves to be citizens of heaven, since from there Christ would come to transform this creation. Because of this, they were not to be "conformed to this age" but transformed in their way of thinking and living (Rom 12:2).

This identification with the coming new age and the corresponding disassociation from the present evil age led to conflict and difficulties for the first believers, who suffered various types of persecution at the hands of both Jews and Gentiles on account of their faith in Christ. For Paul, this persecution was related to the cross, not only because he proclaimed as Messiah one who had been crucified, an idea that was "a stumbling block to Jews and foolishness to Gentiles" (1 Cor 1:23), but because Jesus had been crucified as a "sinner" who violated the law. Thus, when Paul and others were persecuted for supposedly teaching others to "sin" by not observing literally the commandments of the law regarding things such as circumcision, they identified with the cross in that, like Christ at his crucifixion, they were being "counted among the lawless" by many law-observant Jews who found their proclamation that Christ had been crucified as a "sinner" offensive (Gal 5:11; 6:12; cf. Luke 22:37). Similarly, because Christ had been crucified for refusing to conform to the norms of this world, when believers were persecuted for rejecting those norms, it was natural for them to identify with the cross of Christ and speak of themselves as being crucified to the world like Christ (Gal 6:14), and to regard those who set their minds on "earthly things" as "enemies of the cross of Christ" (Phil 3:18–19). While this identification with the cross and Christ's own crucifixion was characteristic of believers in general, it was particularly characteristic of apostles and missionaries such as Paul who were dedicated to proclaiming the gospel and establishing churches. The persecutions and hardships they faced inevitably brought to mind the persecutions and hardships Jesus Christ their Lord had endured because of his own proclamation of the gospel. All of this meant that both believers in general and the apostles in particular *not only identified with the coming age* rather than the present one *but also identified with Christ himself and with the suffering and persecution he endured as a consequence of his own commitment to doing God's will and seeking the salvation of others*, including particularly *the price he had paid* for that commitment, namely, *his death on the cross*. While no doubt distinguishing themselves from Jesus the historical person, they realized that their own commitment to obeying God and attaining God's kingdom inevitably brought the same consequences. In fact, according to the Gospels, Jesus himself had told his followers that they would face persecution, violence, and even death like him, but that like him they should be willing to deny themselves and "take up their cross" for the sake of their Lord and the gospel (Mark 8:34–35; 10:30; Luke 21:12–19). By doing so, however, he claimed that they would attain the glorious life of the coming age, "saving their life" by giving it up. Here again there was a clear analogy between Christ and believers in the early tradition.

Paul's "With Christ" Language

The preceding general observations provide virtually all the background we need to understand Paul's "with Christ" language. On numerous occasions, Paul uses the Greek preposition *syn* (sometimes as a prefix) to speak of believers' suffering, dying or being crucified, being buried, being raised, and being glorified "with" Christ. When Paul speaks in these terms, does he have in mind some type of mystical or ontological participation in these past events?

A close look at a number of Pauline passages would indicate that he does not. Perhaps the most convincing in this regard is Rom 8:17, where Paul writes that believers are "heirs of God and joint heirs with Christ—if, in fact, we suffer with him so that we may also be glorified with him." This latter phrase cannot be understood as an actual participation in the event of Christ's glorification, since for Christ this is a *past event*, while for believers it is a *future* one. It is not that they *have been* "co-glorified" with Christ (*syndoxasthēnai tō Christō*) but that they *will be*, provided they are willing to suffer as Christ did. Thus, to be co-glorified with Christ must involve *coming to participate in the same glorious condition in which he has come to exist.* According to Paul, God will send his Son to raise the dead and give them glorious bodies like that which he received (Phil 3:20–21). Paul repeats this same idea in 2 Cor 4:14, where he writes, "The one who raised the Lord Jesus will raise us also with [*syn Iēsou*] Jesus." Here, while the resurrection of believers is obviously a future event, Jesus' resurrection lies in the past; Paul obviously does not mean that Jesus will be raised at the same time as believers. Thus, he does not have in mind a future participation in a past event on the part of believers but rather a coming to share in Christ's risen condition. As Thrall observes, "It is best to suppose Paul is saying that God will raise him to join Jesus in the resurrection existence."[53]

Similarly, the fact that Paul uses the present tense *sympaschomen* in Rom 8:17 rules out an interpretation according to which believers have actually participated in the same sufferings that Christ once endured in Jerusalem. Paul here is simply saying that they should be willing to suffer as they follow Christ in serving God and sharing the gospel. They suffer with Christ in the sense that they suffer *for the same cause and the same gospel as he did.* This idea is present in 1 Thess 2:14–16, where Paul compares the persecution of the Thessalonian and Judean believers by certain Jews to the persecution Christ endured; both Christ and believers are said to have suffered not just *similar* things but "the *same* things" (*ta auta*). Thus, Paul can say in the same breath that they "killed both the Lord Jesus and the prophets, and drove us out," since he sees the suffering of Christ as being in continuity with the suffering of the prophets preceding him and the apostles who followed him: *it is all one and the same suffering and persecution.* We find precisely the same idea in the Gospel tradition, where Jesus warns his disciples that they will suffer persecution like him, being beaten, tried before authorities, hated, and put to death; just as they malign the "master of the house," so will they malign those of his household (Matt 10:16–25). In fact, as was noted in chapter 3, Jesus tells John and James that they will drink the *same cup* as he will and be baptized with the *same baptism* (Mark 10:38–39), that is, undergoing the same fate as he.

That Paul has this in mind is evident in a number of other passages. In 2 Cor 1:5–7*, he writes, "We share abundantly in Christ's sufferings," and then immediately tells the Corinthians, "You share in our sufferings." Obviously, Paul was not with the Corinthians when he wrote this. Thus, they shared in

Paul's sufferings not in the sense that they were actually mystically suffering there with him but in the sense that together with him they made sacrifices to support his work, making his own cause theirs. In the same way, Paul means that he and the Corinthians share in Christ's sufferings not in the sense that they actually participate in the past events of Christ's passion in some mysterious way but in the sense that they suffer as Christ did for the same gospel. Thus, their sufferings and Christ's are the *same sufferings*, since they all work together (1 Cor 3:9; 16:16; 2 Cor 1:24; 6:1; 8:23; cf. Col 1:24). Similarly, Paul writes of the believers in Rome struggling together (*synagōnisasthai*) with him by praying to God on his behalf (Rom 15:30), and those in Philippi wrestling or struggling (*synathlein*) with him to extend the gospel (Phil 1:27; 4:3), in spite of the fact that he was far away from them when he wrote. He speaks of the *koinōnia* or fellowship of the Philippians in his gospel (1:5) and calls them his coparticipants (*sygkoinōnoi*) of God's grace in his chains and afflictions (1:8; 4:14), not because they were actually chained up in prison with him but because they had made the cause of the gospel for which Paul had been jailed their own, supporting him financially and morally and even sending someone to care for him in jail. In none of these instances does Paul have in mind a common participation in a historical event; nor is his language to be interpreted literally, as if there were some actual mystical participation or union with him that transcended time and space.

For Paul, to undergo tribulations in serving God and Christ is not only to suffer with Christ but to die with him as well. After mentioning his afflictions and persecutions in proclaiming the gospel, he writes to the Corinthians of "always carrying in the body the death of Jesus, so that the life of Jesus may also be made visible in our bodies. For while we live, we are always being given up to death for Jesus' sake, so that the life of Jesus may be made visible in our mortal flesh. So death is at work in us, but life in you" (2 Cor 4:10–12). These words do not imply some type of mystical or ontological presence of the event of Christ's death in believers. Instead, the context plainly indicates that Paul has in mind facing the same type of affliction and persecution that Christ faced and that led to his death.[54] Paul is conscious of going down the same road to a violent death as Christ did, and in this sense carries in his own body Christ's death, since he will die the same death Christ died. Because he is constantly being given up to death, as Jesus had been, he also knows that the same resurrection life attained by Jesus after his death will one day be his.

Paul sees this as true of the Corinthians as well: "You are in our hearts, to die together and to live together" (*synapothanein kai suzēn*, 2 Cor 7:3). While they will undoubtedly not actually die in the same place and moment as Paul, their love for each other and commitment to a common cause mean that they die (and live) with Paul. The same idea is found in 1 Cor 15:31, where Paul affirms, "I die every day!" This is said in the middle of references to being "in danger every hour" (v. 30) and having "fought with animals at Ephesus" (v. 32). Thus, once again the idea is that following Jesus in proclaiming the gospel involves dying or giving up one's life as a constant reality, since one is always in danger of dying and probably will face an early death because of one's commitment to continuing in the same activity. Paul's thought in this regard is thus essentially the same as that which we find in the Gospels; yet *although the basic idea is the same, his way of expressing it is distinct.*

Dying and Being Crucified with Christ

Perhaps the most significant passage for understanding Paul's "with Christ" language is Rom 6:1–12*, which is worth quoting at length:

> ¹What then are we to say? Should we continue in sin in order that grace may abound? ²By no means! How can we who died to sin go on living in it? ³Do you not know that all of us who have been baptized into Christ Jesus were baptized into his death? ⁴Therefore we have been buried with him by [*dia*, "through"] baptism into death, so that, just as Christ was raised from the dead by the glory of the Father, we too might walk in newness of life. ⁵For if we have been jointly planted [*symphytoi*] in the likeness of his death, so also shall we be in the likeness of his resurrection. ⁶We know that our old selves were crucified with him so that the body of sin might be destroyed, and we might no longer be enslaved to sin. ⁷For whoever has died is freed from sin. ⁸But if we have died with Christ, we believe that we will also live with him. ⁹For we know that Christ, being raised from the dead, will never die again; death no longer has dominion over him. ¹⁰The death he died, he died to sin, once for all; but the life he lives, he lives to God. ¹¹So you also must consider yourselves dead to sin and alive to God in Christ Jesus. ¹²Therefore, do not let not sin exercise dominion in your mortal bodies, to make you obey their passions.

This passage has often been interpreted on the basis of many of the ideas considered at the outset of this chapter.[55] Thus, some claim that Paul has in mind here "an event occurring objectively to the baptized," namely, "participation in the salvation-occurrence, the death and resurrection of Jesus."[56] This is said to involve not only a participation in an *event* but a "participation in Christ" himself.[57] Paul is supposedly speaking of a "sharing in [Christ's] death, a sharing in his transition from one era to another."[58] On this basis, it is argued that Paul has in mind some type of incorporation into Christ as an "inclusive person" and into his death and resurrection as "inclusive events." Because the believer "shares in this death, is included in this death," he has "come to share in Christ. Through baptism he has been included in Christ. He has entered Christ as the corporate person of the new aeon."[59]

Likewise, this passage has often been quoted in support of the idea that Paul believed that, as a result of Christ's death and resurrection, some type of mysterious change has occurred, either in the universe as a whole, in the human nature common to all, or in believers in particular. John Ziesler, for example, commenting on v. 10, affirms that "in his death Christ ended the grip of sin on human beings generally" and adds, "We are not talking about the personal biography of Jesus of Nazareth, after death any more than before it, but about the fundamental change in the human condition brought about by his death and resurrection."[60] Similarly, Robert Tannehill views Paul's words here against the background of the Jewish belief in two ages or dominions, so as to claim that an actual change to the new world from the old world "characterized by the reign of certain demonic powers" has "already happened," so that human beings "have already been freed from these powers and placed under a new Lord. . . . It is to this change that Paul refers when he speaks of dying with Christ as a past event."[61]

Others, such as C. E. B. Cranfield, have interpreted Romans 6 in strictly forensic terms, according to which "God's decision to take our sins upon himself in the person of his dear Son was tantamount to a decision to see us as having died in Christ's death."[62] Whether this dying and rising is understood ontologically or forensically, it nevertheless involves an objective change in the human situation. This change is then regarded as the basis for a new ethical life, an idea also attributed to Paul in this passage. In other words, the *indicative* "you died" is followed by the *imperative* "consider yourselves dead" and constitutes its basis.[63] Believers must "become what they are."

A close look at this passage, however, reveals that just as ideas such as these are not to be found in the tradition Paul received, they are not to be found here. According to the early Christian story of redemption, with which Paul could safely assume the Christians in Rome were well acquainted, those who were baptized identified themselves as members of the people living under Christ who would inherit through him the life of the new age. This is the basic idea behind this passage. Paul is reminding his readers of what they already know (6:3, 6), namely, that when they were baptized into the community of those believing in and following Christ, they made a radical break with the "present evil age" characterized by sin and disobedience so as to identify fully with the age to come through Jesus Christ.

According to the early Christian story, this is precisely what Jesus Christ himself had done in opposing sin and evil in all their manifestations throughout his ministry. He too had broken with the present age and had instead dedicated his life to doing God's will and, because of this, had died on a cross. As a result of the fact that he failed to conform to the present age and to the end lived instead to God, he was raised from the dead by God and is now alive. As was noted above, in this risen condition he is and remains forever dead or "crucified" to the old realm in which sin and death reign, as Paul indicates in vv. 9–10. Paul's argument here is that because they have identified with Christ as their Lord, believers are in a similar condition: "So you also must consider yourselves dead to sin and alive to God in Christ Jesus" (v. 11). This idea of being "dead" to sin is the key to understanding the first part of the passage. If Christians are "dead to sin," the question arises, when did they enter into this condition? Obviously, the answer is, when they came to faith and were baptized, identifying themselves with the coming age rather than the present one. If, therefore, in their baptism they *became dead*, it may be said that *they died*.

This means that the idea in Rom 6:1–12 is not that believers have participated in a past *event* (Christ's crucifixion) or in a *person*, as if Christ were some type of incorporative figure. Rather, what they have come to share in is a *present condition* similar to that of the crucified and risen Christ, as a result of their having broken radically with sin together with their Lord in order to live to God. That this is Paul's thought is evident at a number of points in the passage. Particularly noteworthy is Paul's use of the perfect tense (*gegonamen*) in v. 5 to affirm that believers *have become and still are* jointly planted in the likeness of

Christ's death. This is thus an ongoing condition.[64] While throughout the rest of the passage he makes extensive use of the aorist to indicate a specific point of time in the past when believers were buried with Christ (v. 4) and their old self was crucified with him (v. 6), the context clearly indicates that he has in mind the moment they were incorporated into Christ's body through faith and baptism.[65] This was when they had died (become dead) together with Christ and had become jointly buried with him, identifying with his same condition of being *dead to sin* and to the present age.

This is how the prepositional prefix *syn* should be understood throughout the passage. To be buried together with Christ (*synetaphēmen*, v. 4) is to enter into his same condition of being "buried" to this world for good, not to participate in his past burial. To be "jointly planted" to the likeness of his death (*symphytoi*, v. 5) is to have died (become dead) to sin in a way similar to the manner in which Christ died to sin. To say that "our old person [*anthrōpos*] was jointly crucified" (*synestaurōthē*, v. 6) is a metaphorical way of saying that each believer put to death the old way of being in baptism so as to enter into the same condition in which Christ finds himself, that of being "crucified to the world" (Gal 6:14), and to be no longer dominated by the "body of sin" (v. 6). There is no need to understand the old *anthrōpos* and "body of sin" here in terms of some "inclusive reality" or "corporate entity" in which the existence of all believers or even all humanity is "bound up."[66] Such an idea once again reflects the Platonic idealism found in later Christian theology. Even though the word "body" is used in the singular, it is not to be understood in a corporate sense here, any more than it should be in 6:12*, where Paul also uses the singular to tell the Romans collectively, "Therefore, do not let sin exercise dominion in your mortal body" (*en tō thnētō hymōn sōmati*). Just as the Greek singular *sōma* is best translated into English with the plural "bodies" in v. 12 (as in the NRSV), so also the Greek singular *anthrōpos* in v. 6 should be translated into English with the plural "selves" or "persons," since in phrases like these Greek often employs the singular where English normally makes use of the plural.[67] Thus, Paul is not saying that some shared humanity or collective "self" belonging to all human beings was put to death when Christ died on Golgotha, but that the "self" of each individual believer was crucified with Christ when she or he was baptized; likewise, it is the "body of sin" of each believer that is destroyed, rather than some body common to all people (v. 6). That all of this involves entering into a present *condition* together with Christ rather than participating in a past event is particularly evident from v. 8, where Paul says that "if we have died with Christ, we believe that we will also [come to] live with him" (*syzēsomen autō*). The tenses of the verbs here make it plain that Paul does not mean that believers participated in the historical event of his resurrection or will participate in that past event in the future. The idea instead is that they will come to share with Christ his condition of being alive.

Undoubtedly, Paul uses the noun *thanatos* to affirm that believers have been baptized into Christ's death. Yet this should not be understood in the sense that they have been baptized into an *event*. Rather, what one is baptized into is the same way of being and living that was Christ's in death, as well as the suffering and persecution that are the consequence of that way of being. When Paul speaks of Christ's death, *this is what he has in mind*: the love and dedication to God and others that Christ manifested in giving up his life. According to Paul, when believers gather for the Eucharist, they proclaim Christ's death (1 Cor 11:26), not in the sense that they simply recall that he physically died, but in the sense that he gave up his life in love on behalf of others. This must also be Paul's meaning when he speaks of believers' having been "jointly planted in the likeness of his death." Obviously, this likeness is not a physical or biological one, nor did baptism apparently involve any kind of rite that imitated the mode of Christ's death or burial.[68] There is no need to understand this likeness in ontological terms either, since it is clear that believers have not undergone the ontological transformation that Christ underwent when he died and was raised. The likeness, therefore, must be seen in terms of the *ethical aspects* associated with that event, the way of being and living that was Christ's in his death. This is evident as well from the fact that throughout Romans 6, Paul's concern is with *ethical matters*, that is, the way of life that the Roman believers are to have in Christ. They are to live as "slaves (*douloi*) of righteousness" and of God rather than as "slaves of sin" (6:16–22), in the same way that Christ himself practiced righteousness and died to sin by refusing to submit to it (5:18; 6:10). The question is not what type of ontological transformation has occurred in them but to which of the two ways of being they have yielded themselves (6:16). It is by yielding themselves to one or the other that they make themselves slaves of one or the other.

In his epistle to the Galatians, Paul uses language similar to that found in Romans 6. In Gal 2:19, he uses the perfect tense to affirm, "I have been [and remain] crucified with Christ" (*Christō synestaurōmai*). This must involve sharing not in the past event of the crucifixion but in the present condition of the crucified and risen Lord, as is evident from the fact that both immediately before and after these words Paul speaks of living to God, and Christ living in him. What Paul is claiming is that he has come to be crucified to the old realities (such as the law, 2:19; cf. Rom 7:6), as Christ is crucified to them in his present condition: as observed above, he is forever *estaurōmenos* (Gal 3:1). Of course, Paul's being crucified should be understood in a metaphorical and ethical sense, even though undoubtedly in the case of Christ an ontological transformation has occurred. Paul has broken with the present age in order to identify with the new age in Christ. Paul repeats this idea later on in the same letter, writing, "May I never boast of anything except the cross of our Lord Jesus Christ, by which the world has been crucified to me, and I to the world" (6:14). Once more, the perfect tense *estaurōtai* indicates an ongoing condition of being crucified, dead, and buried to the present sinful realities by identifying with Christ in his death.[69]

What believers are to identify with, therefore, is the way of being in relation to God, sin, the law, the world, and others that Christ manifested in his death, as well as the life of which his death was the ultimate expression. Yet, as Paul reminds his readers in Romans 6, this is not merely something they are now to do, "considering" themselves dead to sin and alive to God like Christ and with Christ, and "yielding" themselves to God as slaves of righteousness; it is something *they already did* when they were baptized. This means that when Paul says they have died or been crucified with Christ, he is not claiming that some type of objective change in their condition occurred when Christ died. Nor is he stating that some type of ontological transformation or forensic declaration took place either then or when they were baptized that must now be the basis for a new life, or that the coming new age actually began for them. This would be to understand either Christ's death or his baptism as a magical or mechanical event that in itself effected some alteration of the human situation, an idea found nowhere in the early tradition or Paul's writings. Likewise, there is no basis here for the affirmation that Paul believed that the "old way of being human" or the "old nature" was destroyed with Christ when he died on the cross and a new being or nature subsequently created in him, so that believers might now participate in it. This would involve some type of ontological transformation of a shared human reality, and it is based on an abstract understanding of "humanity" or "human nature" alien to Paul's thought as well as to Judaism and the early Christian tradition. Rather, *from the start*, dying and being buried with Christ involve an *ethical decision and commitment* on the part of believers. The indicative here is not the basis for the imperative; rather, the indicative is used *because they already responded to the imperative when they were baptized*, putting their old selves to death with Christ. Paul's exhortation is thus not to "become what they are" but to continue to become the persons they became committed to being in their baptism, when they manifested their break with sin. To die and be buried with Christ, or to be crucified with him, is not something that passively occurs to believers but *something done actively* as they identify with Christ as their Lord, and with the life of the new age as well, even though it has not yet actually arrived and they have not been "transferred" into it. While in Rom 6:7* Paul states that "our old selves were co-crucified," the idea is that in submitting to baptism believers consciously "put to death" or "put off" their old selves or way of being (cf. Eph 4:24; Col 3:9). For this reason Paul can tell the Galatians in Gal 5:24 *not that their flesh was crucified* (passive voice) but that *they crucified the flesh* (*tēn sarka estaurōsan*, active voice). His thought in the other passages should be interpreted in the same way. Paul, as well as his "flesh" or "old self," is "crucified with Christ" because in essence *he crucified himself or his old way of being* when he came to live under Christ as Lord and began to relate to the world as Jesus himself related to it in the past and relates to it now. In the language of the Synoptics, it might be said that he took up his cross (so as to become crucified with Christ), denied himself (or died to himself), and came to give up or "hate" his life (in the present age) for the sake of Jesus and the gospel (Mark 8:34–35; Luke 14:26–27). *The idea is the same*, though the language is different.

Similar observations must be made with regard to Rom 7:4–6, which also has been used to support the notion that some objective change has taken place in the situation of believers that constitutes the basis for their new ethical life.[70] When Paul writes, "You have died [*ethanatōthēte*] to the law through the body of Christ, so that you may belong to another, to him who has been raised from the dead in order that we may bear fruit for God" (v. 4), he may merely have in mind that by being incorporated into the body of Christ, they put an end to their previous relationship to the law by coming to live as Christ's own under his lordship, where they now live under a new covenant. This would involve understanding the body of Christ as referring to the church.[71] If he is referring to Christ's own body put to death on the cross, however, the idea would be that Christ offered up his life seeking that the members of his community might live under him ("belong to him") in that new covenant, where they would no longer be under the "letter" of the Mosaic law (v. 6), and might now "bear fruit for God" by doing God's will as members of the people living under him. No matter which of these interpretations of dying to the law through Christ's body is preferred, what is involved is a conscious decision on the part of believers to live under Christ as part of the community identifying with him; only those who are members of that community have died to the law.[72] Thus, in either case, the basis for Paul's language is the commitment made by believers to live as members of Christ's people rather than some mysterious change that took place in or for them when Christ died on the cross. Undoubtedly, their situation has been altered by the fact that through faith they are enabled to live according to the Spirit rather than "living in the flesh" (v. 5). Yet the fact that this new life depends on a commitment made by them is evident from Paul's exhortation to believers in Rom 8:4–13 and elsewhere to live according to the Spirit and not according to the flesh.

One other passage frequently used in support of an ontological understanding of dying with Christ is 2 Cor 5:14*, where Paul writes, "For the love of Christ constrains us, because we are convinced that one has died for all; therefore all have died." The relation between these last two phrases has often been understood as an automatic one: the mere fact that Christ "died for all" results in all having died, as if Christ's death had some mysterious effect on all, or effected a change in their condition before God.[73] In this case, an ethical interpretation would need to be ruled out, since it would be difficult to defend the idea that Christ's death "for all" automatically produced an ethical change in believers (or all people if "all" is understood universally). Thus, either an ontological or forensic interpretation would be required. Yet this would once again distance Paul from the early Christian story, which knows of no type of mechanical or magical "effect" of Christ's death on human beings or the human situation.

This verse, of course, is intimately tied to v. 15*, where Paul goes on to say that Christ "died for all, that those who live might live no longer for themselves, but for him who for their sake died and was raised." According to many of the views we have considered, Paul is saying here that Christ died to fulfill some requirement on behalf of others or in their stead, so that once that requirement had been fulfilled and they had thereby been saved, they might come to live in a new way (perhaps out of gratitude for what he had done, or by being enabled to change their behavior thanks to the example he had laid down or the alteration of their human condition he had effected).[74] This involves interpreting the passage on the basis of the objective/subjective distinction discussed previously.

The presuppositions associated with interpretations such as these have blinded interpreters to the fact that Paul himself explains to his readers what the logical connection is between "one has died for all" and "all have died" in v. 14: *all have died precisely because the love of the one who died for all constrains them.* In other words, because they are constrained or controlled by the same love of Christ manifested in his death for all, they have died as Christ did. In the case of believers, this "dying" must therefore be understood in an ethical (as well as metaphorical) sense. This is clear from the fact that in the following verse Paul affirms that the living *"live no longer for themselves* but for him who for their sake died and was raised." To "live no longer" is to "die"; thus to "die" should also be understood here in an ethical sense. This is the point of comparison between their dying and Christ's dying: in both cases, what is involved is giving up one's life for others and for the sake of the gospel. Just as Christ "died for all" in the sense that he went to his death seeking for "all" what he had sought for them throughout his ministry, namely, that they might be delivered by God from the present evil age so as to attain the life of the new age, so also Paul and his coworkers, constrained by the same love shown by Christ, die in the sense of giving up their lives for others by proclaiming the gospel in spite of the fact that by doing so, they constantly face suffering and death. Here Paul appears to be using the same death/dying metaphor found in 4:10–12 in this letter, where the idea is that of putting one's life at risk "for Jesus' sake."

As believers live to Christ, they also die to the present age in the sense that they no longer identify with it. The context makes it clear that this idea is behind Paul's thought in the passage, since he continues in v. 16 speaking of no longer knowing others, as well as Christ himself, "according to the flesh" (*kata sarka*), that is, according to the way of knowing others that is characteristic of the present age.[75] He then writes in v. 17* that whoever is in Christ is a "new creation; the old things have passed away; see, they have become new." Once more, rather than Paul's having in mind some actual ontological transformation of believers or the cosmos here, it seems that he is referring to the fact that believers have ceased to be identified with the old age and instead are now identified with the new. They are new persons who think, see, and know the world and others according to what is coming and will come, rather than according to the present reality, which is soon to pass away (1 Cor 13:9–12). They have died to this age and the way of living that characterizes it, together with Christ, who died for them.

If the passage is understood in this fashion, the "all" who died must refer only to believers, since only they are dead to the old age and alive to the new.[76] This seems to be indicated by the context, since in the previous verses Paul makes the distinction between "you" and "us" in speaking to the Corinthians. He thus uses the word "all" to include both groups; the "all" is the same as the "we" (or "us") several words earlier in this same verse, that is, "all of us." Such a usage is common in Paul, since while undoubtedly on some occasions he does mean "all people" when using the word *pantes*, he also uses it frequently to speak of believers alone.[77]

It is important to note that when Paul says that "all have died" (*apethanon*) here, he is obviously giving a positive value to the notion of death. The idea of dying as *a result of* sin cannot be behind his thought here, since all people die in that sense independently of Christ; such a death is the consequence not of Christ's death for all but of Adam's sin.[78] To say that believers are now spared death because they have already undergone it in and with Christ would raise the difficulty of what type of death they are spared from. They certainly must still undergo physical death (at least in the case of those dying before Christ's second coming), and thus have not been saved from it. One might argue that they are spared from eternal or spiritual death, but when Paul writes that "Christ died for all," it seems highly unlikely that he had in mind primarily Christ's dying an eternal or spiritual death on the cross of Golgotha; such an idea is the product of later Christian theology.

The idea that believers have not only died but also risen with Christ does not appear in the undisputed Pauline letters but is found in both Eph 2:1–7 and Col 2:13; 3:1–4. These passages have also been taken as evidence that either Paul or a Pauline circle thought in terms of an actual "participation in the Christ-event" or an "inclusion of the believer in the death-resurrection event"; it is said that these verses present Christ's death and resurrection as a "representative, comprehensive event," and that believers are "joined to this event by an indissoluble bond" and "taken up into the death and resurrection of Christ," so as to be "transferred into the domain of Christ's rule."[79]

In two of these passages, it is said that believers were dead in trespasses and sins (Eph 2:1; Col 2:13), which is distinct from dying with Christ.[80] The consequent affirmation that they were "made alive" should probably be understood as simply reflecting the idea found in Luke 15:32, where the father in the parable rejoices that his son, who was "dead," had "become alive" (*ezōsen*) when he returned home.[81] When it is said that believers have died and been buried with Christ in baptism (Col 2:12; 3:3; cf. 2:20), the context of these passages makes it clear that the idea is that they have put off their old way of being so as no longer to live and think as they did previously. There is no reason to understand all of this in a literal or ontological sense; the language should instead be seen as metaphorical.

The same observation must be made with regard to the affirmation that believers have been raised with Christ. In Col 2:12, it is said that this occurs in baptism, rather than having occurred when Christ actually died. Thus, there is no reason to posit some type of actual participation in the event of Christ's resurrection, which lies in the past. In Eph 2:5–6 and perhaps Col 3:1, however, the idea may be that believers were raised when Christ himself was raised. Nevertheless, this should still not be understood in terms of some actual "participation in the resurrection of Christ."[82] Instead, according to the early story, God raised his Son from the dead so that the Son might in turn someday raise from the dead those for whom he had offered himself up and give them eternal life. Thus, it can be said that they were in effect raised by God at the same moment that God raised his Son, since God ensured their resurrection by raising Christ. In this case, "believers are the object of the same divine action as Christ himself at his resurrection," yet not because they are "incorporate in him" or constitute an "essential unity" with him,[83] but because God's action in raising up and exalting Christ had as one of its primary objectives the posterior resurrection and exaltation of believers by Christ, now certain to occur.

Christ and Adam

Paul's "in Christ" language has often been interpreted on the basis of his similar language concerning humanity's relationship to Adam in Rom 5:12–21 and 1 Cor 15:21–22, as well as his references to Adam in 1 Cor 15:45–49.

In these passages, Paul makes several contrasts between Adam, the "first man," and Christ. In or through Adam, sin, death, and condemnation came into the world, but in or through Christ comes the free gift of justification and righteousness, as well as the resurrection from the dead (Rom 5:12–17; 1 Cor 15:21–22). By Adam's trespass and disobedience many were constituted sinners and came under condemnation, but through Christ's obedience many will be made righteous and receive life (Rom 5:18–19).

Many Pauline scholars have looked to the same notions of participation, representation, and incorporation to understand Paul's language in these passages. Charles Cousar, for example, claims that for Paul both Adam and Christ are "more than individuals; they incorporate in themselves all people. Each is the progenitor and prototype of all humanity. Through the one person death spreads to all people; through the other person life comes to all."[84] Similarly, Hans Conzelmann looks to the notion of corporate personality in order to claim that in Jewish thought Adam was "the primal man, in whom the whole of mankind is virtually contained. Death proceeds from him because the whole of humanity is contained in him."[85] Douglas Moo rejects the idea of corporate personality, preferring instead that of "corporate solidarity" in order to explain Paul's thought. According to Moo, this idea is rooted in Old Testament thought, in which "the actions of certain individuals could have a 'representative' character, being regarded as, in some sense, the actions of many other individuals at the same time."[86]

Yet there is no reason to believe such ideas are behind Paul's thought in Rom 5:12–14. Instead, he is recalling certain aspects of the ancient Jewish story, telling how sin came into the world through Adam, together with death as its consequence, even among those who did not sin in the same manner as Adam or did not violate God's law, which had not yet been given. In the following verses, he continues to develop the same thought, referring to the manner in which the sin or trespass of Adam brought death and condemnation. Paul here does not go into the question of precisely how Adam's sin leads to the death and condemnation of "all people." Perhaps he believed that some change in Adam's own nature had occurred that affected his descendants, or that the world had fallen under the influence of evil powers or an "evil heart" from that point on, and that this led to human sin and consequently to death, God's judgment upon sin. Ideas such as these seem to have been known in the Judaism of Paul's day.[87] However, Paul may simply have been making a historical observation: Adam's sin was followed by his descendants' sinning and dying, for whatever reason.

Paul is not explicit regarding the precise relationship between Adam's sin and the death of all human beings. It is important to note, however, that the ancient Jewish writings that mention this relationship do not provide any evidence for the idea that there had been some type of universal human participation in Adam's sin, or in Adam himself. Even passages such as 4 Ezra 7:118 and 2 Bar 48:42–43, which have been cited in support of the idea that Adam was "a corporate figure, whose sin could be regarded at the same time as the sin of all his descendants,"[88] actually affirm only that all people suffer the consequences of Adam's sin in that they too now inevitably sin and die. Thus, the idea is not that Adam's sin was also the sin of others, or that Adam was a corporate figure who represented or included those who were to follow him, but simply that Adam's sin led to the present situation in which all of his descendants also sin and die. "All died" in the sense that Adam's act made it certain that they would also die, not in the sense that they somehow actually died when Adam sinned. The notion of some type of common participation in Adam's sin as well as a common sharing in his guilt is not found in Jewish thought but is a later Christian development, present particularly in the writings of Augustine, who was heavily influenced by Platonism. For Augustine, Adam appears to be something like the original "form" or "idea" of "man," in which all "men" participate; since all human beings are "one in him," they all share both in his sin and in his guilt.[89]

The importance of this lies in the fact that it has been common to attempt to establish the same type of relationship between Christ and "all" as that which is posited to exist between Adam and "all." Thus, if Adam's sin leads automatically to the sin and death of all people, then Christ's obedience and act of righteousness must also lead automatically to the justification and salvation of "all." Yet to affirm this would be to read later ideas back into Paul's thought once more. C. E. Hill, for example, commenting on 1 Cor 15:20–22, where Christ is spoken of as the "first fruits" (*aparchē*), claims that Paul looked to "the concept of a union or solidarity between Christ and his people" as well as his "notion of incorporation into Christ" in order to affirm that, on this basis, Christ's resurrection "portends and guarantees the resurrection of others. . . . It is because Christ stands in such a relation to Christians as Adam does to those who die that the historical reality of Christ's bodily resurrection can furnish grounds for the Christians' hope of their own. . . . There will be a bodily resurrection in the future simply and directly on the fact of solidarity with Christ the *aparchē*."[90] In essence, this is an affirmation of an automatic or mechanical relationship between Christ and the "all": they will rise, simply because they are included or incorporated in some mysterious way into Christ and the event of his resurrection.

According to the early Christian story, however, the relation between Christ's resurrection and that of others is based not on any type of incorporation into Christ or participation in the event of his resurrection, but on the idea that, now enthroned in power as a result of his own resurrection, Christ has the authority to return to raise the dead and give them life.[91] The basis for the believers' certainty that this will occur is that Christ gave up his life in love for them; because of his love for them, there can be no doubt that he will return to save them, as Paul states in v. 23. Thus, Christ is the first fruits of those who have fallen asleep, not because they are included in him, but because God raised him in order that others might consequently be raised through him. Paul's thought in this passage, then, is that just as death came as the result of the actions of one man (Adam), so the resurrection will come as the result of the actions of another man (Christ).[92] The preposition *en* used twice in v. 22 should therefore be understood not as implying some type of human incorporation or participation in Adam and Christ but in an instrumental sense: *through* Adam all died, and *through* Christ all will be made alive. The early Christian story understands the relationship between Adam's sin and the death of all, as well as that between Christ's resurrection and the raising of all, in these terms; it knows of no type of mysterious participation or incorporation into Adam or Christ. Believers will rise to new life because Christ as "the last Adam" has become "life-giving spirit," that is, someone who can impart to others the same type of resurrection body he has received, as Paul writes in 1 Cor 15:45–49 (as well as Phil 3:20–21).

Some of the same observations apply also to Paul's words in Rom 5:15–21, where in fact the idea of being "in Adam" or "in Christ" is absent. Instead, Paul employs the preposition *dia* throughout. Here the relation between Christ's act of righteousness and his obedience and the justification of believers is not that believers participate in Christ's own righteousness or obedience but that, on account of his righteousness and obedience in seeking their salvation, he was exalted to God's right hand. This ensures the salvation and justification of those who belong to him.

Other Supposedly
"Participatory" Passages in Paul's Letters

On the basis of what we have seen in this chapter, it should now be clear that many of the passages that are often cited in support of the idea that Paul conceived of the relationship between Christ and believers in mystical or participatory terms are best understood in other ways, according to the early story of redemption told by Paul and the first believers. Nevertheless, a number of other passages have been influential in this regard and cannot be ignored in any discussion of the subject.

In *Paul and Palestinian Judaism*, E. P. Sanders claims that there are two passages in particular that demonstrated "how easily Paul's mind moved into the categories of *participation* and *unity*." The first of these is 1 Cor 6:15–20*, where Paul argues that a man who joins himself to a prostitute becomes "one body with her," but "anyone who joins himself or herself to the Lord becomes one spirit with him." Sanders argued that here "the participatory union is not a figure of speech for something else; it is, as many scholars have insisted, real."[93] Yet a close look at this passage reveals that there is no need to interpret it in this way, since there are two different types of unions spoken of, one bodily and one spiritual. In addition, as Calvin Roetzel has pointed out, if on the basis of Gen 2:24 a bodily union in which a man becomes "one flesh" with a woman rules out a spiritual union with Christ, then union not only with a prostitute but with one's wife would exclude a union with Christ.[94] What is involved, then, are ethical decisions rather than some type of mysterious or ontological union.

The second passage cited by Sanders is 1 Cor 10:16, where Paul writes of the communion (*koinōnia*) of believers with the blood and body of Christ in the cup they drink and the bread they eat. Sanders translates *koinōnia* here as "participation" so as to speak of participating in Christ's body and blood as a "union with Christ."[95] Yet this interpretation requires that we understand Christ's body and blood in a literal sense, so that one becomes joined to the actual substance of Christ's body and blood. Obviously, there are other ways of understanding Christ's body and blood. It has been noted elsewhere that for Paul Christ's "blood" signifies his self-giving for others unto death; in that case, it is this that believers have fellowship with or in which they share. Similarly, Christ's body can be understood to refer either to the offering of himself he made in dying, or to the community of believers who identify with Christ.

That in 1 Cor 10:16 Paul does not have in mind some type of ontological union with Christ through his body and blood is evident as well from the context, where Paul says that those who eat of the sacrifices offered according to the Mosaic law are "partakers [koinōnoi] of the altar" (v. 18*) and then compares this to the manner in which pagans eat of food that has been offered to idols, regarded by Paul as demons (vv. 19–21); this involves the "worship of idols" (v. 14), that is, participation in the service of invocation and intercession offered up to them with the sacrifices. To be "partakers of the altar" does not mean to have some type of real "participation" in the altar, but to participate in the worship offered to God there by eating and drinking of what is sacrificed. Those who ate of the offerings manifested their inclusion among the people on whose behalf the invocation and intercessions to God had been made. In the same way, those who ate of the bread and drank of the cup in the context of the Eucharist were manifesting their inclusion among the people (or "body" of believers) on whose behalf Christ died. For this reason, it was unacceptable for them to partake of the food offered to idols, since this would involve participation in the invocation and worship of demons rather than God. For Paul, then, to have communion (koinōnia) with the body and blood of Christ through the bread and wine is to identify with those on whose behalf Christ offered up his body and shed his blood, the new covenant people.[96]

In addition to these two passages, Sanders also points to Paul's language regarding being baptized into one body in 1 Cor 12:12–13, being baptized into Christ in Gal 3:27 (cf. Rom 6:3), and being "one body in Christ" in Rom 12:5 in order to support his view that Paul thought in terms of a participatory union between believers and Christ. Here again, however, no such interpretation is called for. Paul's affirmation that Christians are one body in Christ is best understood metaphorically: they are all members of the community for which he offered himself up in death.[97] With regard to the idea of being baptized into Christ, a number of Pauline scholars have pointed out that Paul employs a similar phrase in 1 Cor 10:2, where he writes that those who were under the cloud that led Israel and crossed the sea were all "baptized into Moses in the cloud and in the sea."[98] This can hardly mean that Paul viewed Moses as some type of "corporate person" who mysteriously contained others in himself. Rather, the idea is clearly that they were baptized into the community of those under Moses' leadership, or into the covenant established through Moses and thus symbolized by him. Baptism into Christ should be understood in the same way.

This interpretation also provides us with a basis for understanding Paul's *en Christō* language in similar fashion: to be "in Christ" is merely to live under his lordship, as part of his community. As Bultmann argued, the formula is primarily ecclesiological, although it is more than this, since it involves a relation not only between the believer and the community under Christ, but between the believer and Christ himself as well.[99] This relationship is one in which the believer obeys Christ, follows his teaching, and lives under Christ as his or her Lord.[100]

Of course, Paul also speaks of Christ's being and living in believers in passages such as Rom 8:10; 2 Cor 13:5; and Gal 2:20. Yet this need not be understood in a mystical fashion. Paul may mean merely that he is under Christ's guidance or control, doing Christ's will rather than his own. Paul speaks in similar terms to the Corinthian believers in 2 Cor 7:3—"You are in our hearts, to die together and to live together"—where no mystical interpretation is called for. For Christ to be "in" believers may simply mean that he is active in them through his Spirit, speaking through them (2 Cor 13:3), just as God is active in them (1 Cor 14:25; Phil 2:13).

None of these passages, therefore, provides any firm evidence for the claim that Paul understood the relationship between Christ and believers in terms of some type of "mystical participation" or "ontological union." In order to interpret them in such a manner, such an idea must be read back into the texts, and metaphorical language must be taken literally. Yet to understand Paul's thought in those terms raises once again all of the difficulties we saw at the outset. Thus, it is preferable to look to simpler explanations, such as those just considered, which are easily harmonized with other passages in Paul's letters and with the early Christian story as best as we can reconstruct it. *As is true with Paul's "cultic-juristic" language, the story behind his so-called participatory language is the same one found in the early Christian tradition as it appears in the Gospels and Acts.*

Conclusion

If the argument developed throughout this work is correct, then from at least the time of Irenaeus to the present, Paul's letters (together with the other New Testament writings) have been used to support soteriological ideas and interpretations of Christ's death that are fundamentally different from those of Paul. None of the stories of redemption outlined in chapter 1 represents Paul's understanding of salvation and the cross. Rather, biblical scholars and theologians have taken those stories and read adaptations of them back into the biblical texts, claiming that they faithfully reflect the thought of Paul, as well as the other New Testament writers; in this way, they have constructed a Paul who is no longer the Paul we find in his letters.

According to what has been argued here, Paul does not teach that "the situation of the world is fundamentally different" following Christ's death and resurrection,[1] that there is an "objective transformation of reality effected by Christ's death," or that "the death and resurrection of Christ are cosmic-ontological events" that have "inaugurated a new ontological reality" or "changed the nature of historical reality."[2] Nor does he proclaim that the "universe has been reconciled," that "heaven and earth have been brought back into their divinely created and determined order through the resurrection and exaltation of Christ," that creation is "restored," or that "cosmic peace has returned."[3] For Paul as well as the other Christians of his day, the transformation of the world still lay in the future; they did not believe this to have changed as a result of Christ's death. Certainly that event changed the course of human history in many ways, but other events have also changed the course of history. In fact, *every* event alters the course of history in some way, making the world a different place.

Neither does Paul teach that the world has actually been delivered from sin, death, and evil at present as a result of the cross, or that "Jesus' death was the end of humankind under the power of sin and death."[4] Humanity and human nature in general remain exactly as they were before Christ's coming. Christ has not transformed humankind or the human nature common to all through his death and resurrection. "Man" in general is no more and no less united to God or the divine nature than before Christ came. Creation has not actually been restored or delivered from evil, but is still "subjected to futility" and in "bondage to decay" (Rom 8:20–21), as are Christians. According to the early Christian story, what has changed is that the future deliverance from sin, death, and evil is now a certainty through Christ for believers, who will be freed from their present condition so as to participate in the new world to come. Undoubtedly, they are able to participate already to some degree in the blessings of the age to come, since they have received the eschatological gift of the Holy Spirit as an *arrabōn*, and experience in the present a foretaste of the joy, communion, fellowship, and peace that will someday be theirs fully. That Spirit also empowers them to resist and overcome to some degree even now the forces of sin and evil that are active both *in* them and in the structures and powers of the world *around* them. Only in that sense can it be said that they are no longer "in the flesh" (Rom 8:9), since they remain in the "present evil age" (Gal 1:4), just like everyone else, and await their redemption and liberation (Rom 8:23; Phil 3:20–21).

Similarly, Paul's gospel does not proclaim that "God's sentence of condemnation was passed and executed on sin" in Christ's death, or that "in dying Christ exhausted the effects of divine wrath against sin."[5] Like the Jewish belief out of which it developed, the Christian belief was that God's wrath at sin and injustice continued and would finally be manifested at the *eschaton*; only then would God judge all people and do away with sin and evil for good. Of course, the first Christians were convinced that because of their relationship with Christ their Lord, they would be delivered from that wrath, in spite of their sinfulness; and because they would not be under God's wrath in the future, they could rest assured that they were not under that wrath at present either, but instead had peace with God.

Equally foreign to Paul's thought is the notion that through Christ's death God "fulfilled the requirement which humanity could not fulfill" in order for human beings to be saved.[6] In itself, Christ's death was not necessary for sin to be forgiven by God, or for human beings to be saved from the penalty or consequences of sin. According to Jewish and early Christian thought, God is always completely free to grant forgiveness of sins to anyone he wishes, but he desires that human beings repent and change their way of life. At the same time, however, God himself is active to bring about in them repentance and change of life. Similarly, according to both Jewish and early Christian belief, God is free to bring about the destruction of sin, death, and the forces of evil at any time, simply by fiat; it was not impossible for him to do so without Christ's death and resurrection. God evidently was thought to have reasons for letting these forces continue to exist at present, yet nothing was preventing him from redeeming the world whenever he chose.

Paul does not teach that Christ had to die and rise so that others might participate in his death and resurrection.[7] According to the early Christian story, all die independently of Christ and will be raised by God at the *eschaton*. Although God will do this through Christ, the Scriptures never imply that it was impossible for God to raise the dead or "transfer" people into the new age without Christ himself dying and rising first. While believers are said to "die" to the world and to sin in the present in the sense that, together with Christ, they cease to identify with the sin and evil of the present age, this does not involve any type of actual participation or sharing in the past event of Christ's death. Believers do not repeat Christ's actual experiences, participate in his own personal faith or faithfulness, or become one person with him through his "inclusive humanity."[8] Nor have they actually risen with him or participated in the event of his resurrection, which was his alone and not theirs. Rather than constituting an "eschatological and inclusive event,"[9] Jesus' death is consistently seen in the New Testament writings as an event in human history that is in most ways similar to the death of any other human being, including especially those who have been executed unjustly. Undoubtedly, the early story ascribes a unique significance to Jesus' death, but it never claims that this event transcends history, puts an end to the world as it was, or produces some salvific effect for others. In the same way, while Jesus Christ is a uniquely significant figure, according to the early Christian story told by Paul, he always has been and always will be only an individual person, rather than some type of inclusive person or "corporate being" who is "more than individual."[10] What is true of Christ concretely with regard to his passion, death, resurrection, and exaltation is *not* true of anyone else. These events cannot be brought out of the past into the present except by recalling them, just like any other past event.

Undoubtedly, certain ideas from the stories of redemption considered in chapter 1, when understood properly, can be regarded as faithful to the teaching of Paul and the rest of the New Testament. There is a sense in which it can properly be said that sin, death, and the forces of evil have been overcome through Christ's death, and that by giving up his life in faithfulness to his mission, Christ has laid down an example for believers and has kindled in them a greater love—although this was not considered to be the *purpose* of his death. Even though the restoration of human nature and nature as a whole still lies in the future, it can also be attributed to Christ's death, since on account of his faithfulness unto death to his mission, he was exalted so as to be able to bring about that restoration someday. Christ can also be said to have made satisfaction to God and delivered people from God's wrath by undergoing the penalty or consequences of human sin (understood simply as death itself) on their behalf (though not in their stead), in the sense that his obedience unto death to the task given him by God has ensured that God will have the righteous, obedient people God always desired. This satisfied God, who effectively put away his wrath against the sins of his people when he raised Christ from the dead so as to ensure their redemption. These people have now, like Christ, become dead to sin and alive to God, and in that sense can be said to have died and been raised with him. While there is therefore some basis in Paul's letters and the rest of the New Testament for many of the ideas associated with the stories considered in chapter 1, it must still be stressed that in themselves these stories are fundamentally different from the one told by Paul and the first Christians.

In the end, it should be clear that what has been presented here calls for a radical rethinking of the Christian doctrine of the "atonement" (if in fact we can still properly speak of Christ's having "made atonement" for human sin) and the salvific significance of Christ's death. It also calls for a profound revision of the manner in which biblical scholars have interpreted Paul's letters, and especially his soteriology. Rather than continuing to claim that Paul's soteriology and his teaching regarding the cross are essentially different from what we find in the Gospels and the other New Testament writings, and that he looked *outside* of the earliest Christian tradition for the ideas necessary to create a story of redemption that is in many ways unique to him, we must recognize that underlying Paul's teaching is the same basic story of redemption found throughout the rest of the New Testament—a story that continues to be essentially a *Jewish* story, unlike the stories considered in chapter 1. Contrary to E. P. Sanders's claim, it was not Paul but later theologians who made the cross the center and starting point of Paul's soteriology, regarding it as the "solution" so as then to define the human "plight" on that basis. While Jesus' death may have been seen as the center and climax of this story, for Paul and the first believers what was redemptive was the *whole story*, that is, *all* the events making up that story; the cross was redemptive *only to the extent that it formed a part of that story*. Thus, in order to understand what Paul and the other New Testament authors wrote regarding the salvific significance of Jesus' death, and to interpret properly the formulaic allusions they use to speak of that death, we must reconstruct correctly the underlying story of redemption—the "foundation story"—running through the New Testament, including Paul's letters. What is called for, therefore, is a greater appreciation of the continuity between the Jewish and Christian understandings of redemption, as well as renewed efforts at reconstructing a "New Testament theology" that reflects the essential continuity and unity of thought that exists between Paul's letters and the rest of the New Testament writings, in spite of the differences between them. The result will no doubt be the emergence of a Paul who in many ways looks very different from the apostle as he has commonly been portrayed.

Notes

Introduction

1. On the concept of foundation stories, see especially N. T. Wright, *Christian Origins* and the *Question of God,* vol. 1, *The New Testament and the People of God* (Minneapolis: Fortress Press, 1992).

Chapter 1

1. Gustav Aulén, *Christus Victor: An Historical Study of the Three Main Types of the Idea of Atonement,* trans. A. G. Hebert (New York: Macmillan, 1969), 4.

2. Athanasius, *De Incarnatione* 44.4–8. Quotation taken from vol. 4 of *A Select Library of Nicene and Post-Nicene Fathers of the Christian Church,* ed. Philip Schaff and Henry Wace, American Reprint, 2nd ser. (Grand Rapids: Eerdmans, 1952–57).

3. Irenaeus, *Adversus Haereses,* preface to Book 5. Quotations taken from vol. 1 of *The Anti-Nicene Fathers: Translations of the Writings of the Fathers Down to A.D. 325,* ed. Alexander Roberts and James Donaldson, American Reprint (Grand Rapids: Eerdmans, 1950).

4. Ibid., 3.18.7.

5. See, for example, ibid., 3.22.1–2; 5.14.1–2; 5.19.1; 5.20.2; 5.21.1; 5.23.2; Athanasius, *Contra Arianos* 2.47, 69–70; Gregory of Nyssa, *Contra Eunomium* 12.1. On the use of Paul by the other Fathers, see especially vol. 1 of Jean Rivière's work *The Doctrine of the Atonement: A Historical Essay,* trans. Luigi Cappadelta (London: Kegan Paul, Trench, Trübner & Co., 1909).

6. Calvin, *Institutes of the Christian Religion* 2.16.5; see also 2.16.6. Quotations taken from vols. 20–21 of *The Library of Christian Classics,* ed. John T. McNeill, trans. Ford Lewis Battles (Philadelphia: Westminster, 1960).

7. Ibid., 2.12.3; 3.4.30.

8. In the English-speaking world, the most ardent proponent of this view has probably been Leon Morris; see *The Apostolic Preaching of the Cross*, 3rd ed. (Grand Rapids: Eerdmans, 1965); *The Cross in the New Testament* (Grand Rapids: Eerdmans, 1965).

9. Peter Abelard, *Exposition of the Epistle to the Romans*, commentary on Rom 3:19–26. Quotation taken from vol. 10 of *The Library of Christian Classics*, ed. and trans. Eugene R. Fairweather (Philadelphia: Westminster, 1956).

10. See, for example, Jürgen Moltmann, *The Crucified God*, trans. R. A. Wilson and John Bowden (Minneapolis: Fortress Press, 1993), 205; Colin E. Gunton, *The Actuality of Atonement* (Grand Rapids: Eerdmans, 1988), 77–80, 84; David McNaughton, "Reparation and Atonement," *RelSt* 28 (1992): 129–44.

11. Karl Barth, *Church Dogmatics*, ed. and trans. G. W. Bromiley and T. F. Torrance (Edinburgh: T&T Clark, 1956–61), 4.1:215–16, 254.

12. Ibid., 4.2:382, 384.

13. Ibid., 4.2:59.

14. Ibid., 4.1:298.

15. Ibid., 4.2:28.

16. Ibid., 3.2:161–62.

17. Ibid., 4.1:295.

18. Rudolf Bultmann, *Theology of the New Testament*, trans. Kendrick Grobel (New York: Scribner's, 1951), 1:298; see also 295–96.

19. Ibid., 1:299.

20. Ibid., 1:303.

21. Barth, *Church Dogmatics*, 4.1:316; see Bultmann, *Theology*, 1:302–303.

22. See Barth, *Church Dogmatics*, 4.1:285; Bultmann, *Theology*, 1:298.

23. E. P. Sanders, *Paul and Palestinian Judaism* (Philadelphia: Fortress Press, 1977), 453, 502. Among the works influencing Sanders were D. E. H. Whiteley, *The Theology of St. Paul* (Philadelphia: Fortress Press, 1964), esp. 130–52, and Robert C. Tannehill, *Dying and Rising with Christ: A Study in Pauline Theology*, BZNW 32 (Berlin: Alfred Töpelmann, 1966).

24. Morna Hooker, *From Adam to Christ: Essays on Paul* (Cambridge: Cambridge University Press, 1990), 9. See Richard B. Hays, "Crucified with Christ: A Synthesis of the Theology of 1 and 2 Thessalonians, Philemon, Philippians, and Galatians," in *Pauline Theology*, vol. 1, *Thessalonians, Philippians, Galatians, Philemon*, ed. Jouette M. Bassler (Minneapolis: Fortress Press, 1991), 227–46; James D. G. Dunn, *The Theology of Paul the Apostle* (Grand Rapids: Eerdmans, 1998), 207–33, 334–412; N. T. Wright, *The Climax of the Covenant: Christ and the Law in Pauline Theology* (Minneapolis: Fortress Press, 1991), 18–55, 151–53, 193–216.

25. T. L. Donaldson, "The 'Curse of the Law' and the Inclusion of the Gentiles: Galatians 3.13–14," *NTS* 32 (1986): 105.

26. Sanders, *Paul*, 466, referring to Whiteley, *Theology of St. Paul*, 134–37. "Gal. 3.16" should be "Gal. 3.13." Cf. Hooker, *From Adam to Christ*, 26–27.

27. See, for example, Wright, *Climax*, 153 n. 54.

28. See especially Otfried Hofius, *Paulusstudien*; WUNT 51 (Tübingen: Mohr, 1989), 33–49, who traces the distinction to Harmut Gese (41). See also the discussion by Daniel P. Bailey, "Concepts of *Stellvertretung* in the Interpretation of Isaiah 53," in *Jesus and the Suffering Servant: Isaiah 53 and Christian Origins*, ed. William H. Bellinger and William R. Farmer (Harrisburg, Pa.: Trinity Press International, 1998), 223–50. Many German-speaking Pauline scholars do continue to employ the German equivalents *Teilhabe, Teilnahme,* or even *Partizipation,* rather than *inkludiender Stellvertretung.* For a summary of scholarly discussion in German regarding Paul's teaching concerning atonement through Christ, see Martin Gaukesbrink, *Die Sühnetradition bei Paulus: Rezeption und theologischer Stellenwert* (Würzburg: Echter Verlag, 1999), 13–39.

29. See James D. G. Dunn, "Paul's Understanding of the Death of Jesus," in *Sacrifice and Redemption: Durham Essays in Theology*, ed. S. W. Sykes (Cambridge: Cambridge University Press, 1991), 35–56 (esp. 50–52).

30. Dunn, *Theology*, 204.

31. David Seeley, *The Noble Death: Graeco-Roman Martyrology and Paul's Concept of Salvation*, JSNTS 28 (Sheffield: Sheffield Academic Press, 1990), 148; see 104–5, 143–48. For the same type of "moral influence" interpretation of Paul's teaching regarding Jesus' death, see Charles B. Cousar, *A Theology of the Cross: The Death of Jesus in the Pauline Letters* (Minneapolis: Fortress Press, 1990), 181–83.

32. Calvin, *Institutes of the Christian Religion* 2.17.4.

33. Irenaeus, *Adversus Haereses* 5.12.6; 5.14.2.

34. Gregory of Nyssa, *Oratio Catechetica Magna* 16.32. Quotation taken from vol. 5 of *A Select Library of Nicene and Post-Nicene Fathers of the Christian Church*, ed. Philip Schaff and Henry Wace, American Reprint, 2nd ser. (Grand Rapids: Eerdmans, 1952–57).

35. See Irenaeus, *Adversus Haereses* 3.18.7; 3.20.3; 3.23.1; 5.21.3.

36. Anselm, *Cur Deus Homo* 2.18. Quotations taken from vol. 3 of *Anselm of Canterbury*, ed. and trans. Jasper Hopkins and Herbert Richardson (Toronto and New York: Edwin Mellen, 1976).

37. Ibid., 2.16; cf. 2.17.

38. Jürgen Moltmann, *The Trinity and the Kingdom: The Doctrine of God*, trans. Margaret Kohl (Minneapolis: Fortress Press, 1993), 82; see 75–83, including his interpretation of Gal 3:13 and 2 Cor 5:21 on p. 79.

39. Irenaeus, *Adversus Haereses* 3.18.7; 5.1.1; 5.21.3.

40. Ibid., 3.18.7—3.19.1; cf. 3.18.2; 3.22.4. See also Athanasius, *De Incarnatione* 44.4–8; cf. 20.4; Gregory of Nyssa, *Oratio Catechetica Magna* 14.

41. Anselm, *Cur Deus Homo*, preface.

42. Ibid., 1.15.

43. Sanders, *Paul*, 502.

44. Donaldson, "'Curse,'" 94.
45. Dunn, *Theology*, 218.
46. Sanders, *Paul*, 443.
47. Hays, "Crucified," 238.
48. Dunn, *Theology*, 223, emphasis added.
49. Wright, *Climax*, 151–52, emphasis added.

Chapter 2

1. See especially N. T. Wright, *Christian Origins and the Question of God*, vol. 1, *The New Testament and the People of God* (Minneapolis: Fortress Press, 1992), 216–23.

2. Summaries of this foundation story are found in the Hebrew Scriptures itself, in passages such as Deut 6:20–24; Josh 24:2–13; Neh 9:6–37; Ps 78; 105; 106; 136; Ezek 16:3–63; 20:5–44.

3. On the idea that the "punishments" Israel experiences are the attempt of a gracious God to bring the people back to him in obedience, see especially Deut 8:5; Job 5:17; Pss 78:34–38; 81:11–16; 89:31–34; 106:40–46; Prov 3:11–12; Jer 2:30; 5:3; Lam 3:32–33; Ezek 14:22–23; 16:41; Amos 4:6–11; Zeph 3:6–13; 2 Macc 6:12–16.

4. For Scripture references to these promises, see especially Donald E. Gowan, *Eschatology in the Old Testament* (Philadelphia: Fortress Press, 1986).

5. For relevant texts, see Gowan, *Eschatology*, 42–54. On the question of the salvation of Gentiles in ancient Judaism in general, see especially James M. Scott, *Paul and the Nations*, WUNT 84 (Tübingen: Mohr, 1995), 58–120.

6. Wright, *New Testament*, 300; cf. 285–86, 331–33.

7. Ibid., 268.

8. Ibid., 334.

9. Ibid., 169–70; cf. 208, 268–72, 285–86, 299–301, 331–34.

10. Ibid., 272–73; see also N. T. Wright, *Christian Origins and the Question of God*, vol. 2, *Jesus and the Victory of God*; (Minneapolis: Fortress Press, 1996), 271.

11. Wright, *New Testament*, 299–300.

12. E. P. Sanders, *Paul and Palestinian Judaism* (Philadelphia: Fortress Press, 1977), 141.

13. Ibid., 420 (emphasis removed).

14. Ibid., 75; cf. 236.

15. On this problem in Sanders's interpretation of ancient Jewish thought, see especially Friedrich Avemarie, *Tora und Leben: Untersuchungen zur Heilsbedeutung der Tora in der frühen rabbinischen Literatur*, TSAJ 55 (Tübingen: Mohr, 1996), 36–40.

16. See especially Sanders, *Paul*, 81, 93, 125–26, 141, 178–82, 189, 204–5, 236–37, 320, 420–22.

17. On these points see E. P. Sanders, *Judaism: Practice and Belief, 63 BCE–66 CE* (Philadelphia: Trinity Press International, 1992), 247–51; Wright, *New Testament*, 250–51.

18. On these points see Sanders, *Jusaism*, 87–88, 170–72. See also C. G. Montefiore and H. Loewe, *A Rabbinic Anthology* (New York: Schocken, 1974), 202–24; Adolf Büchler, *Studies in Sin and Atonement in the Rabbinic Literature of the First Century*, LBS (New York: KTAV, 1967), 170–211.

19. Sanders, *Paul*, 138–43.

20. Ibid., 147–50, 346, 398–406.

21. Wright, *New Testament*, 271.

22. Ibid., 195–96, 227.

23. Ibid., 221.

24. See Frank Thielmann, *From Plight to Solution: A Jewish Framework for Understanding Paul's View of the Law in Galatians and Romans*, NovTSup 61 (Leiden: E. J. Brill, 1989), 36–45.

25. Wright, *New Testament*, 272.

26. Leon Morris, in particular, has defended this view (see the works cited in chapter 1 above). See also Gordon J. Wenham, "The Theology of Old Testament Sacrifice," in *Sacrifice in the Bible*, ed. Roger T. Beckwith and Martin J. Selman (Carlisle: Paternoster Press, 1995), 75–87; Ben Witherington III, *Paul's Narrative Thought World: The Tapestry of Tragedy and Triumph* (Louisville: Westminster John Knox, 1994), 160–68.

27. James D. G. Dunn, *Romans 1–8*, WBC (Dallas: Word, 1988), 172.

28. James D. G. Dunn, "Paul's Understanding of the Death of Jesus," in *Sacrifice and Redemption: Durham Essays in Theology*, ed. S. W. Sykes (Cambridge: Cambridge University Press, 1991), 50; idem, *The Theology of Paul the Apostle* (Grand Rapids: Eerdmans, 1998), 386; idem, *Romans 1–8*, 170, 182, 439.

29. See, for example, the understanding of sacrifice in Paul S. Fiddes, *Past Event and Present Salvation: The Christian Idea of Atonement* (London: Darton, Longman & Todd, 1989), 63–79.

30. See, for example, Jacob Milgrom, *Studies in Cultic Theology and Terminology*, SJLA 36 (Leiden: E. J. Brill, 1983), 67–95; idem, "Atonement in the OT," "Day of Atonement," and "Sacrifices and Offerings, OT," in *Interpreter's Dictionary of the Bible*, supplementary vol. (Nashville: Abingdon, 1976), 78–83, 763–71. As a basis for interpreting Paul's sacrificial language regarding Christ's death, Robert G. Hammerton-Kelly, in *Sacred Violence: Paul's Hermeneutic of the Cross* (Minneapolis: Fortress Press, 1992), used the ideas of René Girard regarding sacrifice in *Violence and the Sacred* (Baltimore: Johns Hopkins University Press, 1977) and *The Scapegoat* (Baltimore: Johns Hopkins University Press, 1986).

31. Dunn, *Theology*, 218, 223.

32. Dunn, "Paul's Understanding," 43–44.

33. See, for example, Bradley Hudson McLean, "The Absence of Atoning Sacrifice in Paul's Soteriology," *NTS* 38 (1992): 532–42; Stanislas Lyonnet, "The Terminology of Redemption," in *Sin, Redemption and Sacrifice: A Biblical and Patristic Study*, ed.

Stanislas Lyonnet and Léopold Sabourin, AnBib 48 (Rome: Biblical Institute, 1970), 123, 126–36, 169–80.

34. Dunn, "Paul's Understanding," 44.

35. See ibid., 44–46.

36. See Roland de Vaux, *Studies in Old Testament Sacrifice* (Cardiff: University of Wales, 1964), 94.

37. Dunn, *Theology*, 219. See also David P. Wright, *The Disposal of Impurity: Elimination Rites in the Bible and in Hittite and Mesopotamian Literature*, SBLDS 101 (Atlanta: Scholars Press, 1987), 77–78; Wright, *New Testament*, 274–75.

38. N. Kiuchi, *The Purification Offering in the Priestly Literature: Its Meaning and Function*, JSOTS 56 (Sheffield: JSOT Press, 1987), 162.

39. On this point and what follows, see, for example, Kiuchi, *Purification Offering*, 34–37; Milgrom, "Atonement in the OT," 81; idem, "Sacrifices," 767.

40. Sanders, *Paul*, 164. Sanders also observes there that those in the diaspora could obtain forgiveness even though they were unable to present sacrificial offerings under normal circumstances; cf. 298–305.

41. See, for example, Büchler, *Studies*, 341, 456.

42. Wright, *New Testament*, 274.

43. Josephus, *Antiquitates Judaeorum* 8.4.2–3. Quotation taken from vol. 5 of Josephus, *Jewish Antiquities*, trans. H. St. J. Thackeray and Ralph Marcus, LCL (Cambridge, Mass.: Harvard University Press, 1977).

44. On the intimate relation between sacrifice and prayer, see especially the following, which contain further references from Scripture and other ancient sources: Walter Eichrodt, *Theology of the Old Testament*, trans. J. A. Baker (Philadelphia: Westminster, 1961, 1967), 2:446–54, 462; Sanders, *Judaism*, 142–43, 252–56, 271, 276–77; Werner Foerster, *Palestinian Judaism in New Testament Times*, trans. Gordon Harris (Edinburgh: Oliver & Boyd, 1964), 153.

45. Roland de Vaux, *Ancient Israel*, trans. John McHugh (New York: McGraw-Hill, 1965), 357.

46. Ibid., 457.

47. See Sanders, *Judaism*, 142–43.

48. See ibid., 252–56, 271, 276–77.

49. Lyonnet, "Terminology of Redemption," 141–46, 167; Royden Keith Yerkes, *Sacrifice in Greek and Roman Religions and Early Judaism* (New York: Scribner's, 1952), 180–81.

50. Büchler, *Studies*, 430–31; cf. 439–43, 446–47.

51. So claims Morris, for example (*The Apostolic Preaching of the Cross*, 3rd ed. [Grand Rapids: Eerdmans, 1965], 83, 118). See also Wolfgang Kraus, *Der Tod Jesu als Heiligtumsweihe: Eine Untersuchung zum Umfeld der Sühnevorstellung in Römer 3,25–26a*, WMANT 66 (Neukirchen-Vluyn: Neukirchener Verlag, 1991), 161–62.

52. See Jacob Milgrom, "A Prolegomenon to Leviticus 17:11," *JBL* 90 (1971):

149–56; Bradley Hudson McLean, *The Cursed Christ: Mediterranean Expulsion Rituals and Pauline Soteriology,* JSNTS 126 (Sheffield: Sheffield Academic Press, 1996), 30, 36.

53. See especially Eduard Lohse, *Märtyrer und Gottesknecht,* 2nd ed. (Göttingen: Vandenhoeck & Ruprecht, 1963), 78–87.

54. Sanders, *Paul,* 168–76.

55. On this point and what follows, see especially David Seeley, *The Noble Death: Graeco-Roman Martyrology and Paul's Concept of Salvation,* JSNTS 28 (Sheffield: Sheffield Academic Press, 1990), 87–99. Cf. Sam K. Williams, *Jesus' Death as Saving Event: The Background and Origin of a Concept,* HDR 2 (Missoula, Mont.: Scholars Press, 1975), 165–202.

56. Sanders, *Paul,* 169.

57. See Williams, *Jesus' Death,* 85–88.

58. Sanders, *Paul,* 190.

59. See Albert Schweitzer, *The Mysticism of Paul the Apostle,* trans. William Montgomery (Baltimore: Johns Hopkins University Press, 1998), 60: "The Kingdom cannot come until the pre-Messianic tribulation has taken place. If Jesus suffers a death which God can accept as the equivalent of that tribulation, he can thereby bring in the Kingdom at once." See also Wright, *New Testament,* 277–78.

60. Sanders, *Paul,* 180.

61. See, for example, Gen 18:14; 2 Chron 20:6; Job 42:2; Pss 115:3; 135:6.

Chapter 3

1. See Dale C. Allison Jr., "The Continuity between John and Jesus," *JSHJ* 1.1 (2003): 6–19.

2. See Robert L. Webb, "John the Baptist and His Relationship to Jesus," in *Studying the Historical Jesus: Evaluations of the State of Current Research,* ed. Bruce Chilton and Craig A. Evans, NTTS 19 (Leiden: E. J. Brill, 1994), 194–96.

3. James D. G. Dunn, *Christianity in the Making,* vol. 1, *Jesus Remembered* (Grand Rapids: Eerdmans, 2003), 359.

4. See Matt 4:17; 11:20–21; 12:41; Mark 1:15; 6:12; Luke 5:32; 13:3, 5; 15:7, 10; 16:30.

5. On these issues in Matthew, see J. Andrew Overman, *Matthew's Gospel and Formative Judaism: The Social World of the Matthean Community* (Minneapolis: Fortress Press, 1990), 78–94.

6. On this point and what follows, see especially William R. G. Loader, *Jesus' Attitude towards the Law: A Study of the Gospels,* WUNT 2.97 (Tübingen: Mohr, 1997), especially his conclusions on 509–24; Irving M. Zeitlin, *Jesus and the Judaism of His Time* (Oxford: Basil Blackwell, 1988), 73–84; Robert J. Banks, *Jesus and the Law in the Synoptic Tradition,* SNTSMS 28 (Cambridge: Cambridge University Press, 1975),

90–263; Marcus J. Borg, *Conflict, Holiness and Politics in the Teachings of Jesus* (Harrisburg, Pa.: Trinity Press International, 1998), 90–212.

7. See David E. Holwerda, *Jesus and Israel: One Covenant or Two?* (Grand Rapids: Eerdmans, 1995), 130–32.

8. See Alexander J. M. Wedderburn, "Paul and Jesus: Similarity and Continuity," in *Paul and Jesus: Collected Essays*, ed. Wedderburn, JSNTS 37 (Sheffield: Sheffield Academic Press, 1989), 119–43.

9. E. P. Sanders, *Jesus and Judaism* (Philadelphia: Fortress Press, 1985), 153; cf. 271; idem, *The Historical Figure of Jesus* (London: Penguin, 1993), 238.

10. See David Hill, *The Gospel of Matthew*, NCBC (Grand Rapids: Eerdmans, 1981), 207–8.

11. See Sanders, *Jesus*, 208, 240; idem, *Historical Figure*, 236–38. Cf. Leonhard Goppelt, *Theology of the New Testament*, trans. John Alsup (Grand Rapids: Eerdmans, 1981), 1:122.

12. See Ben Meyer, *The Aims of Jesus* (London: SCM, 1979), 137–53.

13. Sanders, *Jesus*, 260, 271, 293, 301.

14. Sanders, *Historical Figure*, 238; see also Dunn, *Jesus Remembered*, 787–90.

15. Jack D. Kingsbury, *Conflict in Luke: Jesus, Authorities, Disciples* (Minneapolis: Fortress Press, 1991), 81. See also his *Conflict in Mark: Jesus, Authorities, Disciples* (Minneapolis: Fortress Press, 1989), 66–67, 86.

16. On these passages, see Frank J. Matera, "Responsibility for the Death of Jesus according to the Acts of the Apostles," *JSNT* 39 (1990), 77–93.

17. See Donald Senior, *Matthew*, ANTC (Nashville: Abingdon, 1998), 240–43.

18. On these points, see Raymond E. Brown, *The Death of the Messiah*, ABRL (New York: Doubleday, 1994), 1:440–44; Robert H. Gundry, *Matthew: A Commentary on His Literary and Theological Art* (Grand Rapids: Eerdmans, 1982), 542–43; R. T. France, *The Gospel of Mark*, NIGTC (Grand Rapids: Eerdmans, 2002), 605–7.

19. On this discussion, see Dunn, *Jesus Remembered*, 638 n. 119.

20. See N. T. Wright, *Christian Origins and the Question of God*, vol. 2, *Jesus and the Victory of God* (Minneapolis: Fortress Press, 1996), 552.

21. See Susanne Lehne, *The New Covenant in Hebrews*, JSNTS 44 (Sheffield: JSOT Press, 1990), 80–82.

22. See Jonathan Klawans, "Interpreting the Last Supper: Sacrifice, Spiritualization, and Anti-Sacrifice," *NTS* 48 (2002): 15–16.

23. See Lehne, *New Covenant*, 84; Kim Huat Tan, *The Zion Traditions and the Aims of Jesus*, SNTSMS 91 (Cambridge: Cambridge University Press, 1997), 198, 215–20.

24. On this discussion, see Dunn, *Jesus Remembered*, 818–24.

25. See ibid., 816–17.

26. On these ideas, see especially Bruce Chilton, *Pure Kingdom: Jesus' Vision of God* (Grand Rapids: Eerdmans, 1996), 125–26.

27. "For the many" here and in Mark 10:45 should be understood as a reference to the community of believers; see Christopher Stephen Mann, *Mark: A New Translation with Introduction and Commentary,* ABC 27 (Garden City, N.Y.: Doubleday, 1986), 415–17.

28. See Brown, *Death,* 2:1098–1118; France, *Mark,* 656–58.

29. See Matt 26:24, 31, 56; 27:9–10; Mark 14:21, 27, 49; Luke 18:31; 22:37; John 13:18; 17:12; 19:24, 28, 36–37.

30. See Darrell Bock, "Scripture and the Realisation of God's Promises," in *Witness to the Gospel: The Theology of Acts,* ed. I. Howard Marshall and David Peterson (Grand Rapids: Eerdmans, 1998), 58–61.

31. Acts 16:9; 19:21; 20:10–11; 23:11; 27:24. See Charles H. Cosgrove, "The Divine *dei* in Luke-Acts" *NovT* 26 (1984): 168–90; John T. Squires, *The Plan of God in Luke-Acts,* SNTSMS 76 (Cambridge: Cambridge University Press, 1993), esp. 166–77.

32. On this idea in Mark's Gospel, see Eduard Schweizer, *The Good News according to Mark,* trans. Donald Madvig (Richmond: John Knox Press, 1970), 241.

33. See Senior, *Matthew,* 245–46; Wright, *Jesus,* 421; Rudolf Schnackenburg, *The Gospel of Matthew,* trans. Robert Barr (Grand Rapids: Eerdmans, 2002), 204–5, 214–15.

34. See Matt 19:26; Mark 14:36; Luke 1:37; 18:22.

35. This idea is alluded to by Justin Martyr in his *Dialogue with Trypho* 40.

36. As F. F. Bruce observes, the author states that "almost everything" had to be purified with blood because there were exceptions to the "rule" (*The Epistle to the Hebrews,* NICNT, rev. ed. [Grand Rapids: Eerdmans, 1990], 226–27).

37. On the centrality of repentance in the early Christian proclamation as presented by Luke, see especially Guy D. Nave, Jr., *The Role and Function of Repentance in Luke-Acts*; SBLAB 4 (Atlanta: Society of Biblical Literature, 2002).

38. See Vincent Taylor, *Forgiveness and Reconciliation: A Study in New Testament Theology* (London: Macmillan, 1956), 3.

39. N. T. Wright, *Christian Origins and the Question of God,* vol. 1, *The New Testament and the People of God*; (Minneapolis: Fortress Press, 1992), 150.

40. On these points, see especially Holwerda, *Jesus and Israel,* 27–112, 177–84; Donald E. Gowan, *Eschatology in the Old Testament* (Philadelphia: Fortress Press, 1986), 30–31.

41. On the origin and antiquity of these canticles, see Raymond E. Brown, *The Birth of the Messiah: A Commentary on the Infancy Narratives in Matthew and Luke* (Garden City, N.Y.: Doubleday, 1977), 346–55.

42. See Jacob Jervell, *The Theology of the Acts of the Apostles,* NTT (Cambridge: Cambridge University Press, 1996), 106–15.

43. See Matt 10:17–21, 38; 16:24; 17:12, 22; 20:18–19; 21:34–39; 23:31–37; 24:9–10; Mark 8:34; 9:31; 10:21, 33; 12:1–8; 13:9–13; Luke 9:23; 13:31–34; 14:27; 20:9–15; 21:12, 16; 23:31; 24:7.

Chapter 4

1. See E. P. Sanders, *Paul and Palestinian Judaism* (Philadelphia: Fortress Press, 1977), 443–47, 554–55.

2. Sanders, *Paul*, 543, 551, emphasis removed.

3. See especially 2 Cor 11:1–23; Gal 1:11—2:16.

4. The discussion of Paul's teaching here and in the following chapters will be based primarily on the undisputed Pauline letters (Romans, 1–2 Corinthians, Galatians, Philippians, 1 Thessalonians, and Philemon), although at times reference will also be made to the deuteropaulines (Ephesians, Colossians, 2 Thessalonians, 1–2 Timothy, and Titus).

5. See Rudolf Bultmann, *Theology of the New Testament*, trans. Kendrick Grobel (New York: Scribner's, 1951), 1:293–94, 298–306; cf. 188.

6. See especially Bultmann, *Theology*, 1:63–4, 141, 175, 298–303.

7. See Gerhard Barth, *Der Tod Jesu im Verständnis des Neuen Testaments* (Neukirchen-Vluyn: Neukirchener Verlag, 1992), 117. See also various essays in *Kreuzestheologie im Neuen Testament*, ed. Andreas Dettwiler and Jean Zumstein, WUNT 151 (Tübingen: Mohr Siebeck, 2002).

8. Sanders, *Paul*, 445.

9. Ibid., 497–502.

10. James D. G. Dunn, *The Theology of Paul the Apostle* (Grand Rapids: Eerdmans, 1998), 212.

11. Richard B. Hays, "Crucified with Christ: A Synthesis of the Theology of 1 and 2 Thessalonians, Philemon, Philippians, and Galatians," in *Pauline Theology*, vol. 1, *Thessalonians, Philippians, Galatians, Philemon*, ed. Jouette M. Bassler (Minneapolis: Fortress Press, 1991), 233, 239. See also Jens Schröter, *Der Versöhnte Versöhner: Paulus als unentbehrlicher Mittler im Heilsvorgang zwischen Gott und Gemeinde nach 2 Kor 2,14–7,4*, TANT 10 (Tübingen and Basel: A. Francke Verlag, 1993), who argues for an ontological interpretation of *kain ̄e ktisis* and claims that wit Christ's death, the old Aeon is done away, and a renewal of the whole cosmos has occurred (286).

12. John Ziesler, *Paul's Letter to the Romans*, TPINTC (Philadelphia: Trinity Press International, 1989), 157, 162. See also Hans-Joachin Eckstein, *Verheissung und Gesetz: Eine exegetische Untersuchung zu Galater 2,15–4,7*, WUNT 86 (Tübingen: Mohr, 1996), who writes that as a consequence of being crucified with Christ, the definite eradication of existence under sin is, for Paul, completed . . . the human being set in opposition to God no longer exists. (71, 73).

13. See, for example, Rom 1:20; 4:13–21; 9:4–18; 11:2–5, 28; 1 Cor 10:1–11; 2 Cor 3:7–13; Gal 3:17–20; 4:21–31.

14. See Rom 2:7; 5:21; 6:22–23; Gal 6:8. On this point, see Don B. Garlington, *Faith, Obedience, and Perseverance: Aspects of Paul's Letter to the Romans*, WUNT 79 (Tübingen: Mohr, 1994), 57. Alan Richardson also observes, "In later Judaism the

conception of 'life' had acquired a markedly eschatological character as a quality of the Age to Come. . . ." Thus, the Greek phrase *zoē aiōnios* "really means 'the life of the Age to Come'" (*An Introduction to the Theology of the New Testament* [New York: Harper & Row, 1958], 71, 73).

15. Don B. Garlington, *"The Obedience of Faith": A Pauline Phrase in Historical Context*, WUNT 2.38 (Tübingen: Mohr, 1991), 236.

16. David Wenham, *Paul: Follower of Jesus or Founder of Christianity?* (Grand Rapids: Eerdmans, 1995), 381. Wenham has also argued that the fact that Paul knew that Jesus had commissioned apostles and that they had been given authority to do miracles makes it "entirely probable" that he knew of Jesus' own miracles as well, since "it is highly unlikely that he associated the apostles but not Jesus himself with working of miracles" (351). See also Michael B. Thompson, *Clothed with Christ: The Example and Teaching of Jesus in Romans 12.1–15.13*, JSNTS 59 (Sheffield: JSOT Press, 1991).

17. On these points, see D. Wenham, *Paul*, 354–55, as well as Christian Wolff, "Humility and Self-Denial in Jesus' Life and Message and in the Apostolic Existence of Paul," in *Paul and Jesus: Collected Essays*, ed. Alexander J. M. Wedderburn, JSNTS 37 (Sheffield: Sheffield Academic Press, 1989), 145–60. Regarding Bultmann's claim that when Paul spoke of Christ's becoming poor and alluded to his ethical qualities, he had in mind Christ's incarnation rather than his ministry, see Wedderburn's response, "Paul and the Story of Jesus," in *Paul and Jesus*, 182–83.

18. Dunn, *Theology*, 206; see 182–206 for his argument as a whole.

19. Bultmann claimed that in 1 Cor 2:6–8 the "rulers" Paul had in mind were "the spirit powers and Satan" (*Theology*, 1:258–59). While this is questionable, even if such a claim is granted, there is no reason to doubt that the reference is also to the Jewish and Roman authorities who had Jesus crucified. The only other mention of "rulers" in the undisputed Pauline letters appears in Rom 13:3, where Paul clearly refers to human authorities. If Paul does have the demonic forces in mind, he may be thinking of something similar to what we find in Luke's Gospel (as well as the Fourth Gospel), where Jesus' betrayal is attributed to Satan's entering into Judas's heart (see Luke 22:3; cf. John 13:2, 27). According to this idea, Satan and the forces of evil were believed to have been active not only through Judas but through all those who were involved in having Jesus crucified. Some have argued that 1 Thess 2:14–16 is an interpolation (see, for example, Neil Elliott, *Liberating Paul: The Justice of God and the Politics of the Apostle* [Maryknoll, N.Y.: Orbis, 1994], 7, 13, 25–27, 110). In part, this argument seems motivated by a desire to deny any biblical or apostolic basis for the anti-Semitism that, unfortunately, some have justified on the basis of this text. Many, however, continue to maintain the authenticity of the passage; see Charles A. Wanamaker, *The Epistles to the Thessalonians: A Commentary on the Greek Text*, NIGTC (Grand Rapids: Eerdmans, 1990), 112–19; Jon A. Weatherly, *Jewish Responsibility for the Death of Jesus in Luke-Acts*, JSNTS 106 (Sheffield: Sheffield Academic Press, 1994), 176–94.

20. On this passage, see Thompson, *Clothed with Christ*, 222–23.

21. On the question of Paul's knowledge of the passion narratives, see Wenham, *Paul*, 125, 276–80, 363–72.

22. See C. F. Evans, *The Resurrection and the New Testament* (London: SCM, 1970), 135–42.

23. See especially Rom 1:1, 8; 10:14–15; 11:13; 15:15–21; 1 Cor 4:9; 9:5; 12:28; 15:9; 2 Cor 2:14–17; 3:6; 10:13–16; Gal 1:16; 2:7–9; 1 Thess 2:2–6.

24. See especially Rom 1:7; 15:25–26, 31; 1 Cor 1:2; 14:33; 2 Cor 1:1; 9:12; 13:13; Gal 1:13; Phil 1:1; 4:21–22; 1 Thess 2:14; 5:27.

25. Behind Paul's allegorical interpretation of the Hebrew Scriptures in passages such as 1 Cor 10:1–4 and Gal 4:21–31 may be this same conviction that even the narrative passages of the Pentateuch point forward to the divine plan.

26. Rom 2:4; 3:25–26; 9:14–26; 11:5–35; 15:9; 16:27; 1 Cor 2:6–13; 2 Cor 4:15.

27. Rom 5:6, 7 (twice); 8:32; 14:15; 2 Cor 5:14, 15, 21; Gal 2:20; 3:13; 1 Thess 5:10; cf. 1 Cor 1:13; 11:24; Eph 5:2, 25.

28. On this point, see especially Wolff, "Humility," 145–60.

29. Brice L. Martin, *Christ and the Law in Paul*, NovTSup 62 (Leiden: E. J. Brill, 1989), 84.

30. C. K. Barrett, *A Commentary on the Epistle to the Romans*, HNTC (New York: Harper & Row, 1957), 30.

31. James D. G. Dunn, *Romans 1–8*, WBC (Dallas: Word, 1988), 183.

32. See particularly Garlington, *Faith*, 156; Klyne R. Snodgrass, "Justification by Grace—to the Doers: An Analysis of the Place of Romans 2 in the Theology of Paul," *NTS* 32 (1986): 72–93.

33. See especially Kent L. Yinger, *Paul, Judaism, and Judgment according to Deeds*, SNTSMS 105 (Cambridge: Cambridge University Press, 1999).

34. Herman N. Ridderbos, *Paul: An Outline of His Theology*, trans. John Richard de Witt (Grand Rapids: Eerdmans, 1975), 180.

35. Heikki Räisänen, *Paul and the Law*, WUNT 29 (Tübingen: Mohr, 1983), 69; cf. 199.

36. Ibid., 201, 267–68.

37. Ibid., 71.

38. See Susanne Lehne, *The New Covenant in Hebrews*, JSNTS 44 (Sheffield: JSOT Press, 1990), 69, 73–4; Frank J. Matera, *II Corinthians: A Commentary*, NTL (Louisville: Westminster John Knox, 2003), 78–82.

39. See Bultmann, *Theology*, 1:330–52.

40. Scott J. Hafemann, *Paul, Moses and the History of Israel: The Letter/Spirit Contrast and the Argument from Scripture in 2 Corinthians 3*, WUNT 81 (Tübingen: Mohr, 1995), 404–6.

41. See Thompson, *Clothed with Christ*, 121–40.

42. See Wenham, *Paul*, 92–94; Thompson, *Clothed with Christ*, 185–99.

43. John M. G. Barclay, *Obeying the Truth: A Study of Paul's Ethics in Galatians* (Minneapolis: Fortress Press, 1991), 125–45. See also Dunn, *Theology*, 654–58, and Graham Stanton, "The Law of Moses and the Law of Christ," in *Paul and the Mosaic Law*, ed. James D. G. Dunn, WUNT 89 (Tübingen: Mohr, 1996), 99–116, who agree that Paul has the Mosaic law in mind.

44. See also Gal 2:17, where Paul argues against the idea that Christ is a "servant of sin." Jesus could be understood in this way according to a literal interpretation of the law, since his teaching that at times it is acceptable to disobey the literal commandments would be seen by some Jews as teaching others to sin. In Rom 3:7–8 and 6:1, Paul also defends himself against the accusation that he teaches others to sin.

45. To say that Paul is applying the same principles applied by Jesus in the Sermon on the Mount is not necessarily to posit some direct relationship between Jesus' words there and Rom 2:21–24. As James D. G. Dunn has argued, even though there is no evidence that the traditions behind passages such as Mark 2:15—3:6 influenced Paul directly, at the least they must have done so indirectly through Paul's precursors (*Jesus, Paul and the Law: Studies in Mark and Galatians* [Louisville: Westminster John Knox, 1990], 28–29).

46. See respectively C. E. B. Cranfield, *A Critical and Exegetical Commentary on the Epistle to the Romans*, ICC (Edinburgh: T&T Clark, 1975), 1:169; Garlington, *Faith*, 32–43.

47. Garlington's concern to "explain adequately how *hierosuleō* can form the counterpoint of *ho bdelussomenos ta eidōla*," since the reference in the latter phrase is clearly to pagan idols (*Faith*, 33–34), can be dealt with by noting that the idea in the passage is that of the Jew *teaching others* not to do things that he himself does. In this case, what is involved is teaching the Gentile to abhor and reject idol worship and instead serve the one true God. Thus, Paul's thought here would be that even the Jew who teaches Gentiles not to dishonor God by worshiping other gods dishonors God himself at times (Rom 2:23) by not offering God what he should in the context of the worship in the Jerusalem Temple. This might involve the Temple tax but also other tithes, offerings, or obligations, or simply the necessary spirit of obedience to God's will in his worship of God.

48. See, for example, Dunn, *Jesus, Paul and the Law*, 194.

49. See ibid., 198.

50. See Räisänen, *Paul*, 190. From Qumran, see 1QS 11:1–5, 9–15.

51. See Matera, *II Corinthians*, 81–82.

52. Space does not permit entering into a full discussion regarding what Paul meant here and elsewhere by the "righteousness of God." This short phrase, like many similar Pauline phrases, is open to all sorts of interpretations, and these are generally defended or rejected on the basis of the theological concerns of biblical scholars. Therefore, rather than reviewing the almost interminable scholarly discussion on this

question in order to argue for one interpretation or another, the position being taken on the basis of the overall argument of this work will simply be stated here, namely, that generally *dikaiosunē theou* means for Paul what it means in Judaism in general and the other New Testament passages where it appears (Matt 6:33; Jas 1:20), that is, the righteous way of life in accordance with God's will. Nevertheless, it would be a mistake to attempt to impose this meaning on all occurrences of the phrase, since it appears that Paul uses it in more than one sense. For the background to the understanding of *dikaiosunē theou* as conduct according to God's will, see especially Benno Przybylski, *Righteousness in Matthew and His World of Thought*, SNTSMS 41 (Cambridge: Cambridge University Press, 1980), 89–104. Przybylski argues against using Paul's understanding of righteousness to interpret Matthew's teaching; it seems, however, that we should actually do the opposite, namely, use the understanding of righteousness found in Matthew's Gospel as well as ancient Judaism in general to interpret Paul's thought.

53. Bultmann, *Theology*, 1:292.

54. The idea that the Holy Spirit enables believers to fulfill the law may also be behind Paul's thought in 2 Corinthians 3; see Jens Schröter, "Schriftauslegung und Hermeneutik in 2 Korinther 3: Ein Beitrag zur Frage der Schriftbenutzung des Paulus," *NovT* 40 (1998): 231–75.

55. Sanders, *Paul*, 494.

56. Garlington, *Obedience*, 251. Mark A. Seifrid makes the same observation regarding the concept of righteousness in the Qumran manuscripts, where it is consistently conceived in "behavioral" terms and "regularly coupled with 'perfection of way' and 'holiness' as in 1QS as a description of the ideas of conduct for the members of the community" (*Justification by Faith: The Origin and Development of a Central Pauline Theme*, NovTSup 68 [Leiden: E. J. Brill, 1992], 97).

57. Douglas A. Moo, for example, claims that "'being justified' alludes to the past declaration of acquittal pronounced over the sinner who believes in Christ. . . . Justification language is legal, law-court language, picturing the believer being declared innocent by the judge" (*The Epistle to the Romans*, NICNT [Grand Rapids: Eerdmans, 1996], 310–11).

58. See Garlington, *Faith*, 15–31, 56–71.

59. Yinger notes that "the role of the Spirit in enabling obedience, while not absent in Judaism, is certainly heightened significantly in Paul" (*Paul*, 289).

60. See Rom 3:22, 26; Gal 2:16; 3:22; Phil 3:9; cf. Eph 3:12. The phrase "faith in Christ Jesus" appears only in Gal 3:26 (although it is also present in Eph 1:15 and Col 1:4).

61. Although this interpretation goes back to the nineteenth century, it became influential once more thanks largely to Thomas F. Torrance ("One Aspect of the Biblical Conception of Faith," *ExpT* 68 [1957]: 111–14, 221–22), who developed Karl Barth's view of Christ as both substitute and representative so as to claim that

believers participate in Christ's own faith/faithfulness, as well as other aspects of his past historical existence. See, for example, *The Mediation of Christ*, rev. ed. (Edinburgh: T&T Clark, 1992), 83–98. It was then developed further by biblical scholars who were also proponents of participatory understandings of salvation. See especially Arland J. Hultgren, "The *Pistis Christou* Formulation in Paul," *NovT* 22 (1980): 248–63; Richard B. Hays, *The Faith of Jesus Christ: An Investigation of the Narrative Substructure of Galatians 3:1—4:11*, 2nd ed., Biblical Resource Series (Grand Rapids: Eerdmans, 2002), 141–62; Morna D. Hooker, "ΠΙΣΤΙΣ ΧΡΙΣΤΟΥ," *NTS* 35 (1989): 321–42; Ian G. Wallis, *The Faith of Jesus Christ in Early Christian Traditions*, SNTSMS 84 (Cambridge: Cambridge University Press, 1995).

62. For references as well as Dunn's views on this question, see especially Dunn, *Theology*, 379–85, and his debate with Richard Hays in the two appendixes of the 2002 edition of Hays, *Faith*, 249–97.

63. See Rom 10:17; 15:19; 16:25; 1 Cor 1:6–7; 9:12; 2 Cor 9:13; Gal 1:7, 12; Phil 1:27; 3:8; 1 Thess 1:3; 3:12. Hays notes that a few scholars, especially O. Schmitz, have understood *pistis Christou* in terms of "Christ-faith," but he does not explore the possibility further in *Faith*, 142–44.

64. Johan Christiaan Beker, *The Triumph of God: The Essence of Paul's Thought*, trans. Loren T. Stuckenbruck (Minneapolis: Fortress Press, 1990), 84.

65. For the relevant passages from Paul's epistles in this regard, see especially Dunn, *Theology*, 461–82.

66. 1 Cor 1:7–8; 5:5; 11:26; 15:23; 2 Cor 1:14; Phil 1:6, 10; 2:16; 1 Thess 1:10; 2:19; 3:13; 4:15–16; 5:2, 23.

67. Dunn, *Theology*, 313.

68. David J. Lull, "Salvation History," in Bassler, *Pauline Theology*, 1:264.

69. The same observations must be made with regard to Ephesians and Colossians, where language reflecting a realized eschatology is found. See Clinton E. Arnold, *Ephesians, Power and Magic: The Concept of Power in Ephesians in Light of Its Historical Setting*, SNTSMS 63 (Cambridge: Cambridge University Press, 1989), 145–58; John M. G. Barclay, *Colossians and Philemon*, NTG (Sheffield: Sheffield Academic Press, 1997), 26, 89–90. Because these epistles also speak of salvation and deliverance as a future hope, the expressions of realized eschatology should be understood in terms of a present certainty regarding the coming salvation as well as a present experience of many of the blessings associated with the age to come, rather than some type of actual change of aeons or ontological transformation in the present. Similarly, in Titus 3:4–7, there is no reason to ascribe to the author the notion that some "changeover" has been "activated by the Christ event in history" so that there is a "disruption in the present age" (P. H. Towner, "The Present Age in the Eschatology of the Pastoral Epistles," *NTS* 32 [1986]: 434), since the idea is merely that believers have been "saved" in the sense of being incorporated into the church through baptism and receiving the Holy Spirit so as to become "heirs in hope of eternal life," which is yet to come.

70. For this understanding of *arrabōn*, see A. J. Kerr, "*Arrabōn*," *JTS* 39 (1988): 92–97; Kurt Erlemann, "Der Geist als *arrabōn* (2 Kor 5,5) im Kontext der paulinischen Eschatologie," *ZNW* 83 (1992): 202–23.

71. See Phil 3:9, 12–15; cf. 1 Cor 2:6; Col 1:28; 4:12.

72. See especially the argument of Moyer V. Hubbard, *New Creation in Paul's Letters and Thought*, SNTSMS 119 (Cambridge: Cambridge University Press, 2002). See also Margaret E. Thrall, *A Critical and Exegetical Commentary on the Second Epistle to the Corinthians*, ICC (Edinburgh: T&T Clark, 1994), 1:421–22, although Thrall herself argues against the view that "new creation" simply refers to the individual who enters the believing community (whether Jewish or Christian).

73. See respectively Robert C. Tannehill, *Dying and Rising with Christ: A Study in Pauline Theology*, BZNW 32 (Berlin: Alfred Töpelmann, 1966), 65; Beker, *Triumph*, 159; Schröter, *Der Versöhnte Versöhner*, 286.

74. See Barclay, *Obeying*, 202–15, who argues that Paul uses flesh to designate "what is merely human," or "merely human behavior," characterizing "human beings who have not been transformed by the Spirit" (206–7). The fact that life in the present age is not *entirely* evil means that at times Paul can speak of "flesh" in a neutral sense as well; see Rom 1:3; 4:1; 9:3, 5; 1 Cor 15:39; 2 Cor 5:16; Gal 1:16; Phil 1:22–24. On the Palestinian Jewish background to Paul's thought here, see Jörg Frey, "Die paulinische Antithese von 'Fleisch' und 'Geist' und die palästinisch-jüdisch Weisheitstradition," *ZNW* 90 (1999): 45–77.

75. See, for example, Walter Schmithals, *The Theology of the First Christians*, trans. O. C. Dean (Louisville: Westminster John Knox, 1997), 64–65, 76.

76. On these points, see especially Dunn, *Theology*, 266–93. On ancient Jewish beliefs regarding the preexistence of the Torah, see Werner Foerster, *Palestinian Judaism in New Testament Times*, trans. Gordon Harris (Edinburgh: Oliver & Boyd, 1964), 184–86; W. D. Davies, *Paul and Rabbinic Judaism*, 2nd ed. (London: SPCK, 1965), 147–76.

Chapter 5

1. Rudolf Bultmann, *Theology of the New Testament*, trans. Kendrick Grobel (New York: Scribner's, 1951), 1:84, 295, 298–300; cf. 46–47.

2. E. P. Sanders, *Paul and Palestinian Judaism* (Philadelphia: Fortress Press, 1977), 520.

3. Ibid., 507.

4. Ibid., 506.

5. Ibid., 520.

6. Richard B. Hays, "Crucified with Christ: A Synthesis of the Theology of 1 and 2 Thessalonians, Philemon, Philippians, and Galatians," in *Pauline Theology*, vol. 1,

Thessalonians, Philippians, Galatians, Philemon, ed. Jouette M. Bassler (Minneapolis: Fortress Press, 1991), 232.

7. Paul's version of Jesus' words is most similar to the version presented by Luke in his Gospel; see Susanne Lehne, *The New Covenant in Hebrews,* JSNTS 44 (Sheffield: JSOT Press, 1990), 80–82.

8. See James D. G. Dunn, *The Epistle to the Galatians,* BNTC (Peabody, Mass.: Hendrickson, 1993), 254–55.

9. See James D. G. Dunn, *The Theology of Paul the Apostle* (Grand Rapids: Eerdmans, 1998), 147–48, 643–44.

10. See Richard B. Hays, *First Corinthians,* Int (Louisville: Westminster John Knox, 1997), 57.

11. So suggests James D. G. Dunn, *Christianity in the Making,* vol. 1, *Jesus Remembered* (Grand Rapids: Eerdmans, 2003), 515.

12. On this idea in Paul and Paul's sacrificial language regarding himself and other believers, see especially Michael Newton, *The Concept of Purity at Qumran and in the Letters of Paul,* SNTSMS 53 (Cambridge: Cambridge University Press, 1985), 52–78.

13. See Gordon D. Fee, *The First Epistle to the Corinthians*; NICNT (Grand Rapids: Eerdmans, 1987), 562–64; John Ziesler, *Paul's Letter to the Romans*; TPINTC (Philadelphia: Trinity Press International, 1989), 174.

14. See Rom 5:6–8; 8:32; 14:15; 1 Cor 11:24; 2 Cor 5:14–15, 21; Gal 2:20; 3:13; 1 Thess 5:10; cf. 1 Cor 1:13.

15. See, for example, Bultmann, *Theology,* 1:296.

16. In the Pauline letters, see Rom 8:27; 10:1; 15:30; 2 Cor 1:11; 9:14; Phil 1:4; cf. Eph 1:16; 6:19; Col 1:3, 9; 4:12.

17. Alexander J. M. Wedderburn, "The Theology of Colossians," in *The Theology of the Later Pauline Letters,* ed. Andrew T. Lincoln and A. J. M. Wedderburn, NTT (Cambridge: Cambridge University Press, 1993), 38.

18. For interpretations of this variety, see, for example, Irenaeus, who understands 1 Cor 15:3 in the sense of the reformation of "man" and the victory over the powers of sin and evil (*Adversus Haereses* 3.17.2–3, 6–7), and Athanasius, who sees Christ's death as "for sins" in that he delivers our mortal flesh from its fallen condition, thereby ransoming the human race (*Epistola* 59.8–9). Johan Christiaan Beker claims that Christ's death is "for sins" because it brings an end to the dominion of the law and thus saves believers from the condemnation due them because of their sins, as well as breaking sin's power (*The Triumph of God: The Essence of Paul's Thought,* trans. Loren T. Stuckenbruck [Minneapolis: Fortress Press, 1990], 261–62). And Calvin J. Roetzel interprets 1 Cor 15:3 as part of a Pauline story according to which one can "participate in Christ and share in his salvific act," so as to be liberated from sin, death, and the principalities and powers (*Paul: The Man and the Myth* [Minneapolis: Fortress Press, 1999], 66).

19. Gordon D. Fee, "Toward a Theology of 1 Corinthians," in *Pauline Theology*, vol. 2: *1 and 2 Corinthians*, ed. David M. Hay (Minneapolis: Fortress Press, 1993), 49.

20. On the differences between the Hebrew and Septuagint versions of Isaiah 53, see David A. Sapp, "The LXX, 1QIsa, and MT Versions of Isaiah 53 and the Christian Doctrine of Atonement," in *Jesus and the Suffering Servant: Isaiah 53 and Christian Origins*, ed. William H. Bellinger and William R. Farmer (Harrisburg, Pa.: Trinity Press International, 1998), 170–92.

21. See Jacob Milgrom, *Studies in Cultic Theology and Terminology*, SJLA 36 (Leiden: E. J. Brill, 1983), 76.

22. See ibid., 70.

23. For this interpretation, see Paul S. Fiddes, *Past Event and Present Salvation: The Christian Idea of Atonement* (London: Darton, Longman & Todd, 1989), 80–81, who claims that through the servant's sufferings the people are "brought to confess their guilt and receive healing. . . . God has burdened the servant with suffering in order to create a change in their perception of themselves, to make them aware of their perilous condition before God."

24. George A. F. Knight, for example, considers the vicarious suffering of the servant "participative" (*Deutero-Isaiah: A Theological Commentary on Isaiah 40–55* [New York: Abingdon, 1965], 237). See also Daniel P. Bailey, "Concepts of *Stellvertretung* in the Interpretation of Isaiah 53," in Bellinger and Farmer, *Jesus and the Suffering Servant*, 223–50.

25. See, for example, Athanasius, *Orationes contra Arianos* 26.31–34, as well as the quotes from various Fathers in Jean Riviére, *The Doctrine of the Atonement: A Historical Essay*, trans. Luigi Cappadelta (London: Kegan Paul, Trench, Trübner & Co., 1909), 1:186, 193–94, 206–8, 230–31.

26. Leonhard Goppelt, *A Commentary on 1 Peter*, trans. John Alsup (Grand Rapids: Eerdmans, 1993), 212–13.

27. Paul J. Achtemeier, *A Commentary on 1 Peter*, Hermeneia (Minneapolis: Fortress Press, 1996), 247, commenting on 1 Pet 3:18.

28. See, for example, Calvin, *Institutes of the Christian Religion*, 2.16.12–13; Leon Morris, *The Cross in the New Testament* (Grand Rapids: Eerdmans, 1965), 47–49; Wolfhart Pannenberg, *Jesus—God and Man*, trans. Lewis L. Wilkins and Duane A. Priebe (Philadelphia: Westminster, 1968), 260–69.

29. David Wenham, *Paul: Follower of Jesus or Founder of Christianity?* (Grand Rapids: Eerdmans, 1995), 391.

30. See James D. G. Dunn, "Jesus Tradition in Paul," in *Studying the Historical Jesus: Evaluations of the State of Current Research*, ed. Bruce Chilton and Craig A. Evans, NTTS 19 (Leiden: E. J. Brill, 1994), 169–70. See also Michael B. Thompson, *Clothed with Christ: The Example and Teaching of Jesus in Romans 12.1–15.13*, JSNTS 59 (Sheffield: JSOT Press, 1991), 210–11.

31. See Douglas A. Moo, *The Epistle to the Romans,* NICNT (Grand Rapids: Eerdmans, 1996), 288; Walter Schmithals, *Der Römerbrief: Ein Kommentar* (Gütersloh: Gütersloher Verlagshaus Gerd Mohn, 1988), 148–49.

32. See James D. G. Dunn, *Romans 1–8,* WBC (Dallas: Word, 1988), 422.

33. See Herman N. Ridderbos, *Paul: An Outline of His Theology,* trans. John Richard de Witt (Grand Rapids: Eerdmans, 1975), 188–90.

34. See James D. G. Dunn, "Paul's Understanding of the Death of Jesus," in *Sacrifice and Redemption: Durham Essays in Theology,* ed. S. W. Sykes (Cambridge: Cambridge University Press, 1991), 42–51.

35. See Ridderbos, *Paul,* 191; C. E. B. Cranfield, *A Critical and Exegetical Commentary on the Epistle to the Romans,* ICC (Edinburgh: T&T Clark, 1975), 1:382.

36. See, for example, Cranfield, *Romans,* 1:382; Brice L. Martin, *Christ and the Law in Paul,* NovTSup 62 (Leiden: E. J. Brill, 1989), 112; N. T. Wright, *The Climax of the Covenant: Christ and the Law in Pauline Theology* (Minneapolis: Fortress Press, 1991), 207–9; Stephen H. Travis, "Christ as Bearer of Divine Judgment in Paul's Thought about the Atonement," in *Jesus of Nazareth, Lord and Christ: Essays on the Historical Jesus and New Testament Christology,* ed. Joel B. Green and Max Turner (Grand Rapids: Eerdmans, 1994), 332–45. Such an idea was fundamental for Karl Barth, for whom Christ was the "Judge judged in our place" (*Church Dogmatics,* trans. and ed. G. W. Bromiley and T. F. Torrance [Edinburgh: T&T Clark, 1956–61], 4.1: 211–83).

37. Whether Paul has in mind in this verse the Mosaic law or some general law or principle for our purposes here is not an issue. On this question, see Dunn, *Romans 1–8,* 436–37; Heikki Räisänen, "Das 'Gesetz des Glaubens' (Röm 3.27) und das 'Gesetz des Geistes' (Röm 8.2)," *NTS* 26 (1980): 101–17.

38. On these questions, see Dunn, *Romans 1–8,* 164–83; Sam K. Williams, *Jesus' Death as Saving Event: The Background and Origin of a Concept,* HDR 2 (Missoula, Mont.: Scholars Press, 1975), 24–56.

39. Ziesler, *Romans,* 112–13; see also Dunn, *Theology,* 213–14.

40. So, for example, Cranfield, *Romans,* 1:210–17.

41. So Dunn, *Romans 1–8,* 180–81.

42. See Stanislas Lyonnet, "The Terminology of Redemption," in *Sin, Redemption and Sacrifice: A Biblical and Patristic Study,* ed. Stanislas Lyonnet and Léopold Sabourin, AnBib 48 (Rome: Biblical Institute, 1970), 155–66.

43. For the various alternatives, see especially Williams, *Jesus' Death,* 34–38.

44. See Cranfield, *Romans,* 1:208–9.

45. See Dunn, *Romans 1–8,* 172.

46. See Cranfield, *Romans,* 1:211–14.

47. See Sam K. Williams, "The 'Righteousness of God' in Romans," *JBL* 99 (1980): 260–65; Dunn, *Romans 1–8,* 173.

48. This is essentially how the Epistle to the Hebrews understands Christ's expiatory work: as the Jewish priests took sacrificial blood into the Holy of Holies, imploring

God's forgiveness for the sins of his people on the Day of Atonement, so Christ made expiation by offering up himself and his own blood with the petition that God forgive and redeem the members of his community. Because God accepted his sacrifice for their sins by receiving him into heaven, the "true sanctuary," they can now confidently draw near to God and have access to him through Christ and through his past and present intercession on their behalf. In this way, through his death or blood, Christ attained "once and for all" their forgiveness and redemption, since it is now certain that he will return one day from heaven, "not to deal with sin, but to save those who are eagerly waiting for him" (Heb 9:28; see 1:4; 2:17; 5:1–10; 6:19–20; 7:15–27; 9:11—10:22). These same basic ideas are behind Rom 3:24–25 and other passages from Paul's letters; there is thus no need to look to a notion such as substitution to understand the thought of either Paul or Hebrews regarding Jesus' sacrificial death.

49. One of the few to do so is Williams, *Jesus' Death*, 33–34.

50. On the question of the participation of Gentiles in the sacrificial worship at the Jerusalem Temple in the first century, see Daniel R. Schwartz, *Studies in the Jewish Background of Christianity*, WUNT 60 (Tübingen: Mohr, 1992), 102–16.

51. See Léopold Sabourin, *Rédemption Sacrificielle: Une Enquête Exégétique* (Paris: Desclée de Brouwer, 1961), 323, 360–61.

52. See Williams, *Jesus' Death*, 27–34. On the background of the phrase *en tē anochē tou theou* in Rom 3:26, see especially Wolfgang Kraus, *Der Tod Jesu als Heiligtumsweihe: Eine Untersuchung zum Umfeld der Sühnevorstellung in Römer 3,25–26a*, WMANT 66 (Neukirchen-Vluyn: Neukirchener Verlag, 1991), 112–49.

53. The Greek text, *to pascha hēmōn*, does not explicitly mention a "lamb," but virtually all commentators agree that the reference is in fact to the Passover lamb that is sacrificed (*etuthē*).

54. See, for example, C. K. Barrett, *The First Epistle to the Corinthians*, BNTC (Peabody, Mass.: Hendrickson, 1968), 128.

55. On the Passover lamb in first-century Judaism and its application to Jesus in early Christian thought, see especially Robert J. Daly, *The Origins of the Christian Doctrine of Sacrifice* (Philadelphia: Fortress Press, 1978), 38–41.

56. On this point and the following, see Newton, *Concept of Purity*, 90–93.

57. This type of symbolism is found explicitly in Justin Martyr's *Dialogue with Trypho* 40, 111.

58. On this point and the "righteous/sinners" distinction in ancient Judaism and the New Testament in general, see especially Severino Pancaro, *The Law in the Fourth Gospel: The Torah and the Gospel, Moses and Jesus, Judaism and Christianity according to John*, NovTSup 42 (Leiden: E. J. Brill, 1975), 30–44.

59. See N. T. Wright, "Putting Paul Together Again," in Bassler, *Pauline Theology*, vol. 1, 202–3.

60. The phrase *en tō haimati autou* here can be understood either in the instrumental sense, "by means of," or in the sense of "at the cost of" (C. K. Barrett, *A*

Commentary on the Epistle to the Romans, HNTC [New York: Harper & Row, 1957], 107).

61. On these views, see respectively Anselm, *Cur Deus Homo* 1.9; 2.19, 21; George Eldon Ladd, *A Theology of the New Testament,* rev. ed. (Grand Rapids: Eerdmans, 1993), 482–91; Council of Trent, Sixth Session, *Decree concerning Justification* 7; Peter Stuhlmacher, *Paul's Letter to the Romans: A Commentary,* trans. Scott Hafemann (Louisville: Westminster John Knox, 1994), 119–20; Don B. Garlington, *Faith, Obedience, and Perseverance: Aspects of Paul's Letter to the Romans,* WUNT 79 (Tübingen: Mohr, 1994), 102–4; Morna Hooker, *From Adam to Christ: Essays on Paul* (Cambridge: Cambridge University Press, 1990), 9; David Seeley, *The Noble Death: Graeco-Roman Martyrology and Paul's Concept of Salvation,* JSNTS 28 (Sheffield: Sheffield Academic Press, 1990), 102–4.

62. The "all" in this passage and in 1 Cor 15:22 should be understood as referring to believers, Jews and Gentiles, rather than all people in general, as Sanders claims (*Paul,* 473); see also Moo, *Romans,* 343–44; Ziesler, *Romans,* 151.

63. Dunn, *Romans 1–8,* 298.

64. See, for example, Charles B. Cousar, "Continuity and Discontinuity: Reflections on Romans 5–8," in *Pauline Theology,* vol. 3, *Romans,* ed. David M. Hay and E. Elizabeth Johnson (Minneapolis: Fortress Press, 1995), 203–4; Robert C. Tannehill, *Dying and Rising with Christ: A Study in Pauline Theology,* BZNW 32 (Berlin: Alfred Töpelmann, 1966), 26–30; Garlington, *Faith,* 78–109.

65. Ralph P. Martin, *Reconciliation: A Study of Paul's Theology* (Atlanta: John Knox, 1981), 98, 102. Ladd also understands the passage in terms of penal substitution (*Theology,* 468–69).

66. See Dunn, *Theology,* 212–23, who also speaks of the "mechanism" whereby sin is removed and sinners are forgiven (219). See also Frank J. Matera, *II Corinthians: A Commentary,* NTL (Louisville: Westminster John Knox, 2003), 142–44.

67. See Margaret E. Thrall, *A Critical and Exegetical Commentary on the Second Epistle to the Corinthians,* ICC (Edinburgh: T&T Clark, 1994), 1:442–43.

68. See Sanders, *Paul,* 443, for whom this verse in particular provides support for the idea that Paul proceeded from "solution" to "plight."

69. For these interpretations of Paul's teaching regarding reconciliation, see respectively James Denney, *The Death of Christ* (London: Tyndale, 1951), 84–110, 159–61, 186–205; Auguste Sabatier, *The Doctrine of the Atonement,* trans. Victor Leuliette (London: Williams & Norgate, 1904), 126–27; Gustav Aulén, *Christus Victor: An Historical Study of the Three Main Types of the Idea of Atonement,* trans. A. G. Hebert (New York: Macmillan, 1969), 4–5; cf. 55–59, 70–72; Barth, *Church Dogmatics,* 4.1: 222–30, 241–42, 250–59, 306–12, 316–17; 4.2: 6, 28, 69–70.

70. On these ideas in the Old Testament, see especially G. K. Beale, "The Old Testament Background of 2 Corinthians 5–7 and Its Bearing on the Literary Problem of 2 Corinthians 6.14—7.1," *NTS* 35 (1989): 553–75.

218 Notes to Chapter Six

71. On these distinctions, see especially Ladd, *Theology*, 493–98; Dunn, *Theology*, 626–31.

72. Thrall, *Second Corinthians*, 1:430–31; see also Bultmann, *Theology*, 1: 286–87.

73. See Alister E. McGrath, *Iustitia Dei: A History of the Christian Doctrine of Justification* (Cambridge: Cambridge University Press, 1986), 2:48.

74. See Otfried Hofius, *Paulusstudien*, WUNT 51 (Tübingen: Mohr, 1989), 9.

75. On this question, see especially Alan F. Segal, "Universalism in Judaism and Christianity," in *Paul in His Hellenistic Context*, ed. Troels Engberg-Pedersen (Minneapolis: Fortress Press, 1995), 1–29.

76. See David E. Holwerda, *Jesus and Israel: One Covenant or Two?* (Grand Rapids: Eerdmans, 1995), 150–76.

77. On the background of these ideas in ancient Jewish and Hellenistic thought, see especially Lyonnet, "Terminology of Redemption," 80–97, 105–18.

78. See Leon Morris, *The Apostolic Preaching of the Cross*, 3rd ed. (Grand Rapids: Eerdmans, 1965), 36–61.

79. See Peter Stuhlmacher, *Reconciliation, Law and Righteousness*, trans. Everett Kalin (Philadelphia: Fortress Press, 1986), 16–29, 40–43; Morris, *Apostolic Preaching*, 51.

80. See Morris, *Apostolic Preaching*, 21–22.

81. On the textual difficulties in this passage, see I. Howard Marshall, *The Acts of the Apostles*, TNTC (Grand Rapids: Eerdmans, 1980), 334.

82. See Lyonnet, "Terminology of Redemption," 110–12.

83. On this idea, see Bernard Sesboüé, *Jésus-Christ l'unique Médiateur* (Paris: Desclée, 1988), 1:152.

84. For examples of these interpretations, and for much of what follows, see my article "The Cross and the Curse: Galatians 3.13 and Paul's Doctrine of Redemption," *JSNT* 81 (2001): 5–8.

85. Bradley Hudson McLean, *The Cursed Christ: Mediterranean Expulsion Rituals and Pauline Soteriology*, JSNTS 126 (Sheffield: Sheffield Academic Press, 1996), 125.

86. Richard B. Hays, *The Faith of Jesus Christ: An Investigation of the Narrative Substructure of Galatians 3:1—4:11*, 2nd ed., Biblical Resource Series (Grand Rapids: Eerdmans, 2002), 112–13.

Chapter 6

1. Adolf Deissmann, *Paul: A Study in Social and Religious History*, trans. William Wilson (London: Hodder & Stoughton, 1926), 140.

2. Ibid., 136, 138.

3. Ibid., 182.

4. Albert Schweitzer, *The Mysticism of Paul the Apostle*, trans. William Montgomery (Baltimore: Johns Hopkins University Press, 1998), 19.

5. Ibid., 118.

6. Ibid., 128.

7. John A. T. Robinson, *The Body: A Study in Pauline Theology* (London: SCM, 1952), 51–53.

8. Karl Barth, *Church Dogmatics*, trans. and ed. G. W. Bromiley and T. F. Torrance (Edinburgh: T&T Clark, 1956–61), 4.2: 48.

9. Rudolf Bultmann, *Theology of the New Testament*, trans. Kendrick Grobel (New York: Scribner's, 1951), 1:302.

10. Ibid., 1:303.

11. Ibid., 1:311.

12. Ibid., 1:140–51.

13. Ibid., 1:299.

14. See D. E. H. Whiteley, *The Theology of St. Paul* (Philadelphia: Fortress Press, 1964), 130–65; Robert C. Tannehill, *Dying and Rising with Christ: A Study in Pauline Theology*, BZNW 32 (Berlin: Alfred Töpelmann, 1966), 1–134; E. P. Sanders, *Paul and Palestinian Judaism* (Philadelphia: Fortress Press, 1977), 442–556; Morna Hooker, *From Adam to Christ: Essays on Paul* (Cambridge: Cambridge University Press, 1990), 1–185; James D. G. Dunn, *The Theology of Paul the Apostle* (Grand Rapids: Eerdmans, 1998), 199–233, 390–412; N. T. Wright, *The Climax of the Covenant: Christ and the Law in Pauline Theology* (Minneapolis: Fortress Press, 1991), 18–55, 157–267; Richard B. Hays, *The Faith of Jesus Christ: An Investigation of the Narrative Substructure of Galatians 3:1—4:11*, 2nd ed., Biblical Resource Series (Grand Rapids: Eerdmans, 2002), 150–77, 206–9, 247–66.

15. See, for example, Wright, *Climax*, 48; James D. G. Dunn, "Paul's Understanding of the Death of Jesus," in *Sacrifice and Redemption: Durham Essays in Theology*, ed. S. W. Sykes (Cambridge: Cambridge University Press, 1991), 40; Tannehill, *Dying*, 25.

16. This understanding of participation was adopted almost universally by the church fathers, and through them has continued to influence biblical scholarship. See especially Friedrich Normann, *Teilhabe, ein Schlüsselwort der Vätertheologie*, MBT 42 (Münster: Aschendorff, 1978).

17. Schweitzer, *Mysticism of Paul*, 118.

18. Bultmann, *Theology*, 1:299.

19. Sanders, *Paul*, 482, 507, 547, 549. He seems to have borrowed this phrase from Tannehill, *Dying*, 20.

20. Johan Christiaan Beker, *The Triumph of God: The Essence of Paul's Thought*, trans. Loren T. Stuckenbruck (Minneapolis: Fortress Press, 1990), 309.

21. Bultmann, *Theology*, 1:303.

22. Sanders, *Paul*, 522.

23. Ibid., 522–23.

24. Hays, *Faith*, 260, 262.

25. Richard B. Hays, "Crucified with Christ: A Synthesis of the Theology of 1 and 2 Thessalonians, Philemon, Philippians, and Galatians," in *Pauline Theology*, vol. 1, *Thessalonians, Philippians, Galatians, Philemon*, ed. Jouette M. Bassler (Minneapolis: Fortress Press, 1991), 233, 239.

26. Hooker, *From Adam to Christ*, 40–45, 91–92.

27. Dunn, *Theology*, 400.

28. Ibid., 410; cf. 393.

29. Wright, *Climax*, 41, 46–49.

30. Markus Barth and Helmut Blanke, for example, claim that for Paul baptism was "understood only as proclamation, thanks and praise of that which has already occurred in Christ" (*Colossians*, trans. Astrid Beck, ABC 34B [New York: Doubleday, 1994], 369). Similarly, Ian G. Wallis attributes to Paul the idea that "baptism is the acknowledgment or demonstration that Christ's death and its salvific implications encompass—and always have done—the person baptized" (*The Faith of Jesus Christ in Early Christian Traditions*, SNTSMS 84 [Cambridge: Cambridge University Press, 1995], 126).

31. C. E. B. Cranfield, *A Critical and Exegetical Commentary on the Epistle to the Romans*, ICC (Edinburgh: T&T Clark, 1975), 1:311.

32. Barth, *Church Dogmatics*, 4.1: 230.

33. Ibid., 4.1: 222, 285.

34. Ibid., 4.1: 294–95. Barth rejects an entirely forensic view, which for him would involve "an exchange only in appearance" (4.1: 237).

35. Dunn, "Paul's Understanding," 50–52; *Theology*, 211.

36. Wright, *Climax*, 153 n. 54.

37. See, for example, Sanders, *Paul*, 443, 506–11; Tannehill, *Dying*, 8, 39–43; Dunn, *Theology*, 223; Wright, *Climax*, 151–56, 239.

38. Bultmann, *Theology*, 1:140, 164–83, 298–314.

39. John A. Ziesler, *Pauline Christianity*, rev. ed. (Oxford: Oxford University Press, 1983), 61. Ziesler also presents a couple of other common arguments against the idea that Gnosticism influenced Paul's soteriology there.

40. Dunn, *Theology*, 393, 550–51.

41. Alexander J. M. Wedderburn, *Baptism and Resurrection: Studies in Pauline Theology against Its Graeco-Roman Background*, WUNT 44 (Tübingen: Mohr, 1987), 396.

42. For summaries of these and other arguments, in addition to Wedderburn's book and his article "The Soteriology of the Mysteries and Pauline Baptismal Theology," *NovT* 29 (1987): 53–72, see Everett Ferguson, *Backgrounds of Early Christianity*, 2nd ed. (Grand Rapids: Eerdmans, 1993), 279–82; David Seeley, *The Noble Death: Graeco-Roman Martyrology and Paul's Concept of Salvation*, JSNTS 28 (Sheffield: Sheffield Academic Press, 1990), 67–82.

43. Ziesler, *Pauline Christianity*, 56.

44. Dunn, *Theology*, 82, 94.

45. Wright, *Climax*, 48; see also 19–25.

46. Ziesler, *Pauline Christianity*, 52.

47. Ibid., 62–63.

48. Ibid., 63. On this point, see also J. W. Rogerson, "The Hebrew Conception of Corporate Personality: A Re-examination," *JTS* 21 (1970): 1–16.

49. Ferguson, *Backgrounds*, 279.

50. See James D. G. Dunn, *The Epistle to the Galatians,* BNTC (Peabody, Mass.: Hendrickson, 1993), 152.

51. See David Wenham, *Paul: Follower of Jesus or Founder of Christianity?* (Grand Rapids: Eerdmans, 1995), 364.

52. See Wolfgang Kraus, *Zwischen Jerusalem und Antiochia: Die "Hellenisten", Paulus und die Aufnahme der Heiden in das endzeitliche Gottesvolk,* SB 179 (Stuttgart: Verlag Katholisches Bibelwerk, 1999), 106–30. On the relation between Christian baptism and that of John, see especially R. T. France, "Jesus the Baptist?" in *Jesus of Nazareth, Lord and Christ: Essays on the Historical Jesus and New Testament Christology,* ed. Joel B. Green and Max Turner (Grand Rapids: Eerdmans, 1994), 94–111.

53. Margaret E. Thrall, *A Critical and Exegetical Commentary on the Second Epistle to the Corinthians,* ICC (Edinburgh: T&T Clark, 1994), 1:343.

54. See Paul Barnett, *The Second Epistle to the Corinthians,* NICNT (Grand Rapids: Eerdmans, 1997), 235–36.

55. On the interpretations given to this passage in the first three centuries C.E., see Robert Schlarb, *Wir sind mit Christus begraben: Die Auslegung von Römer 6,1–11 im Frühchristentum bis Origenes,* BGBE 31 (Tübingen: Mohr, 1987).

56. Bultmann, *Theology,* 1:312–13.

57. Sanders, *Paul,* 506–7.

58. James D. G. Dunn, *Romans 1–8,* WBC (Dallas: Word, 1988), 327.

59. Tannehill, *Dying,* 22–24, 27.

60. John Ziesler, *Paul's Letter to the Romans,* TPINCT (Philadelphia: Trinity Press International, 1989), 162.

61. Tannehill, *Dying,* 15.

62. Cranfield, *Romans,* 1:316.

63. See, for example, ibid., 1:316–17; John A. Ziesler, *The Meaning of Righteousness in Paul: A Linguistic and Theological Inquiry,* SNTSMS 20 (Cambridge: Cambridge University Press, 1972), 202.

64. On this meaning of the perfect tense here, see Dunn, *Romans 1–8,* 331.

65. See Ziesler, *Romans,* 157, 159.

66. Tannehill, *Dying,* 24, 29–30.

67. Cf. Rom 1:21; 2 Cor 3:15; 4:10; 6:11; Phil 3:21.

68. See Wedderburn, *Baptism,* 343.

69. On Gal 6:14–15, see especially Moyer V. Hubbard, *New Creation in Paul's Letters and Thought,* SNTSMS 119 (Cambridge: Cambridge University Press, 2002), 188–232.

70. See, for example, Douglas A. Moo, *The Epistle to the Romans,* NICNT (Grand Rapids: Eerdmans, 1996), 417–18; Dunn, *Romans 1–8,* 368–74; Peter Stuhlmacher, *Paul's Letter to the Romans: A Commentary,* trans. Scott Hafemann (Louisville: Westminster John Knox, 1994), 103–4.

71. This is the proposal of Robinson, *Body,* 47.

72. The idea of having died to the law together with Christ also appears in Eph 2:14–16, and perhaps Col 2:14–15, if the *cheirographon* nailed to the cross is understood as something such as a "promissory note," as A. J. M. Wedderburn has argued ("The Theology of Colossians," in *The Theology of the Later Pauline Letters,* ed. Andrew T. Lincoln and Alexander J. M. Wedderburn, NTT [Cambridge: Cambridge University Press, 1993], 43–44). In this case, the idea is that believers are no longer obligated to live under the law, since by giving his Son over to death, God has brought a new covenant and new dispensation into existence. However, even if the *cheirographon* is taken to refer to a document certifying some debt owed to God on account of human sinfulness, there is no need to understand the passage in substitutionary terms, as if "the weight of human guilt fell upon Christ and was crucified with him" (Eduard Schweizer, *The Letter to the Colossians,* trans. Andrew Chester [Minneapolis: Augsburg, 1982], 143). Rather, the idea would merely be that when Christ died, God put away his wrath at the sins of those who would come to faith, in essence letting the righteous claims he had against them on account of their disobedience to his regulations perish permanently with Christ on the cross. The reason for this, however, would be that through Christ's death a new covenant would be established in which they would receive God's promises of forgiveness and a new life of righteousness as members of a community into which entrance is now through baptism rather than circumcision (Col 2:11–12).

73. See, for example, Thrall, *Second Corinthians,* 1:410–11; Dunn, *Theology,* 210–11; Tannehill, *Dying,* 67.

74. See George Eldon Ladd, *A Theology of the New Testament,* rev. ed. (Grand Rapids: Eerdmans, 1993), 473–74.

75. See Thrall, *Second Corinthians,* 1:418–20.

76. See Barnett, *Second Corinthians,* 290.

77. See Moo, *Romans,* 343–44.

78. Dunn seems to confuse these two ideas; see *Theology,* 211.

79. See respectively Rudolf Schnackenburg, *Ephesians: A Commentary,* trans. Helen Heron (Edinburgh: T&T Clark, 1991), 95; John M. G. Barclay, *Colossians and Philemon,* NTG (Sheffield: Sheffield Academic Press, 1997), 84; Clinton E. Arnold, *Ephesians, Power and Magic: The Concept of Power in Ephesians in Light of Its Historical Setting,* SNTSMS 63 (Cambridge: Cambridge University Press, 1989), 136–37; Markus Barth, *Ephesians 1–3,* ABC 34 (Garden City, N.Y.: Doubleday, 1974), 235; Eduard Lohse, *Colossians and Philemon,* trans. R. J. Karris and W. R. Poehlmann,

Hermeneia (Philadelphia: Fortress Press, 1971), 103, 105, 141–42.

80. See Wedderburn, "Colossians," 51.

81. See M. Barth, *Ephesians 1–3*, 233.

82. C. Leslie Mitton, *Ephesians*, NCBC (London: Marshall, Morgan, & Scott, 1976), 88.

83. Martin Kitchen, *Ephesians*, NTR (London: Routledge, 1994), 60.

84. Charles B. Cousar, *A Theology of the Cross: The Death of Jesus in the Pauline Letters* (Minneapolis: Fortress Press, 1990), 203.

85. Hans Conzelmann, *A Commentary on the First Epistle to the Corinthians*, trans. James W. Leitch, Hermeneia (Philadelphia: Fortress Press, 1975), 268–69.

86. Moo, *Romans*, 327.

87. See Dunn, *Theology*, 84–90.

88. Moo, *Romans*, 328.

89. Augustine, *De Civitate Dei* 13.14.

90. C. E. Hill, "Paul's Understanding of Christ's Kingdom in 1 Cor. 15:20–28," *NovT* 30 (1988): 303–7.

91. See Gordon D. Fee, "Toward a Theology of 1 Corinthians," in *Pauline Theology*, vol. 2, *1 and 2 Corinthians*, ed. David M. Hay (Minneapolis: Fortress Press, 1993), 57–58.

92. It is important to note that Paul does not employ any verb in 1 Cor 15:21, which literally reads: "For as through a man death, so also through a man resurrection of the dead." The idea is thus not that the resurrection of the dead has already come through Christ, as translations such as the KJV, RSV, and NRSV infer, but that it *will* come through him, as v. 22 makes clear.

93. Sanders, *Paul*, 454–55.

94. Calvin J. Roetzel, *Paul: The Man and the Myth* (Minneapolis: Fortress Press, 1999), 112–13.

95. Sanders, *Paul*, 455.

96. See Kim Huat Tan, *The Zion Traditions and the Aims of Jesus*, SNTSMS 91 (Cambridge: Cambridge University Press, 1997), 218.

97. On the church as the body of Christ, see especially Dunn, *Theology*, 548–52.

98. See Wedderburn, *Baptism*, 58–80; cf. Ziesler, *Romans*, 156–57.

99. Bultmann, *Theology*, 1:311.

100. Ziesler correctly observes that the Greek preposition *en* can properly be translated as "under" in certain contexts, so that the basic idea is that of living "under" Christ (*Pauline Christianity*, 63–64).

Conclusion

1. Rudolf Bultmann, *Faith and Understanding*, trans. Louise Pettibone Smith (New York: Harper & Row, 1969), 1:234. Cf. Robert C. Tannehill, *Dying and Rising with*

Christ: A Study in Pauline Theology, BZNW 32 (Berlin: Alfred Töpelmann, 1966), 67.

2. Raymond Pickett, *The Cross in Corinth: The Social Significance of the Death of Jesus,* JSNTS 143 (Sheffield: Sheffield Academic Press, 1997), 157; Johan Christiaan Beker, *The Triumph of God: The Essence of Paul's Thought,* trans. Loren T. Stuckenbruck (Minneapolis: Fortress Press, 1990), 196.

3. Eduard Lohse, *Colossians and Philemon,* trans. R. J. Karris and W. R. Poehlmann, Hermeneia (Philadelphia: Fortress Press, 1971), 59–60 (commenting on Col 1:19–23).

4. James D. G. Dunn, *The Theology of Paul the Apostle* (Grand Rapids: Eerdmans, 1998), 223; Brice L. Martin, *Christ and the Law in Paul,* NovTSup 62 (Leiden: E. J. Brill, 1989), 70, 112; Beker, *Triumph,* 215.

5. Martin, *Christ,* 112; I. Howard Marshall, *Jesus the Saviour: Studies in New Testament Theology* (London: SPCK, 1990), 264.

6. Bradley Hudson McLean, *The Cursed Christ: Mediterranean Expulsion Rituals and Pauline Soteriology,* JSNTS 126 (Sheffield: Sheffield Academic Press, 1996), 46.

7. So, for example, James D. G. Dunn, *Romans 1–8,* WBC (Dallas: Word, 1988), 329; E. P. Sanders, *Paul and Palestinian Judaism* (Philadelphia: Fortress Press, 1977), 507, 511.

8. Ian G. Wallis, *The Faith of Jesus Christ in Early Christian Traditions,* SNTSMS 84 (Cambridge: Cambridge University Press, 1995), 69, 124–25.

9. Tannehill, *Dying,* 71.

10. James D. G. Dunn, *The Partings of the Ways between Christianity and Judaism and Their Significance for the Character of Christianity* (Philadelphia: Trinity Press International, 1991), 191.

Index of Subjects and Names

Index of Scripture Citations

OTHER EARLY CHRISTIAN WRITINGS